HISTORICAL

SOUTHERN FAMILIES

VOLUME XVIII

Edited by Mrs. John Bennett Boddie

CLEARFIELD COMPANY

Publishers

Genealogical Publishing Company

Baltimore   1973

Library of Congress Catalog Card Number 67-29833

International Standard Book Number 0-8063-0565-7

Reprinted for
Clearfield Company, Inc. by
Genealogical Publishing Co., Inc.
Baltimore, Maryland
1994

TABLE of CONTENTS

****

EXPLANATION of ABBREVIATIONS

C. & P.	Cavaliers & Pioneers by Nugent
D.B. or D.Bk.	Deed Book
d.s.p.	Died single person
D. & W.	Deeds and Wills
Harl.	Harleian Society Publications
H.S.F.	Historical Southern Families, by Boddie
Hotten	Original Lists of Immigrants to America, by Hotten
Ibid or id.	Reference as above
O.B. or O.Bk.	Order Book
P.Bk.	Patent Book
P.Reg.	Parish Register
17th Cent.	Seventeenth Century Isle of Wight Co.
S.V.F.	Southside Virginia Families, by Boddie
V.M.	Virginia Magazine of History
W.B. or W.Bk.	Will Book
Wm. & M. Q.	William & Mary Quarterly

LATER DESCENDANTS OF THE DEES FAMILY

Note: See Historical Southern Families,
      Vols. XVI, XVII, for previous
      generations.

Descendants of Harman Dees #14 (William,Emanuel)

The family of Harman Dees is treated in H.S.F.
Vol.XVI, pp.195,196. His children were:
68. James Dees. 69. Jacob Dees. 70. Arthur
Dees. 71. John Dees. 72. Jesse Dees. 73.Ran-
som Dees. 74. Edward Dees. 75. Susannah Dees.
76. Mary Dees. Nothing further is known of the
sons of Jacob and Edward, nor of the daughters,
but the following is known in regard to the
other five sons.

James Dees #68, son of Harman #14, does not
appear in the Census of 1810 for Sumter County,
S.C., and was probably identical with a James
Dees who was granted land in East Feliciana
Parish, Louisiana in 1807, as shown by the La.
State Land Office. The Census records of this
parish show that James Dees was born 1775-80,
died 1830-40, and that his wife Charlotte was
born in South Carolina in 1784 (from the Census of 1850).
     The Census returns of 1820 and 1830 show that
James Dees's family consisted of 2 males and 1
female born 1784-94, 1 son born 1802-4, 1 female
born 1804-10, 3 males and 4 females b. 1810-20,
amd 1 female born 1820-25. The years 1840 and

1

1850 show Charlotte Dees as head of the family.

Among the children of James and Charlotte were the following: 68a. A Joseph Dees who appears in the adjoining parish of St. Helena in 1820, with himself and wife born 1794-1804, and a son born 1810-20. 68b. William Dees, born 1810 in Louisiana, shown in the 1860 Census of St. Helena Parish with wife Ann (born 1812) and the following children, all born in Louisiana: Zederic born 1841, Charles born 1845, and John born 1852. 68c. A daughter,probably, who married a Carroll and died prior to 1850, when Anderson Carroll b.1830, Tilman Carroll b.1835, and Amanda Carroll b. 1844 are all shown in the family of Charlotte Dees. 68d. James Dees b.1818 in Louisiana, single in 1850 and living with his mother and the Carroll children. 68e. Charlotte Dees, who married John E. Smith, Jan.25,1849 in E.Feliciana Parish. A John W.Dees who married Melissa Yarborough in E.Feliciana Parish Nov.29,1866 was probably a grandson of James Dees #68.

Arthur Dees #70, son of Harman Dees #14, was born 1775-80, judging by the Census, and probably died in Covington County, Mississippi 1830-40. He is shown with his family in Sumter County,S.C. in 1810 with himself and wife born 1765-84, 1 son and 1 daughter b. 1794-1800, 2 sons and 2 daughters born 1800-1810; he served in the War of 1812 from Sumter County, S.C. in 1814 and 1815 (File #380, Adjutant-General's Office in Washington), seeing the same service as his brother John Dees #71. He must have moved to Georgia right after 1815, and his first wife (name unknown) having apparently died, he was probably the Arthur Dees who married (2) Lucy Terrell on Dec.23,1816 in Liberty County, Georgia. By 1820 he had moved to Covington County, Mississippi, and is shown there in the Census with himself born 1775-94, a female born before 1775, a female born 1794-1804, and a daughter born 1810-1820. The Census of 1830 for Covington County shows two Arthur Deeses, probably himself and his son Arthur, one born 1770-80 with wife born 1790-1800, 2 males born 1820-25, 1 male born 1825-30, and three other females, apparently daughters; and the other Arthur born 1790-1800, with wife the same age, a daughter born 1815-20, a son born 1820-25, and a son and a daughter born 1825-30. The same Census of 1830 shows a Calvin Dees born 1800-10 with wife the same age, and a daughter born 1825-30, and a Leasey Dees, both in Covington County, and probably sons of Arthur Sr.; and a Ransom Dees, a single man b. 1810-20 in Amite County, Mississippi, probably another son of Arthur Sr., named for his uncle Ransom Dees #73. The probable children of Arthur Dees #70 were as follows:

70a. Arthur Dees Jr., shown in Covington Co. Mississippi above in 1830. A William Dees, born 1822 in Mississippi, shown in the 1850 Census of Kemper Co., Mississippi in 1850, with wife Sarah born 1830, and children William b. 1847 and Sarah born 1849, all born in Mississippi, may have been a son of Arthur Dees Jr. In William's family were Mary Dees born 1802 in North Carolina, and Catherine Dees born 1828 in Mississippi, who may have been the widow and daughter of Arthur Dees #70a.

70b.   Calvin Dees, born 1806 in South Carolina (Census of 1850) is shown in 1830 in Covington County, Mississippi, but had moved to Jasper County, Mississippi by 1850, when the Census shows him as born above, apparently a widower with children: Harriet born 1834, William J. born 1836, John E. born 1838, Mary M. born 1839, and Martha J. born 1842.

70c.   Leasey Dees, shown in Covington County, Mississippi in 1830.

70d.   Ransom Dees, shown in Amite County, Mississippi, in 1830.

The following were possibly sons of Arthur Dees #70 by his second wife Lucy Terrell, though one or more of them could have been sons of Arthur Jr.:

70e.   Crawford Dees, b. 1822 in Mississippi, shown in the 1850 Census for Simpson County, Miss. with wife (or older sister?) Elizabeth, born 1808 in Georgia, and children, Mary A. born 1834 in Mississippi, Joseph born 1841 in Texas, and Emily born 1846 in Texas.

70f. John T. Dees, born 1825 in Mississippi, shown in the 1850 Census of Covington Co., Miss. as born above, with wife Elizabeth b.1828 and son Calvin born 1849, both born in Mississippi.

70g. J.W.Dees, born 1827 in Mississippi (date almost illegible, but probably 1827), shown in the 1860 Census of Neshoba Co., Miss. with wife Jemima born 1830 in Alabama, and children, all born in Mississippi: Mary J.,born 1847, Nancy T., born 1854, John H. born 1857, Erma or Emma M. born 1858, and Laura E.H. born 1860 (six months old).

John Dees #71, son of Harman Dees #14, called "Jacky" in his father's 1800 deed to his children, was born probably 1774 (see later), and seems to have died after 1860 in Conecuh County, Alabama, where in that year John Dees b. 1774 and his wife Alice b. 1786, both born in South Carolina, were living. Judging by the births in the families of his probable sons, shown in Conecuh Co., Alabama, John Dees and his sons lived for many years in South Carolina, though no record of them has been found there as yet. John Dees #71 served in the War of 1812 from Sumter County, South Carolina in 1814 and 1815, in the same company as his brother Arthur #70 (Folder #381, South Carolina Militia, in the Adjutant-General's Office in Washington). This is the only record of him in South Carolina, but he was living in the Muscogee County, Georgia, in 1850 and 1855, as shown by his application for a bounty, though not shown in the 1850 Census there. The bounty applications are in the Department of National Archives (Act 55-80, Wt. #3854). One application, dated Oct.22,1850 gives his age as 81, which would put his birth in 1769; the other dated March 26,1855 gives his age as 75, which would put his birth in 1780. If identical with the John Dees in the 1860 Census of Conecuh Co., Alabama, 1774 is probably the correct date of his birth. His sons were probably the following men:

71a.   A son, name unknown, who was the father of John S. Dees, born 1835 in South Carolina, shown next to John #71 in Conecuh County in 1860 with wife Nancy born 1844 and daughter Mary born 1860 (three months old), both born in Alabama.

71b.   John P. Dees, born 1809 in South Carolina, shown in the Censuses of 1850 and 1860 in Conecuh County, Alabama, with wife Elizabeth b. 1816 in South Carolina and the following children: Sarah born 1833, Lucinda born 1836, Elly born 1838 (male), Mary Ann born 1840, Herrick born 1842, Laura born 1844, John born 1849, and William born 1855 (born in Alabama).

71c.   Hardy Dees, born 1816 in South Carolina, shown in the Conecuh County Census of 1860 and right next to John Dees #71, with wife Sarah born 1824 in South Carolina, and the following children, all born in Alabama: Joseph born 1846, John born 1851, Mary born 1853, and Julian born 1856.

71d.   Probably another son, whose children, all born in South Carolina, are shown in the 1850 Census of Conecuh County in the family of Robert R. Smith and wife Martha: David Dees b. 1840, Martha Dees b. 1842, Robert A. Dees b. 1843, and Sarah Ann Dees b. 1846. It seems likely that Martha Smith was this son's widow who had married (2) Robert R. Smith.

Jesse Dees #72, son of Harman Dees #14, was born 1788 in South Carolina (Census of 1850 for Monroe County, Alabama) and died 1860 in Monroe County (from his tombstone in Polar Springs Cemetery, Uriah, Alabama). He is shown in the 1810 Census of Sumter County, S.C. with himself and wife, born 1784-94, and a son born 1800-1810. He had moved to Georgia by 1814, as his daughters Martha and Priscilla were born in that State in 1814 and 1817 respectively. While living in Georgia he served in the Seminole War of 1817-1818, enlisting at Hartford, which was in Pulaski

County, Georgia (Folio 19 in the Adjutant-General's Office in Washington). By 1820 he was living in Franklin County, Alabama, where he is shown in the Census with 2 sons under 21 and 3 daughters under 21. In 1830 and 1840 he is shown with his family in Monroe County, Alabama. The Monroe Co. Census for 1850 shows him, his wife Mary, and his daughters still living in Monroe County, where he died in 1860. The wife Mary is shown in 1850 as born 1798 in South Carolina, but in the Census of 1860 as born 1795. The Census of 1850 shows a Thomas Smith, born 1842 in Alabama, in Jesse Dees's family, but that of 1860 shows him as Thomas Dees, born 1843, in Mary Dees's family. The following were the known children of Jesse Dees #72:

72a.   A son born prior to 1810, as shown by the 1810 Census of Sumter County, South Carolina. It is possible that this son was John Dees, born 1803, died 1864, buried in the Uriah, Alabama, cemetery along with Jesse Dees's family, but if so, Jesse must have been born much earlier than 1788, the date given him in the Census of 1850, and this John could hardly have been the son of Jesse's wife Mary (born 1795 or 1798) but would have been the son of an earlier marriage. William Dees, born 1835, died 1855 (from his tombstone in Uriah Cemetery, which states that he was born in South Carolina) may have been a son of this John Dees.

72b.   Martha Dees, born 1814 in Georgia (in her father's family in 1850, but does not show up in her mother's family in 1860, so probably died before that date).

72c.   Martin Dees, born 1816 in Georgia, died 1898 in Alabama, aged 82 years (from his tombstone in Uriah Cemetery, Alabama). His wife was Elizabeth Dees who died in 1901 aged 66 years (from her tombstone in Uruah Cemetery). The tombstone shows her birth as 1835, but the Census of 1860 in Monroe County, Alabama shows her as born 1827 in Alabama, along with her husband, born 1816 in Georgia. The children of Martin and Elizabeth Dees, as shown by the Census of 1860, all born in Alabama, were: Webster Dees, born 1849, Emeline Dees born 1853, James Dees born 1855, and Nancy and Mary Dees, born 1858. If Martin Dees's wife was not born until 1835, as her tombstone states, whe could hardly have been the mother of the earlier of Martin's children, as shown in this Census. Apparently, then, she was a second wife; and if this is the case, then a William Dees, born 1837 in Alabama, with wife Mary born 1839, living near Martin Dees in the Census of 1860, was probably a son of Martin by his first marriage.

72d.   Priscilla Dees, born 1817 in Georgia, in her father's family in 1850, but does not appear in 1860.

72e.   Epsy or Hephziah Dees, born 1821 in Alabama, in her father's family in 1850 and in her mother's in 1860, died 1870 (from her tombstone in Polar Springs Cemetery, Uriah, Alabama).

72f.   "Nancy Dees, born in Alabama, died 1832" (from Polar Springs Cemetery) was probably another daughter of Jesse Dees #72.

72g.   "James Dees, 1833" (tombstone in the above cemetery) was probably another son, 1833 being probably his death date.

Thomas H. Dees, b.1842-3, called Thomas Smith in 1850 and Thomas Dees in 1860, was perhaps a grandson of Jesse Dees #72, but more probably an adopted son. He was Postmaster at Jeddo, Monroe County, Alabama, and served in the Confederate Army. His granddaughter, Mrs. Ruby D. Sessions of Monroeville, Alabama, thought that Thomas H. Dees was either a nephew or a son of Martin Dees #72c, but also thought that he might have been an adopted child. Mrs. Sessions said that Thomas H. Dees married (1) Ella Hollinger and had 3 children: (1) William T. Dees, Postmaster at Jeddo, married, and died about 1930 leaving 5 sons; (2) Arthurine Dees, m. Rufus Harrison and had a daughter; and (3) Charles Swanee Dees born 1870, died 1835, married 1902-3 Pauline Bell, had 3 daughters (one of whom was Mrs. Sessions) and 1 son. Mrs. Sessions states that

Thomas H. Dees married a second time and had 1
son by the second marriage. Thomas H. Dees died
about 1920 or 1925.

Ransom Dees #73, son of Harman Dees #14, was
born in Sumter County, South Carolina ca 1776
(his age, given in the Census of 1860, is almost
illegible but appears to be 74 years). He moved
to Georgia, but no trace of him is found there
until 1860. His eldest son was probably a Ransom
Dees, born 1810-20, living as a bachelor in
Jones County, Georgia in the Census of 1840.This
Ransom Dees of Jones County drew land in the
Cherokee Land Lottery of 1832-35 (though the
Ransom of the Land Lottery could have been his
father, who moved away from Jones County prior
to 1840). Ransom Dees #73 appears himself in the
Census of 1860 of Clay County, Georgia, with age
as given above, wife Mary A., born 1807 in South
Carolina, and children: John born 1840 in S.C.,
James born 1845 in Alabama, and Mary A., born
1847 in Georgia.

****

Descendants of John Dees #15 (John, Emanuel)

John Dees #15 has a very brief paragraph on
him in H.S.F., Vol.XVI, p.184, and his descendants are very uncertain. He may be the John Deas
who was granted 500 acres in the 96th District,
South Carolina, Sept.30,1774, and was the John
Dees shown in Edgefield County, South Carolina
in 1790, with a family consisting of himself,
4 sons born 1774-90, a wife and 2 daughters. By
1800 he was living as "John Deas Sr." in Abbeville District, S.C., which adjoins Edgefield,
with himself and wife born before 1755, a son
and a daughter born 1774-84, a daughter born
1784-90, and a son born 1790-1800. His son,John
Deas Jr., also appears in Abbeville District in
1800, born 1755-74, with 2 females born 1755-74,
1 female born 1784-90, and 5 females born 1790-
1800. The families of two others of John Dees's
(#15) older sons seem to have been living in
Barnwell District, S.C. (another county adjoining

Edgefield) in 1800. Elizabeth Dees, a widow,
born 1774-84, probably widow of an older son,
name unknown, was living in Barnwell District
in 1800 with a large family, probably not all
of them Deeses, 1 male born 1774-84, 2 males
and 2 females born 1784-90, and 3 males born
1790-1800. Another son was probably Abner Deas
shown as born 1755-74, with wife born 1774-84,
and children: 1 male born 1784-90,and 3 females
born 1790-1800. The sons of John Dees #15 were,
then, apparently: 77. John Dees. 78. A son who
died before 1800 and was the husband of Elizabeth Deas of Barnwell County, S.C. 79. Abner
Deas of Barnwell County, in 1800. 80. James
Dease, born 1780-90, who was living in Mobile
County, Alabama in the Census of 1840 near
John Dees #77, with a large family consisting
of himself and wife, born 1780-90, 2 sons and
1 daughter born 1810-20, 2 sons and 2 daughters
born 1820-25, 1 son and 1 daughter born 1825-30
and 4 young children, probably grandchildren, a
girl born 1830-35, and 2 boys and a girl born
1835-40. 81. Joseph Deas, born 1790-1800,living
in Mobile, Alabama in 1850 with 2 sons born
1810-20, his wife perhaps being dead. James G.
Dees #80 corresponds pretty well to the son b.
1774-84 in John Dees #15's family in Abbeville
District, S.C. in 1800, and Joseph Dees #81 to
the son born 1790-1800 in John Dees #15's family
in 1800. The whole of the preceding data are
very uncertain, except that it is certain that
John Dees #15 had a son, John Dees Jr., #77,
who was living in Abbeville District with John
#15 in 1800, with a large family of girls, but
no sons born before 1800.

John Dees #77, son of John Dees #15, was born
before 1770 and seems to have died 1840-50 in
Mobile County, Alabama, a very old man. He may
have wandered off to Louisiana, where the Census
of 1830 shows an aged John Dees, born 1760-70 in
St.Helena Parish, living alone. By 1840 he
seems to have moved to Mobile Co., Ala., and
appears near his probable brothers there,James
G. Dease #80 and Joseph Dease #81, living alone,
born 1760-70. Two of John Dees's sons, both born
after 1800, were perhaps: (1) States G. Deas,

shown in Mobile County, Alabama, in 1840 with a
family consisting of 2 males born 1810-20, 1
female born 1800-10, 1 female born 1810-20, and
1 female born 1835-40; and (2) W.C.Dease,shown
in the same Mobile County Census with a family
consisting of 1 male and 1 female born 1810-20,
and 1 male and 1 female born 1830-35. The Deeses
were numerous in Mobile County, Alabama in 1840,
there being five families in all, but they had
dwindled to the following descendants in 1850:
(1) Cressy Dees born 1775, with three children,
probably her grandchildren, in her family,namely
Rollo Dees, born 1840, Juliana Dees born 1845,
and Jane Dees born 1847; (2) Emeline Dees, a
widow, born 1818, with children, Susan born 1841,
Eleanor born 1844, Hopp born 1847 (all born in
Alabama), and Sarah George, born 1775 in Georgia,
and Isaac George born 1832 in Alabama, in her
family; (3) Caroline Dees, born 1837, shown with
a number of other females in what was probably a
girls school.

****

Descendants of Joel Dees #16 (John, Emanuel)

The family of Joel Dees #16 is treated fairly
fully in H.S.F., Vol.XVI, pp.184-5. Nothing much
can be added to that, except that Joel's claim
to a Revolutionary Pension in Baldwin County,
Alabama, is to some degree given additional sub-
stantiation by the fact that "J.Dees", otherwise
unidentifiable unless he was Joel, saw service
in the Revolution in North Carolina (Revolutionary Accounts at Raleigh, Vol.VIII, p.13, fol.1).
The Census of 1800 shows Joel Dees in Edgefield
County, S.C. with a family consisting of 1 male
and 1 female born 1755-74 (too late for Joel's
real birth, which was in 1749), 1 son and 2 daughters born 1784-90, and 1 son born 1790-1800.
Nothing further is known of the two daughters,
but the two sons were: 82. Joel Dees Jr., and
83. James Dees.

Joel Dees #82, son of Joel Dees #16, was born
in Johnston County, N.C., or Edgefield Co.,S.C.
about 1790, and died apparently 1840-50 in Bald-

win County, Alabama. His wife was Susan Williams born 1793, of Edgefield County, S.C., who also seems to have died prior to 1850. Joel Dees's service in the War of 1812 was in 1813 and 1814 in South Carolina (Folder #271 in the Adjutant-General's Office in Washington). He was living in Baldwin County, Alabama with his father and his brother James in 1830 and 1840. Information about his family comes not only from the records of Edgefield County, S.C., and the Census records in Alabama, but also from a great-granddaughter, Mrs. Floyd John (Opal Beals John) of Arizona,who seems to know a great deal about the family. The ten children of Joel Dees #82 are shown in H.S.F. Vol. XVI, but the following is a fuller account of some of them and their descendants:

82a. Lucinda Dees, born ca 1816 in South Carolina, married a Mr. Calahan.

82b. John Dees, born March 4, 1818 in Edgefield County, S.C., died Nov.30,1885 in Washington County, Alabama (date given by Mrs. John), or Dec.21, 1887 (date given by Mrs. John's mother, Mrs. Mary Frances Dees Beals of Arizona). Descendants will be given later.

82c. William Dees, born 1820, married Eliza Roster, b. 1825. This couple is shown in the 1850 Census for Hancock County, Miss., he being born in Alabama and she in Mississippi, with a son, Jackson Dees born 1837 in Mississippi, and Polly Ann Roster, probably a relative of the wife, born 1840 in Mississippi.

82d. Wiseman Dees, born 1821 in Alabama, m. Emily (born 1828 in Florida), shown with the above birth dates in the 1850 Census of Baldwin County, Alabama, with the following children, all born in Alabama: Edward born 1844, James born 1846, Lewis born 1848, and Ann E. Dees, born 1850.

82e. Ellen Dees, said to have been born ca. 1822 by Mrs. John.

82f. George Dees, born 1828 in Alabama, with wife Ann, born 1830 in Alabama, shown in the Census of Baldwin Co., Ala., of 1860, with two child-

ren, both born in Alabama: George born 1852 and
Catharine born 1854.

82g.   Crecie Dees, born ca 1824 according to
Mrs. John, married George Brown.

82h.   Betsy Dees, married George Harvison.
82i.   Simmie Dees, married Sarah Carpenter.

82j.   Thomas Dees married Martha Burch,
according to a descendant, Mr. Bowen C. Dees of
Washington, D.C., and had the following child-
ren: (1) Susan A. Dees, born 1862; (2) Arrena R.
Dees, born 1865;   (3) Sarah Isabel Dees, born
1867;   (4) Sophronia Ann Dees, born 1870;   (5)
Thomas Jefferson Dees born 1872; (6) John Simeon
Dees, father of Mr. Bowen C. Dees;   (7) Martha
Lazina Dees, born 1877;   (8) Harriet Victoria
Dees, born 1880;   and (9) Joseph Michael Dees,
born 1882.

John Dees #82b above, son of Joel Dees #82,
married (1) Martha Ann Reynolds, who died in
Washington County, Alabama, April 20, 1849. Mrs.
Opal Beals John, who gave information about this
family, was not sure whether this first wife's
name was Coker or Reynolds, but it seems to have
been Reynolds, for John Dees had three children
by his first marriage and they were living in
Washington County, Alabama in the Census of 1850
with Nancy Reynolds (born 1806 in Georgia), probably his mother-in-law, and her children, Sarah
born 1836, Milly J. born 1839, and Martha Reynolds born 1840. By this first marriage, John
Dees had:

1.   Elizabeth Dees, born 1841, married
Richard Weaver.
2.   Lucinda Erettie Dees, born 1844, married
Loud Layton, and died June 23, 1903.
3.   Henry Isom Dees, born Feb.13,1847 at State
Line, Alabama, or Mississippi; his family is
given below.

John Dees #82b. married (2) Jan.4, 1855 in
Washington County, Alabama, Margaret Merchant,
born 1840, died 1903, daughter of James and Hester (East) Merchant. Their children were:

4.   Mary Jane Dees, born 1855, married John Johnson and lived in Florida.

5.   James Thomas Dees, born April 1, 1858 in Santanima Parish, La., married three times and had children, names not given.

6.   John Wesley Dees, born June 12, 1861, died Feb.1926 in Washington Parish, La., married Mrs. Susan (Stuart) Farr, lived at Poplarville, Miss., and had two children: Nellie who married Mr. King, and Brose Dees.

Henry Isom Dees, son of John Dees #82b, was born Feb.13,1847 at State Line, Alabama, and died Nov.13, 1902 at Stafford, Arizona. He was married three times: (1) to Mary Sanford; (2) to Salina Smith; and (3) to Nancy Missouri Calhoun (b. Feb.22, 1847 in Washington Parish, La., d. June 30, 1900 at Pima, Arizona), daughter of Dougal and Mary (Peters) Calhoun. By his first marriage, Henry Isom Dees had children: 1. a daughter who died young; and 2. John Wesley Dees, born 1870, died July 30,1955 at Summerall, Mississippi, married Lola Belle Bryant and had seven children, Bessie, Ida, Thelma, Eunice, Anna, Vardie, and Clyde (the only son) of Hattiesburg, Miss. By his second marriage Henry Isom Dees had: 3. a daughter who died young; and 4. Charles Milton Dees, born 1879, died Sept.1954 in Baxterville, Miss. By his third marriage Henry Isom Dees had:

5.   Albert Alexander Dees, born Sept.3, 1881, d.s.p. Dec.26, 1954.

6.   Alfred Leander Dees, born Sept.3, 1881 (twin of Albert) died unmarried June 30, 1950.

7.   Mary Frances Dees, born June 2, 1883 in Washington Parish, La., married Nov.16,1904 Charles Mitchell Beals, son of John Simpson and Elizabeth Frances (Dyer) Beals. Issue: (1) John Henry Beals, b. Aug.31,1905 at Pima, Arizona, m. Gladys McKinnie; (2) Charles Solon Beals, b. Jan.13,1907, m. Roziel Cluff; (3) Opal Beals, b. Oct.4, 1911, m. Floyd John; (4) Joseph Erving Beals, b. Dec.18, 1915, d. at birth; (5)

Arthur Reeve Beals, b. Oct.2, 1918, m. Zola
Fuller; and (6) Nancy Mildred Beals, b. Jan.5,
1923, m. Laron Waldo DeWitt.

8.   Bessie Dees, born ca. 1885, died young.

9.   Rozeal Preston Dees, born May 26, 1891,m.
Adele Harper and had: (1) Preston Varis Dees;
(2) Veral Naris Dees; (3) Arthilla Dees who m.
a Berg; (4) Darwin Dees, d.y.; (5) Naydall Dees
who m. Mr. Ball; (6) Ludena Dees, who m. Mr.
Carling; and (7) Joanna Rozeal Dees who m. a
Mr. Lovett.

   James Dees #83, son of Joel Dees #16, was
born ca 1792-3 in Edgefield County, S.C. and
died some time after 1850, when he and his family are shown in Baldwin County, Alabama in the
Census, either in Baldwin or in Monroe County,
where his son William was living in 1870. His
wife was Martha Ingram, born 1794 in South Carolina (Census), and died June 7,1867 (from the
family Bible of William Dees, owned by Mrs.H.L.
Dees of Repton, Alabama). Mrs. W.E. Dees of
Evergreen, Alabama, has sent much information
about the family of James Dees #83, including
the family Bible record of his son William,
which includes many other records of his sisters,
brothers, etc., as well as William's own family.
There is a record in the Bible: "J.L.Dees, died
July 7, 1866", which may possibly refer to James
Dees #83, but this is doubtful, as the other records never show James #83 with a middle initial.
Judging by the family Bible and the Census and
other records, the ten children of James Dees
#83 were as follows:

83a. Allen Dees, born 1814 (Census), died June
19,1866 (the William Dees family Bible). The
1850 Census of Baldwin County shows Allen Dees
born in South Carolina, with birth-date as above
and a probable second wife Fanny (born 1833 in
an unknown State), also children: (1) Martha
born 1840, (2) David born 1845, and (3) Virginia
born 1848, all the children born in Alabama.

83b. Perhaps a daughter, who married Joseph
Brady, as the death of Joseph Brady, Dec.25,1850

is recorded in the William Dees Bible. The
Bible also records, without giving the date, the
marriage of Fannie Dees and Jim Brady, but this
Fannie Dees was probably a daughter of William
Dees himself.

83c. Ingram Dees, recorded as dying Nov.13,1850
in the William Dees Bible.

83d. Joel Dees, recorded in the Bible as dying
July 8, 1881. The Clarke County, Alabama "Demo-
crat", Grove Hill, Alabama, under date of July
21, 1881, states: "Joel Dees died at his home
near Monroeville last week". Mrs. W.E.Dees probably refers to Joel Dees #83d when she states
in a letter: "There is a Floyd Dees, son of
James Dees, and James Dees was the son of Joel
Dees". Her letter indicates that she had seen
this Floyd Dees recently, though the letter was
dated some years ago.

83e. Rev.Abner Dees, born 1825 (from the Monroe
County, Alabama Census of 1850, which shows
"Abner Dees, born 1825, Baptist minister", living
in the family of Andrew and Rebecca Lambert).
Abner died Jan.1, 1896 (from the William Dees
family Bible).

83f. Willis Dees, married Mary Brady, Feb.19,
1851 (from the William Dees Bible).

83g. William Dees, born 1829 (Census of 1850)
or 1820 (Census of 1870). Probably 1829 is the
more correct date. His children will be given
later.

83h. Isabella Dees, born 1833 (from the Baldwin County Census of 1850, when she was living
in her father's family), married William Haynes
Feb.19,1851 (from the William Dees Bible).

83i. Richard Dees, born 1836, living in his
father's family in 1850.

83j. Mary Dees, born 1838, also living in her
father's family in 1850.

   <u>William Dees #83g, son of James Dees #83</u>,
was born, probably in 1829, in Alabama, and died
April 27,1898, probably in Monroe County, Alabama, where he appears with his family in the
Census of 1870 (date of death from the family
Bible). He married Sept.15, 1851 Clarissa Watson
(b. Dec.20, 1831, d. July 4, 1882). Their child-
ren, as gathered from the family Bible and the
1870 Census of Monroe Co., Ala., were: (1) J.
Richard Dees, born Oct.1, 1853; (2) John L.Dees
born Oct.11, 1855; (3) Frances M. Dees, born
Dec.12,1858, probably the Fannie Dees who married
Jim Brady (family Bible, with no date of marriage); (4) William J. Dees, born Jan.30,1860, d.
Aug.13, 1931, m. Nettie Wilborn who died May 26,
1936 (family Bible); (5) James T. Dees, born
June 30, 1862, may be the Jim F. Dees who died
Feb.26, 1899 of the family Bible; (6) Mary S.
Dees, born Nov.20, 1864, probably married a Pate
and was the Mamie Dees Pate recorded in the family Bible as dying April 16, 1932; (7) Georgia
Ann Dees, born Feb.27, 1867; (8) Henry L. Dees,
recorded in the family Bible as born Dec.4,1874,
but born 1869 seems to be the correct date, as
shown in the Census of 1870; he married Rowena
Martin and was the father-in-law of Mrs. W.E.
Dees previously referred to; "A.R.Dees, b. June
19, 1874, d. Feb.24, 1928", shown in the family
Bible, was probably this Rowena Martin Dees;
(9) J.I.Dees, born Jan.7,1875.

                    ****

<u>Descendants of Shadrack Dees #17(John, Emanuel)</u>

   The family of Shadrack Dees is dealt with in
H.S.F. XVI, pp.195-6. The Census of 1790 shows
Shadrack (or Shade) in 96th District, S.C.,with
4 sons and 4 daughters. However, the deed of his
heirs in 1816 in Edgefield County, S.C., shows
only 3 sons and 3 daughters, in addition to
Shadrack's widow, Grace. One of the daughters
had obviously died before 1816 and nothing is
known of her. However, the fourth son was probably Benjamin Dees, who in H.S.F.XVI was put
down as a son of Shadrack's brother, Bolling
Dees #18. However, the Census records show that

Bolling was born after 1755, while Benjamin was born 1774 or earlier, so that it looks as though Benjamin was the eldest son of Shadrack Dees, who was older than Bolling and born ca 1751-3. The children of Shadrack Dees #17 were, then: 84. Benjamin Dees. 85. Noah Dees. 86. Shadrack Dees Jr. 87. Daniel Dees. 88. Rebecca Dees, wife of Nehemiah Posey. 89. A daughter, wife of William Holland in 1816.90. Easter or Esther Dees, unmarried in 1816.

Benjamin Dees #84, probably eldest son of Shadrack Dees #17, was probably born ca 1773-4. He was granted land in Edgefield County, S.C. in 1803 and 1804, was deeded land there in 1800, which he deeded away in 1804, and appears in the Census of 1800 in that county with himself born 1755-74, his wife born 1774-84, and 2 daughters born 1790-1800. After this, the family disappears from the records and probably died out or moved away before Shadrack Dees's remaining heirs in Edgefield County deeded away their father's land in 1816.

Noah Dees #85, son of Shadrack Dees #17, was born in North Carolina, probably ca 1775-6, and died in Bibb County, Georgia about 1834. The Census of 1820 shows him still in Edgefield Co. with a family consisting of himself and wife, born 1775-94, 1 son and 2 daughters b. 1804-10, and 1 son and 5 daughters born 1810-20. He moved to Georgia some time in the 1820's and had died in Bibb County, Georgia prior to Sept.29,1834, on which date P.P.Atwell was appointed guardian to Missouri Ann, Jane, Martin, Marshall and Ann Dees, orphans of Noah Dees, decd. (Bibb County Minute Book 2, p.28). The name of Noah Dees's wife is unknown, but he seems to have had the following children:

85a. Benjamin Dees, b. 1799 (Census) in South Carolina, seems to have been the eldest son of Noah Dees. Benjamin's uncle-in-law, Nehemiah Posey, husband of his aunt Rebecca Dees #88, moved to Pulaski County, Georgia,prior to 1820, and Benjamin seems to have accompanied him there, and appears in the 1820 Census of Pulaski Co. with himself, b. 1794-1804, a wife b. 1804-

1810, and a son born 1810-20. He appears in
the Census of Dooly County, Georgia, of 1830,
having moved there with his numerous rather dis-
tant Dees relatives from Pulaski County. By
1850 he was living in Sumter County, Georgia,
where the Census shows him with birth date as
given above, wife Nancy born 1800 in South Carolina, and children, all born in Georgia:
(1) James R. Dees, born 1829; (2) Martha H.Dees,
b.1827; (3) Milbra H. Dees (female) b.1836;
(4) Miranda Dees, b.1838; and (5) Benjamin F.
Dees, b. 1842.

85b.   Labron Dees, born 1802 in South Carolina, was almost certainly the second son of
Noah Dees #85, as he named his first son Noah
Posey Dees, obviously for his father and his
uncle-in-law, Nehemiah Posey. He may have accompanied his uncle and his brother Benjamin to
Pulaski County as early as 1820. However, he
does not show up there until 1827, when he was
appointed Second-Lieutenant in the 350th District of Pulaski Militia;   and he was still living in Pulaski in the Cherokee Land Lottery,
1832-35, in which he drew land. Labron Dees m.
(1) Nov.23, 1834 Mary Bellflower in Houston Co.,
Ga., which adjoins Pulaski, and by her had one
child, Georgia Caroline Dees, b. 1835, d.1840.
He married (2) in Houston County, Aug.24,1837
Jane Wall (born April 16,1818 in Twiggs Co.,Ga.)
probably a daughter of King D. Wall of Twiggs
Co., Ga. who was the son of Henry Wall, a Revolutionary veteran from Orangeburgh District,
S.C., who drew land in Twiggs County, Georgia,
at a very early date.   Labron Dees moved from
Pulaski Co. to Randolph Co., Ga., where he died
about 1847.   His widow, Jane (Wall) Dees, married
Richard Jacobs in 1856 in Randolph County, Ga.,
and the Jacobses had three children:Mary Jane,
Alonzo, and John Jacobs. The family finally
moved to Louisiana, where Jane (Wall) Jacobs
died May 10, 1911. The children of Labron Dees
and Jane Wall were: (1) Noah Posey Dees, b.
Jan.6,1841, whose descendants will be given
below; and (2) John William Harrison Dees, b.
1846, d. June 19,1875 in Texas.

Noah Posey Dees, son of Labron Dees #85b. was born in Georgia, Jan.6, 1841, and died April 6, 1900 at Eagle Creek, Arizona.His first wife was Marium Watson, nee Glenn, who was born ca 1845 and died in Texas about 1873. By her he had 5 children: 1. Theodosia Dees, b. June 9,1866, d. Nov.7, 1922, m. John R. Ransome. 2. Alva Roe Dees, b. March 3,1869, d. Nov.7, 1922, m. Alice M. Watley. 3. Labron Dees. 4. Watson Dees. 5. Robert Harrison Dees.

Noah Posey's second wife was Margaret Ann Short, b. March 25, 1858 in Texas, d. Dec.5,1940 in Arizona, by whom he had the following children:

6. James Gibson Dees, b.June 20, 1877 in Texas, d. Dec.4, 1902 in Stafford, Arizona.

7. Auti Franklin Dees, born Dec.7,1880, died Sept.28,1942 in Phoenix, Arizona, m. Hilda Karchner and had issue: (1) Melba b. June 4,1907; (2) James Henry, b. June 26, 1909, d.Aug.1909; (3) Alvin Franklin, b. Dec.12, 1910, d.1912;(4) Mary b. April 19, 1913; (5) Oscar Culver, b. July 10, 1917; (6) Veral Fay, b. Nov.17,1922; and (7) Floyd b. July 11, 1930.

8. William Henry Arthur Dees, b. Sept.17,1884, m. (1) Laura Alma Parry, and (2) Ruby Dees, widow of Noah Posey Dees Jr.

9. Noah Posey Dees Jr., b. April 18, 1891, d. March 4, 1949 in Oregon, m. Ruby L. Lee.

10. John Thomas Dees, b. Dec.9, 1895 in Texas, d. Aug.10, 1950 at Duncan, Arizona, m. Hallie Elizabeth Craig and had issue: (1) Willis Reid Dees, b. Nov.12, 1918, m. Jean Rebecca Hall Robinson and had children: Margaret, Brian, Russell, John and Quenton; (2) Harry Craig Dees,b. Dec.5, 1921, m. Donna Myrtle Bean (b.April 13, 1926), and had children: Harry Craig and Deanna; Harry Craig Dees has been much interested in the Dees genealogy and gathered much of the information in this chapter; (3) Thomas Edwin Dees,b. Aug.3, 1932, m. Peggy Lucile Hill, and had issue Deborah Lynn and Carol Ann.

11. Leonard Benjamin Dees, b. Jan.2,1898, m. Edna Perry and had Noah Raymond, b.1920, Maburn

Perry, b. 1922, and a baby girl b. and d. 1923.

85c.   Grace Dees who married Samuel Slate Dec.29,1822 in Edgefield County, S.C., was probably the eldest daughter of Noah Dees #85.

85d.   Thomas Dees, a very fat man when mature, remembered as a brother of Labron Dees #85b. by his descendants.

85e.   James Dees, another brother of Labron remembered by his descendants, thought to have died unmarried near Carson City, Nevada.

85f.   Martha Dees, who married Jeremiah Hammock, March 27,1830 in Bibb County, Georgia, was probably another of Noah Dees's children.

The following were the orphans of Noah Dees #85, mentioned in Bibb County, Ga., in 1834:

85g.   Missouri Ann Dees, no further information.
85h.   Jane Dees, probably identical with a Jane S. Dees who married John Romaggi, July 24, 1842, in Bibb County, Georgia.

85i.   Martin Dees, perhaps identical with a Martin Dees, b. 1820 in South Carolina, in the Census of 1860 for Sebastian County, Arkansas, which shows him with wife Catherina, b.1823 in New York, and children: (1) Adolphus Dees, b. 1847 in Missouri; (2) Susannah Dees, b. 1850 in Missouri; (3) Martin Dees, b. 1853 in Arkansas; and (4) Josephine Dees, b. 1856 in Arkansas.

85j.   Marshall (or John Marshall) Dees, son of Noah Dees #85, seems to have been the grandfather of Dr.J.H.Dees of Vidalia, Ga., who wrote years ago that his father was named John Martin Dees, his grandfather was John Marshall Dees, and his great-grandfather was Noah Dees. Marshall Dees died July 8, 1868 (from his tombstone in Toombs Co., Ga. Cemetery). Other members of Marshall Dees's family, buried in the same cemetery, seem to have been: (1) Anaida Dees, b.Jan. 27,1855, d. March 8, 1926, wife of Elias Croseley;   (2) J.E.Dees, b. Feb.2, 1869, d. Nov.7,

1928; (3) J. Preston Dees, b.1865, d.1935; (4)
John Jackson Dees, b. May 1,1875, d.Nov.2,1882.

85k. Ann Dees, orphan of Noah Dees #85 in
1834, no further information.

Shadrack Dees #86, son of Shadrack Dees #17,
was born in South Carolina in 1782 (Census) and
died, probably in Henry County, Alabama, after
1856. His wife was named Celia (Cealy) and she
was born in South Carolina in 1790 (Henry Co.
Census of 1850). Shadrack Dees is shown still
living in Edgefield Co., S.C. in the Census of
1820 with a family consisting of himself and
wife, born 1775-94, a female born 1794-1804
(hardly a daughter if Shadrack's wife was not
born until 1790), and 2 sons and a daughter b.
1810-20. The family had moved to Henry County,
Alabama, by 1840, where it is shown in the
Census of that year. They were still living
there in 1850, when the Census shows Shadrack
and wife Cealy, with birth-dates as given above,
a daughter Easter or Esther Dees, b.1814 in S.C.
and a son Square Dees b.1817 in S.C., also Joel
Dees b.1834 in Alabama, who was a son of Esther
Dees. Esther gave her consent March 30, 1854
to the marriage of her son Joel to Clarka Holl-
and, and the couple were married the same day
(Henry County Marriage Book, 1822-58, p.162).
Esther Dees herself married Lewis Graves Jan.6,
1856 "at the residence of S.Deese" in Henry Co.,
Alabama (same marriage book, p.208). Shadrack's
son, Square Dees, married Lavinia Kirkland in
Henry County April 13,1852 (ibid, p.86). A dau-
ghter Emily married Shadrack Quattlebaum.

Daniel Dees #87, son of Shadrack Dees #17,was
born in South Carolina in 1789 (Census) and died
after 1860, probably in Choctaw Co., Alabama.His
wife was Polly (Mary), born 1795 in S.C.(Census).
Judging by the Census records, Daniel Dees #87
had a large family. In 1820 he is shown in
Edgefield Co., S.C. along with his brothers Noah
and Shadrack, with a family consisting of himself and wife b.1794-1804 (obviously inaccurate
as to Daniel's birth-date), 1 son b.1804-10, and
1 son and 1 daughter b. 1810-20. By 1830 he had
moved to Pulaski Co., Ga., where so many other

Deeses moved. The Census of 1830 in that County shows him and his wife as born 1780-90 (the right birth-date for him, apparently, but not for his wife), 1 son and 1 daughter b.1815-20, 2 sons and 1 daughter b. 1820-25, and 1 son b.1825-30. By 1840 he had moved to Henry County, Alabama (again where so many other Deeses had settled), where the Census shows him with some of the older children in his family, but additional ones born after 1830, 1 son and 1 daughter b. 1830-35, and 1 daughter b. 1835-40. The records of Henry Co., Ala., indicate that the family was still living there around 1850, but Daniel is not shown in the Census of 1850 there, and possibly moved in that year to Choctaw Co., Ala., with his youngest son Wiley, where both are shown in the Census of 1860, Daniel and his wife Polly with the birth-dates given previously, and an unmarried daughter, Zilpha Dees b. 1825 in Georgia, in their family. The records show the following as probably or certainly children of Daniel Dees #87:

87a. Chesley Dees, probably, who was granted land in 1855 in Henry Co., Ala., but nothing further is known of him.

87b. Nancy Dees, b. 1821, married William Renfroe in Henry Co., Ala., Sept.26,1841 (Marriage Book 1822-68, p.44). The Census of Dale County, Alabama of 1850 shows William E. Renfroe b. 1816 in Georgia, wife Nancy b. 1821 in S.C., and the following children, all born in Ala.: Reuben Renfroe b. 1842; Jefferson Renfroe b. 1843; Elizabeth Renfroe b. 1845; Joseph Renfroe b.1846; and Tabitha Renfroe b.1847.

87c. Zilpha Dees, b. 1825, unmarried in 1860.

87d. Shadrack Dees, b. 1831 in Georgia,shown in the 1860 Census of Henry Co., Ala. with birth date above, wife Margaret b. 1835, and children, all born in Alabama: Wiley Dees b. 1853; Catherine Dees b. 1855; Haseltine Dees b. 1857; and Cilla Jane Dees, b. 1859-60 (7 months old).

87e. Amanda Dees, b. 1834, married Washington Love in Henry Co., Ala., April 26,1850. This

couple was living in Henry County in 1850 with
no children, Washington Love being b. 1829 and
Amanda with birth-date as above.

87f. Clarky Dees, m. Calvin Whitehead, Jan.
4,1852 (Henry Co. Marriage Book, p.83).

87g. William Wiley Dees, b. 1836 in Alabama,
m. Elva Whitehead in Henry Co., Ala., Feb.1,
1855, with consent of William Whitehead for his
daughter to marry William Wiley Dees, and consent of Daniel Dees, father of Wiley, for the
marriage (Henry Co. Marriage Book, p.187). Wiley
Dees is shown near his father in 1860 in Choctaw
County, Ala., with wife Elvey, b.1837, and children: Zachariah b. 1856 and Margaret A.M. b.1857,
all b. in Alabama.

****

Descendants of Bolling Dees #18 (John,Emanuel)

Practically all that is known of Bolling Dees
#18 is shown in the paragraph on him in H.S.F.
Vol. XVI, p.186. Benjamin Dees, assigned to him
as a son in Vol.XVI, was probably too old to
have been his son, as he was born in 1774 or
earlier, and the Census records show that Bolling was born 1760-65. It was indicated in the
preceding section that Benjamin was probably the
eldest son of Bolling's elder brother, Shadrack
Dees #17. Bolling Dees is shown in deeds in
Edgefield County, S.C. from 1795-1801. A deed in
1795 calls him Bolling Dees Sr., indicating a
son Bolling Jr. The Census of 1800 in Edgefield
County shows him with 2 sons b. 1774-84 and 1
daughter b. 1784-90; that of 1810 shows in addition a son b. 1794-1800 and another son b. 1800-
1810. Bolling was apparently living in the adjoining county of Barnwell in 1817, when he
deeded away land in that county, and had moved
to Jackson Co., Ga. by 1830, when the Census
shows him with an additional son and daughter,
b. 1810-15. The Census of 1810 shows him as born
before 1765, that of 1830 as born after 1760,
so that his birth-date was apparently 1760-65.

In addition to Bolling Dees Jr., indicated in
the 1795 deed, Bryant Dees of Jackson County,
Georgia, who drew land in the 1827 Land Lottery
and Daniel R. Dees of Jackson Co., Ga., who
drew land in the Cherokee Land Lottery of 1832-
1835, were probably other sons. Nothing further
has yet been discovered about Bolling Dees's
descendants after these records. Thus Bolling
Dees's sons were: 91. Bolling Dees. 92. Bryant
Dees. 93. Daniel Dees.

****

Descendants of Arthur Dees #19 (James, Emanuel)

Arthur Dees #19 was born ca 1741-42 and died
in Marion Co., S.C., probably ca 1819-20, at an
advanced age. His family is dealt with in HSF
Vol.XVI, pp.187-8.
Arthur Dees is shown in the 1790 Census of
Robeson Co., N.C. with 4 males born before 1774,
1 male born 1774-90, 4 females and 2 slaves.
This indicates three sons born before 1774, and
one son born after 1774. The three sons born
prior to 1774 were (probably) Arthur Dees Jr.
(called Matty Dees Jr. in the Census of 1800 in
Marion Co., S.C.), and certainly Malachi Dees
(born before 1765, Census of 1850), and Levi
Dees (born 1768, Census of 1850). The younger
son was Abraham Dees, born before 1780 (Census).
By 1800 Arthur Dees #19 had moved to Marion Co.,
S.C., and he and his wife are shown in that year
in the Census, living alone, and born before
1755. Strange to say, he is not shown in the
Census of 1810, but before that time his first
wife, name unknown, had died, and he had married
a second wife, Anne, as shown by extant records.
These show that Arthur was still living in 1818,
but he had apparently died by 1820, when the
Census shows the widow, Anne Dees, with her 3
children.
In 1811 Mark Turner deeded land to Arthur
Dees himself, which Arthur a few days later
deeded away. The will of Arthur Dees #19, dated
March 21,1817, was not probated until June 23,
1829, in Marion County, though as mentioned,
Arthur himself seems to have died before 1820.

The will mentions his wife, Susannah Dees (other records call her simply Ann); sons Malachi, Abraham, and Levi Dees; daughters Selety Turner, Mary Lowry, and Sarah Garrett (these 3 sons and 3 daughters being issue of his first marriage obviously); grandson Archibald Dees (he was probably son of the deceased son Matty Dees Jr., of the 1800 Census); and "my three young children", Susannah, Charity, and Curtis Dees, residuary legatees and to be schooled (these were obviously children of the second marriage). On Aug.20, 1821 Susannah Dees, eldest of the three children, had married Thomas Melton, for on this date Thomas Melton and Susannah his wife "for parental affection" (supposedly meaning filial affection) made a gift to Anne Dees during her lifetime of the land conveyed by Mark Turner to Susannah Dees. The Census records of Marion County are somewhat confusing regarding Anne or Susannah Dees, widow of Arthur. The 1820 Census shows: (1) Susannah Dees, born before 1775, with 1 female b. 1775-94, 1 female b. 1804-10, 1 male and 1 female b. 1810-20; and an Ann Dees with 2 females born before 1775, 2 females born 1804-10, and 1 male born 1810-20. The 1830 Census shows two Ann Deeses, one born 1780-90 with a daughter born 1815-20, the other born 1790-1800 with a son born 1815-20. The 1840 Census shows a Nancy Dees born 1770-80, with 1 female born 1810-20, and a male (presumably a grandson) born 1835-40. One of these Anns, Nancys or Susannahs was the widow of Arthur Dees #19, the other is uncertain. The above records show that Arthur #19 had ten children, seven by his first marriage and three by his second, as follows:

94. Arthur or "Matty" Dees, Jr.
95. Malachi Dees.
96. Levi Dees.
97. Abraham Dees.
98. Seleta Dees, m. a Turner.
99. Mary Dees, married a Lowry.
100. Sarah Dees, married a Garrett.

All the above were children by the first wife and the following by the second wife, Anne:

101. Susannah Dees, b. probably ca 1804, married to Thomas Melton by 1821.
102. Charity Dees.

103. Curtis Dees, shown in the Census of 1850
      in Marion County as born in 1818, but
      this is obviously too late for his birth
      as he is mentioned in his father's will
      in 1817, and was probably born at least
      as early as 1815-17. Curtis Dees was
      married to a wife Jemima, b.1810, in the
      Census of 1850, but no children are
      shown.

   Nothing further is known of the above children except the first four sons, #94-#97. The
posterity of the family of Arthur Dees #19 is
very confusing, too, as Arthur's younger brothers, John #25 and Moses #26, seem to have
moved finally to Marion Co., S.C., and the later
Census records are somewhat ambiguous.

   <u>Arthur Dees Jr., #94, probably the eldest
son of Arthur Dees #19</u>, was probably born ca
1762-3 in Anson County, N.C., and seems to have
died prior to 1810 in Marion Co., S.C. He appears only once, in the 1800 Census of Marion
Co., S.C. as "Matty Dees,Jr.", with a family
consisting of himself and wife, born 1755-74,
2 sons and 2 daughters born 1784-90, and 1
son born 1790-1800. His wife was perhaps an
Isabella Dees, b. 1760-70, who appears in the
Census returns of Marion Co., S.C., in 1830 and
1840. The Census of 1830 shows her with a son
and a daughter born 1800-1810, a son born 1815-
1820, and a female born 1820-25, perhaps a
granddaughter. The year 1840 shows her still
as born 1760-70, with a female born 1810-20, a
female born 1820-25, a male born 1825-30, and a
female born 1830-35.
   Arthur or "Matty" Dees Jr. was almost certainly the father of Archibald Dees, the grandson mentioned in the will of Arthur Dees #19,
who was born in 1790 (Census). Other sons were
perhaps Rayford Dees, b.1785 (though Rayford
could have been a son of Arthur #94's brother,
Malachi Dees #95), and probably of Levi born
1797 and of Wiley born 1803, both appearing in
Marion Co., S.C. in the Census of 1850 near
Archibald Dees. What is known of these four
men is as follows:

Rayford Dees #94a, perhaps a son of Arthur Dees #94, was born 1785 in North Carolina, in either Anson or Robeson County probably (Census of 1850), and died after 1850 in Marion County, S.C. The Census of 1810 shows him in Marion County with himself and wife, born 1784-94, and a daughter born before 1810. The year 1820 shows him still in the same county, himself and wife born 1775-94, a male born 1794-1804 (perhaps his brother Wiley, b.1803), 3 sons and 1 daughter born 1810-20. The Census returns of 1830 and 1840 show Rayford Dees in the adjoining county of Darlington, S.C. The Census of 1830 shows him as born 1780-90 and married to a new wife, born 1800-10, along with a son and a daughter born 1810-15 (probably by the first marriage), a son and a daughter born 1820-25, and a son and a daughter born 1825-30. The Census of 1840 shows him as born 1770-80 (too early) with some of the same children as shown in 1830, and two additional daughters born 1830-35, and two more born 1835-40. By 1850 Rayford Dees had returned to Marion County, S.C., and the Census of that year shows him as born in North Carolina in 1785, with his second wife Isabella born 1806 in North Carolina, and his younger children, Ann b.1830, Eliza b. 1832, Margaret b. 1835, Salina b. 1838, Barzilla b.1841, Robert b. 1842, and Harrington Dees b. 1824, an older son. Nothing further is known at present of these children. One of Rayford Dees's elder sons was probably Emanuel Dees b. 1814 in South Carolina, who was living in Pike County, Alabama, in the Census of 1880, and whose sons were born in Marion County, S.C. Emanuel Dees was probably the son of Rayford Dees, born 1810-15, shown in the Census of 1830 above.

Emanuel Dees, probably the son of Rayford Dees #94a, is shown in 1880 in Pike Co., Ala., as born 1814 in South Carolina, living with his wife Elizabeth (born 1830, obviously a second wife), and no children in his family at that time. His sons seem to have been as follows:

1. Benjamin N. Dees, who married Fanny Blackman Dec.13,1869 in Pike County, Alabama. In spite of the variation in the initials, this Benjamin N. Dees would seem to be identical with

a "D.B.Dees", born 1840, shown in 1880 on the same page as Eli and John Deese in Pike County, Alabama, with wife Fanny born 1845, and children Abie b.1870, Charles b. 1872, Gus b.1878, and an unnamed male b. 1880 (two months old).

2.   John C. Deese of Shellham, Alabama, born Oct.6,1842 in Marion District, S.C., was a Confederate soldier who enlisted in 1861 at Troy, Alabama, and served throughout the war (from "Confederate Soldiers Resident in Alabama, 1907", now at Montgomery). He seems to be the John O. Deese, born 1842, shown in the Pike County, Ala. Census of 1880, with wife Martha b. 1844, and children, Nettie b.1866, Gerona b.1871, Emanuel b. 1874, Delula (Talulah?) b.1876, and Timothy Deese b.1879.

3.   Eli Deese of Brundage, Alabama, enlisted in the Confederate Army in 1862 at Montgomery, Ala., was born June 10,1844 in Marion District, S.C., and served throughout the war (from the above 1907 list of Confederate soldiers living in Alabama,at Mongomery). Eli Deese was living in Pike County, Ala., aged   35, in the Census of 1880. He married Malinda M. Rogers Jan.23,1869 in Pike County, and the Census of 1880 shows her as born 1850, and hers and Eli's children as Emanuel, b.1870, Fanny b. 1872, Lizzie b.1874, Emma b.1876, and an unnamed female b.1879-80 (7 months old).

A younger brother of Emanuel Dees and another son of Rayford Dees was probably James W.Deese of Pike County, born 1830 (Census), who married probably as his second wife, Elizabeth Davis, April 30,1858 in Pike County. She seems to have died prior to the Census of 1880, which shows James W.Dees, b.1830, with children in his family, Cassandra b. 1855, Franklin b.1857, William b. 1859, Emma b. 1869, Mamie b. 1872, and Sugar (f.) b. 1877. Another daughter of James W. Dees was probably Ann Dees, b.1854, living alone in 1880 on the same page as James W. Dees.

Archibald Dees #94b, son of Arthur Dees #94, born 1790, was living alone in the Marion Co. Census of 1850 right next to his brother Wiley Dees #94d. It is uncertain whether he was ever

married. He was given in the Census of 1820 as
head of a family consisting of 2 males b.1794-
1804 (the second male being probably his brother Wiley), 1 female b.1794-1804 who may have
been his wife, a female born 1804-10 (perhaps
a sister), and a male and a female born 1810-20,
who could possibly have been his children. He
does not appear in the Census of 1830, and the
Census of 1840 is very perplexing, showing Archibald Dees born 1800-10 (much too young) and a
female b.1810-20. It is barely possible that
this 1840 record shows a son, Archibald Jr., b.
ca 1810 with his wife or sister.

Levi Dees #94c, son of Arthur Dees #94, born
1797, is shown in the Marion County Censuses
with his family in 1830 and 1840, and 1850
shows him with the above birth-date, not far
from Archibald Dees #94b and Wiley Dees #94d,
with the following children, his wife apparently
being dead: Mary b.1827; Jane b.1829; Simon b.
1833; Eunice b. 1836; James b.1838; Ann b. 1840;
George b. 1842; and Elizabeth b. 1847.

Wiley Dees #94d, son of Arthur Dees #94, born
1803, is shown in the 1850 Census of Marion Co.,
S.C., next to Archibald Dees #94b, with wife
Jane (b.1810) and the following children: James
b. 1838; Alexander b. 1847; and Sarah b. 1849.

Malachi Dees #95, son of Arthur Dees #19, was
probably born ca 1763-4 (he and his first wife
both being shown in the Marion County Census of
1810 as born before 1765). The wife seems to
have died before 1820, for in that year Malachi
Dees is shown only with his two youngest children, and so continues in the 1830 Census. The
year 1830 shows him as much too old, b. 1750-60.
The Census returns of Marion County, 1800-1830,
show him with 2 sons and a daughter, born 1784-
90, a daughter born 1794-1800, and in 1820 and
1830 a daughter born 1810-15 and a son born
1815-20 (perhaps by a second marriage). One of
the sons born 1784-90 could have been Rayford
Dees #94a, whom we have put down as a son of
Malachi's brother, Arthur Dees #94. Malachi
died in Marion County in 1833, his will, dated

Jan.21,1832 and probated Feb.25,1833 (W.Bk.1, p.232), leaving all his property to his son Malachi Dees Jr., probably the youngest son, born 1815-20. Nothing further is known of Malachi Dees #95's descendants.

Levi Dees #96, son of Arthur Dees #19, was born in 1768 and died after 1850, probably in Baker County, Georgia, where he was living in 1850. His wife was named Nancy (b.1772 in North Carolina), and she was still living in 1850. Levi Dees #96 did not live in Marion Co., S.C. but in the adjoining county of Robeson, N.C., where he is shown in the Census returns of 1800, 1810, and 1830 with varying ages, but all after 1770, and too young for his actual age. The Census of 1800 shows him with only 2 daughters, b. 1790-1800. The Census of 1810 shows in addition 1 son and 3 daughters, b.1800-1810 (also 2 males b. 1794-1800, who must have been other relatives of the family). The year 1830 shows in addition 2 sons and a daughter b. 1810-15, 3 daughters b. 1815-20; and younger children: 1 male b. 1820-25, 1 male and 2 females b. 1825-30, who may have been grandchildren, as they would have been born when Nancy Dees was 50 or more. In addition, the Robeson County Census of 1830 shows the son David Dees, just married. Levi Dees and his wife Nancy deeded land in Marion Co., S.C. in 1834, and he made another deed there in 1839. He must have moved soon after this to Baker County, Georgia, where the Census of 1850 shows him and wife Nancy living alone, with the birth-dates given above, along with his sons David, William and Moses.

David Dees #96a, son of Levi Dees #96,was b. in Robeson County, N.C. in 1804, married his wife Nancy (b.1816 in N.C.) about 1830, and was living in Baker Co., Ga. in 1850 with the following children: Henry, born 1832 in North Carolina, though the rest of the children were born in Georgia, indicating that their father moved to Georgia 1833-35; Mary Ann, b. 1836; Nathan, b. 1839; Sarah b. 1844; Appy, b. 1846 (male); and Jemima, b. 1849.

William Dees #96b, son of Levi Dees #96,was
born 1811 (Census of 1850) or 1810 (Census of
1860). He and his wife Susannah (b.1816,Census
of 1850) or 1818 (Census of 1860) were living
in Baker County, Georgia in 1850 near his father,
and in Miller County, Ga., in 1860 near his
brother Moses. Both were born in North Carolina
and apparently had no children, at least as far
as the Censuses show.

Moses Dees #96c, son of Levi Dees #96, is
shown in Early County, Ga., in 1840 (Census),
but was in Baker County, Ga., in the Census of
1850, and in Miller County, Ga., in the Census
of 1860. The Census of 1850 shows both him and
his wife Mary Ann as born 1814 in North Carolina; that of 1860 shows him as born 1813 and
his wife as born 1819. Their children, as shown
by the Censuses of 1850 and 1860 were: Monroe
b.1839; John b. 1840 or 1841; Elizabeth b. 1842
or 1843; Washington b. 1844 or 1845; William b.
1847; Lucinda b. 1849; Sarah b. 1851; Abner b.
1853; E. Dees (male) b. 1854; and Moses b.1856.

The following families from Lee County, Ga.,
not far from Baker County,in the Census of 1850
may have been descendants of Levi Dees (#96):

1. Dicey Dees, b. 1811 in North Carolina, Tim-
    othy Dees b. 1832 in Georgia, and Frances
    Dees b. 1829 in Florida.
2. Thomas H. Dees, b. 1829 in Florida, Jane
    Dees b.1825 in N.C., and Sarah Dees b.1849
    in Georgia (11 months old).
3. Cornelius Dees, b.1829 in N.C., Sarah Dees
    b. 1831 in Georgia, William B. Dees b.1849
    in Georgia, and David H. Dees b. 1833 in
    North Carolina.

Martin Dees, shown in Appling County, Georgia
in 1830 with a family consisting of 1 male and 1
female b. 1800-1810, 1 daughter b. 1820-25, 2
sons and a daughter b. 1825-30, may have been a
son of Levi Dees #96. Another son may have been
James Dees, b.1810 in North Carolina, shown in
Webster County, Ga. in 1850 with wife Saleda b.
1810 in North Carolina, and children: Atha Dees
(female, b.1843,) Saleda Dees b. 1845, Greenwood

Dees b. 1842, and Dret (Duet?) Dees b.1849, all
the children being born in Georgia.

Abraham Dees #97, son of Arthur Dees #19,was
still living when his father wrote his will in
1817, but strange to say, appears only once, in
the Census of Marion County, 1810. This shows
him with a family consisting of himself and wife
born 1765-84, and 2 sons born 1800-1810. Nothing
further is known of him.

DEESES in DARLINGTON and MARLBORO Counties,S.C.

The following families, shown in Darlington
and Marlboro Counties, S.C., which were adjacent
to Marion County, are uncertain, but may have
been connected with the families of Arthur Dees
#19 or his younger brother, Moses Dees #26 (of
whom later):

1.   The Darlington Co. Census of 1840 shows
Catherine Dees, 1 female born 1780-90, and 1
female born 1825-30.

2.   The same Darlington County Census of 1840
shows Nancy Dees, 1 female b. 1810-20, with a
son born 1830-35, and a son and a daughter born
1835-40.

3.   The Marlboro County Census of 1820 shows
Warren Dees, b. 1794-1804, with wife b.1804-10,
and a son and a daughter b. 1810-20. A Warren
Dees was granted land in Dale County, Alabama
in 1840, which may be the same man.

4.   The Marlboro County Census of 1830 shows
Jenny Dees, b. 1780-90, with 1 daughter b. 1800-
1810, 1 daughter b. 1820-25, and 2 daughters b.
1825-30.

5.   Henry Dees, b. 1800 in South Carolina, with
wife Catherine b.1799, is shown in Marlboro Co.,
S.C. in the Censuses of 1830, 1840, and 1850.
The 1830 Census shows him with a son b. 1820-25
and a daughter b. 1825-30. The 1840 Census shows
him with additional children, a son and three
daughters b. 1835-40. The 1850 Census shows him

and his wife Catherine, with birth-dates given above, and children: Nathan b.1832 and Drucilla b. 1834. In this Census a young widow, Minty Dees b. 1824, with son James W. Dees b. 1848,is shown, and she may have been the widow of Henry Dees's son, shown in the 1830 Census as born 1820-25. Other young Dees females shown in the Marlboro County Census of 1850, all in families named Smith, may have been connected with Henry Dees: (a) Jane Dees, b. 1836, in the family of Edward and Elizabeth Smith; (b) Lucy Dees b. 1843, in the family of David and Sarah Smith; and (c) Mary Dees, b. 1846, in the family of Elizabeth Smith.

6.   The 1860 Census of Darlington County, S.C. shows the following, who may or may not have been connected with Henry Dees above: (a) Catherine Dees, b.1805, Dorcas Dees, b.1832, and Elmira Dees b. 1856; and (b) John Dees b.1829, with wife Eliza b. 1823.

****

Descendants of Benjamin Dees #20 (James,Emanuel)

The family of Benjamin Dees #20 is shown in H.S.F. Vol.XVI, pp.188-9. Payment for his Revolutionary services is found in the North Carolina Revolutionary Accounts at Raleigh, Vol.IX, p.98, folio 2, and Canceled Voucher #1607. These show that he was living in Richmond County, N.C. and the payment was from the Lower Board of the Salisbury District. The 1790 Census of Richmond County, N.C. shows Benjamin Dees and wife, with 2 sons born before 1774, 4 sons born 1774-90, and 3 daughters. The 2 sons born before 1774 were probably George and Benjamin Dees Jr., for George was married by 1800 (Chesterfield Co., S.C. Census), and Benjamin Jr. had 2 daughters born in the 1790's apparently. The 4 sons born 1774-90 were Roderick, Willoughby and Gaddy Dees and perhaps Silas Dees, for whom letters were listed at the Claiborne, Alabama, Post Office, along with Roderick, George and Benjamin and Willoughby Dees, Dec.31, 1818, after the family had moved to Alabama (Territorial Papers of the United States, Vol.18, p.538). This Silas Dees must have died before his father, for he is not listed among Benjamin Dees's heirs in 1821. The Census of 1810 in Chesterfield County,S.C.lists Benjamin Dees #20 with an additional son, born 1790-1800, and the Census of 1810 in the same county shows that this son was born before 1794. This youngest son was Zion Dees, who did not marry until 1819. The three daughters of Benjamin Dees were Hannah Dees, b.1774, who married William Cassity and died in Mississippi in 1858; Dorcas Dees who married a MacDonald and shared Benjamin Dees's estate; and probably a Jane Dees, remembered by Mrs. Eugenia C. Hurlbutt of Terry, Mississippi as having been mentioned by her grandmother, Hannah Cassity, as a sister. Benjamin Dees's whole family, after living in Chesterfield County, S.C. until the Census of 1810, moved in the same year (or at least some of them did, and were soon followed by the others) to the Territory of Mississippi, but the vicinity in which they settled became, a few years later, Clarke County,Alabama. The first to go were the sons George and Gaddy Dees, who on Dec.31, 1810 were granted passports to go through the State of Georgia, both from Chesterfield County,S.C. At the time, George had a wife, 3 children and 10 slaves. Gaddy had a wife and 2 children. The son George Dees and the son-in-law William Cassity signed a petition of the inhabitants of Mississippi Territory, Dec.30,1812, and George signed a petition of the inhabitants east of the Pearl River, Dec.14, 1815 (Territorial Papers of the U.S., pp.569 and 601). The 1816 Territorial Census of Clarke County, Alabama, shows Benjamin Dees Sr. with 2 males over 21 and 2 females over 21; Benjamin Dees Jr. with 1 male and 1 female over 21, 1 male and 1 female under 21; and George Dees with 1 male and 1 female over 21, 1 male and 2 females under 21. Benjamin Dees #20 died in Clarke County, Alabama in 1821, and the account and settlement of his estate by George Dees, the administrator, beginning Nov.26,1821, shows the wife, Nancy Dees (whose maiden name, according to her daughter, Hannah Cassity, was Stout),and all the children, except the two deceased, Silas and Jane Dees. The complete list of the children

from all the records is: 104. George Dees. 105.
Benjamin Dees Jr., b. 1770-73. 106. Hannah Dees
b. 1774, m. William Cassity. 107. Dorcas Dees
m. a MacDonald. 108. Roderick Dees. 109. Willoughby Dees. 110. Gaddy Dees. 111. Jane Dees,
who died before her father (apparently unmarried).
112. Silas Dees, who also predeceased his father.
113. Zion Dees, b. 1790-94.

George Dees #104, son of Benjamin Dees #20,
seems to have been the second son, b. ca 1772,
as his brother Benjamin Dees Jr. is recorded as
born 1760-70 in the Census of 1840. George was
married to a first wife, name unknown, in Chesterfield County, S.C. in 1800, but they had no
children in that year. The Chesterfield Co.
Census of 1810 shows him as head of a large family, consisting of himself and wife b.1765-84,
3 males b. 1794-1800, and 3 males and 3 females
b. 1800-10. The males b. 1794-1800 were certainly not his children, and some of the children b.
1800-10 were probably not either, for his Ga.
passport in Dec.1810 shows him with only three
children, who were apparently 1 male and 2 females under 21 in his family in the Territorial
Census of 1816 in Clarke County, Alabama. He
married (2) in Clarke County July 28,1815 Rachel
Phillips, and is shown in the Clarke Co. Census
of 1830 with himself b. 1770-80, his wife b.1780-
1790, an aged female b. 1750-60, who was probably
Nancy Dees, his mother, and the following children: 2 males and 1 female b. 1815-20, 1 male and
2 females b. 1820-25, and 1 female b. 1825-30.
George Dees #104 moved to Sumter County,Ala.
some time after 1830, and died there in 1841 or
1842, the date of his appraisement being Jan.24,
1842 (Orphans Court Book, p.373). His heirs
(same book, p.425) were William Dees of Clarke
Co., Ala., Samuel Dees of Sumter County, Mary
Ann Dees wife of Alfred Pace of Sumter County,
Martha Dees, Nancy Shamburger wife of Joshua
Shamburger of Sumter Co., Elizabeth Moore wife
of William Moore of Copiah Co., Miss., and minor
heirs: Rebecca aged 13, James aged 18, and Eliza
aged 11, who were put under the guardianship of
their brother William, May 19, 1842. The name of
the son given as Samuel in the above record was
probably really Lemuel Dees, who was bondsman

for the marriage of John Curry to Jane L. Weaver
in Sumter County, Alabama, July 9,1844, and is
mentioned as one of the children of George Dees
(instead of Samuel) in Rev.T.H.Hall's "A Glance
into the Great Southeast", published in 1882,
p.522.

The following were the children of George
Dees #104:

104a.   Nancy Dees, b.1804 (Census) in South
Carolina, m. March 9, 1822 in Clarke Co., Ala.
Joshua Shamburger, who d. prior to 1850, and she
is shown as a widow in Choctaw Co., Alabama in
the Census of that year, with the birth-date
above, and the following children: 1. Martha
Ann Shamburger, b. Jan.17, 1824, d. Aug.7, 1885,
m. Calvin Dees, son of Willoughby Dees #109;she
is not shown in her mother's family in 1850,
being already married; 2. Elbert Shamburger,b.
1826; he m. March 20, 1845 Patience Woodall (b.
Jan.7, 1831, d. Aug.22,1894);   3. Sarah Shamburger, b. 1830, m. Sam Johnson; 4. Patience
Shamburger, b.1830;   5. Eliza Shamburger, b.1838,
m. (1) Frankie Licha, and (2) a Taylor; 6.Rachel
Shamburger, b.1840;   7. Amanda Shamburger, b.
1844; 8. James Shamburger, b. 1846;   9. Lorre
Shamburger, b. 1848.

104b.   Mary Ann Dees, m. Alfred R. Pace,
Dec.30, 1831 in Clarke County, Alabama.

104c.   Elizabeth Dees m. William Moore and
was living in Copiah County, Miss., in 1842.

The above were probably George Dees #104's
children by his first wife; certainly Nancy Dees
was; The following were children of the second
marriage:

104d.   Lemuel Dees (though he may have been
a son of the first marriage).

104e.   William Dees, b. 1818 in Alabama, d.
after 1860, probably in Clarke County, Alabama,
m. Nov.27,1839 in Clarke Co. Martha York (born
1814 in N.C. or S.C.). William Dees and his
wife are shown with the above birth-dates in
Butler County, Ala., in 1850, and in Choctaw Co.,

Alabama, in 1860, with children as follows:
(1) George W. Dees, b. 1840 or 1841, m. Rebecca
Cox in Clarke County Jan.16, 1867; (2) Rachel
Dees, b. 1841 or 1842, m. James H. Perry Jan.30,
1867 in Clarke Co., Ala.; (3) James M. Dees,
b. 1844, m. Laura Shamburger Dec.13, 1869 in
Clarke County, shown in the 1880 Census of Choctaw County, Ala., with his wife Laura (b.1849)
and children: Walton, b.1873, Johnny b. 1874,
Cornelia b.1875, Carrie b. 1876, and Lula b.1879;
(4) John L. Dees, b.1845; (5) Shubal Dees, b.
1847; (6) Amanda Dees b.1848; (7) William Dees
b. 1850, m. Barbara Everlins in Clarke County
Dec.15,1875; (8) Mary Dees, b.1852, probably
the Mamie Dees who m. R.H.Portis, Feb.29,1872 in
Clarke County; (9) Eliza J. Dees, b.1854.

104f.   James Dees, b. 1823-4, 18 years old
in 1842.

104g.   Martha Dees, b. ca 1825, m. Peter K.
McMillan, May 11,1843, her brother-in-law,Joshua
Shamburger, certifying that she was over 18.

104h.   Rebecca Dees, b.1828-9, aged 13 in
1842.

104i.   Eliza A. Dees, b.1830-31, aged 11 in
1842, m. William L. Scruggs, Jan.15,1856, in
Clarke County, Alabama.

104j.   Sarah Dees, mentioned as a daughter
of George Dees #104, who died young, in Rev.
T.H.Hall's book, cited above.

The following Dees marriages in Clarke County
Alabama may refer to later descendants of George
Dees #104: (1) Samuel Dees and Mrs.Fanny Marant,
Oct.6, 1868; (2) James S. Dees and C. Orlin
Mobley, Feb.17,1875; (3) A.E.Dees (the bride)
and R.G.Fountain, Nov.18, 1875; (4) Alice N.Dees
and A.M.English, Oct.9, 1878; (5) E.A.Dees(bride)
and E.B.Moseley, Jan.10,1887; (6) Walter Dees and
Alma Matthews, Nov.13, 1887; (7) W.M.Dees and
Sarah Rivers, Dec.1,1887; (8) Alsoza Dees and
Katie Rivers, Nov.24, 1888; (9) James S. Dees
and Mary B. Cleveland, June 16, 1887; (10)Lizzie
Dees and B.A.Calhoun, Nov.29,1889.

   Benjamin Dees #105, son of Benjamin Dees #20, was apparently born ca 1770, the eldest son, as his birth is given as 1770-80 in the Census of 1830, and 1760-70 in that of 1840, both these Censuses in Butler County, Alabama. The Census of 1810 shows "Benjamin Dees Jr." in Chesterfield County, S.C. with himself and wife, born before 1784, 2 daughters b.1794-1800, and a son b.1800-1810. Apparently the wife had died before the Territorial Census of 1816 in Clarke County,Ala., as this Census shows him with a family consisting of a male and a female over 21, and a male and a female under 21. The female over 21 was probably not his wife but his daughter Sarah, who was born in 1793. Benjamin Dees was living alone in Butler County, Ala., in 1830, so was still a widower. He may have married a second time before 1840, for the Census of that year shows him still in Butler County, but with a female b. 1770-80 in his family. His only son, George J. Dees, is shown near Benjamin #105 in Butler County in both 1830 and 1840. The following seem to be the three children of Benjamin Dees #105:

   105a.   Sarah Dees, b.1793 in North Carolina, died 1866 in Union County, Arkansas, m. Jonas Jones in Clarke County ca 1819 or 1820 (this from Arkansas records). The Marriage Register of Clarke County shows <u>Sallie</u> Dees m. George Oprey Jan.9,1818 and that <u>Nancy</u> Dees m. Jonas Jones on the same date. The names of the brides seem to have been confused on these marriage licenses, for it was Sarah or Sallie Dees who married Jonas Jones. The confusion was easy as the marriages occurred on the same day.

   105b.   Nancy Dees, m. George Oprey, Jan.9, 1818 in Clarke County, Alabama.

   105c.   George J. Dees is shown in the Butler County Census of 1830 as born 1800-1810, his wife as born 1810-1815, and with 3 daughters b. 1825-30. The Census of 1840 shows him in the same county with additional children: 1 son and 1 daughter b.1830-35, and 1 son and 1 daughter b. 1835-40. By 1850 he had moved to Union Co., Arkansas, where the Census shows him as born in 1803 in South Carolina, his wife Isabella as b.

1808 in Kentucky, and children, all born in Ala.:
(1) William G. Dees, b. 1833; (2) Eliza E. Dees
b. 1835; (3) Pruda Dees b. 1837; (4) James A.
Dees, b.1839; and (5) Sarah M. Dees b.1841.

Hannah Dees #106, eldest daughter of Benjamin
Dees #20, was born 1774 and died in Mississippi
in 1858. Her granddaughter, Mrs.Eugenia Cassity
Hurlbutt of Terry, Mississippi, knew her grandmother well as a child, and used to hear her talk
about her father's services in the Revolution.
Mrs.Hurlbutt (now deceased) contributed years ago
a good deal of information about the line of
Benjamin Dees #20, but nothing further is known
about the Cassitys.

Roderick Dees #108, son of Benjamin Dees #20,
was born 1780-90, according to the Censuses of
1830 and 1840, and his wife (name unknown) is
given the same birth-date in these Censuses. The
Census of 1830 shows him in Clarke County, Ala.,
with a daughter b. about 1810, a son b. 1810-15,
2 sons b. 1815-20, 1 son b. 1820-25, and a daughter b. 1825-30. The 1840 Census shows him in
Washington County, Ala., with a daughter b. ca
1810 still in the family, and the 2 youngest
children shown in 1830. Roderick Dees was deeded land in Sumter County, Ala. in March,1840 by
the U.S.Government (Sumter Co. D.Bk."E", p.379),
though still living in Washington County at the
time. After that, he and his family disappear
and it is uncertain what became of him. The
following are possible children of his, since
many Deeses went to Louisiana and Arkansas, but
this is by no means certain:

108a. Mary Dees, who m. Absalom Shamburger
Jan.10,1833 in Clarke County, Alabama.

108b. William Dees, born 1813 in Georgia,
shown with his wife Permelia, b.1828 in Alabama,
in Union County, La., Census of 1850, and children: (1) Oliver b. 1839 in Alabama;(2) Ellen b.
1841 in Alabama; (3) William b. 1848 in Louisiana. If the above records are correct and Wm.
Dees was a son of Roderick, he must have been
born in Georgia while the family was moving to
Alabama, for only George Dees #104, and Gaddy

Dees #110 among Benjamin Dees's children seem to have left Chesterfield County, South Carolina, as early as 1810.

108c.   Martin Dees, b.1819 in Alabama, with wife Rebecca J., b.1829 in Alabama, living in Montgomery Co., Arkansas in the Census of 1850, with children: (1) Mourning E., b.1844; Sarah Ann J., b.1846; and Melissa Ann, b.1849. The first two children were born in Alabama.

108d.   Robert Dees, b.1824 in Alabama, living near the above Martin Dees in 1850 in Montgomery County, Ark., with wife Sarah, b.1823 in Miss., and children, both b. in Alabama: (1) Elizabeth b. 1844 and (2) Catherine b. 1846.

Willoughby Dees #109, son of Benjamin Dees #20, was born 1780-90, and died in Sumter County, Ala., in 1840. His wife, name unknown, seems to have predeceased him. The Census of 1830 shows Willoughby Dees in Butler County, Ala., with himself and wife born 1780-90, 1 son and 3 daughters b. 1815-20, 2 sons and 1 daughter b. 1820-25, and 1 daughter b. 1825-30.The death of Willoughby Dees in 1840 and the distribution of his estate to his six surviving children are shown in Sumter County, Ala., Orphans Court Book #2, (pp.226,264,277, and 386), and Book #3 (pp.160 and 193). The children who shared his estate were as follows:

109a.   Calvin Dees, b.1817 (Census), m.April 4,1841 Martha Shamburger, daughter of Joshua Shamburger and Nancy Dees #104a. For his family, see later.

109b.   Rosanna Dees, m. Enoch James in Sumter County, Ala., Dec.31,1838.

109c.   Elizabeth Dees, m. David Henderson.

109d.   William M. Dees, b.1822, shown by the records to have been a minor in 1842, but an adult heir of Willoughby Dees in 1843. He married Martha Owens in Sumter County, Oct.19,1843 and d. in 1847 (Orphans Book #5,p.287). It is uncertain whether he had children.

109e. Mary Ann Dees, b. 1824-25 (aged 35, Census of 1860), married (1) in Sumter County, Alabama, Nov.4,1845 (probably an error for 1840, as her two Craft children were both born before 1845), and had two sons, Willoughby Webster Craft b. 1841, and William Wiley Craft b. 1844. She married (2) David Daniels (b.1815 in Alabama)and by him had 3 children before the Census of 1860: Calvin b. 1850, Felix b.1854, and Elizabeth b. 1847. All the above dates are from the Census of the Daniels family in Choctaw County, Ala., 1860. A descendant of Mary Ann Dees, Mrs. J.B. Chapman (nee Myrtis Lott) of Baton Rouge, La., sent in her line of descent some years ago. She stated that Willoughby Webster Craft, son of Mary Ann Dees by her first marriage, was born in 1843 and died 1926. He married Margaret Melissa Mitchell (1845-1914) and they had 10 children, among them Mrs. Chapman's mother, Caroline Z. Craft, who married George Franklin Lott (1872-1954), and they had 7 children, including Mrs. Chapman.

109f. Jane H. Dees, b.1826 (17 years of age when she was put under the guardianship of her brother Calvin, June 9, 1843), m. Hezekiah W. Bishop in Sumter County, Ala., April 11, 1844.

Calvin Dees #109a, a son of Willoughby Dees #109, who married his cousin, Martha A.Shamburger April 4,1841, is shown with his family in Choctaw County, Ala., from 1850 through 1880. The date of his birth is given variously as 1814, 1816, 1817, and 1818. Probably 1817 is about right. His wife's date of birth is given as 1824, 1825, and 1827. Her tombstone in the Eutaw Cemetery, Greene County, Ala., shows that she was born Jan.17,1824 and died Aug.7,1885. Her husband seems to have died 1880-85. Their children seem to have been the following, as gathered from the various records:

1. Willoughby J. Dees, shown in his father's family 1860-1880, and apparently never married. The Census returns show his birth as about 1843, but he was probably identical with a W.J.Dees, b. March 7, 1842, d. Oct.6,1900, whose tombstone is in the Eutaw Cemetery along with his mother

and his sister Delia.

2.   Joshua S. Dees, b.1844, shown in the family in 1850 and 1860.

3.   Delia Ann Dees, b. Dec.14,1845, d. June 23, 1902 (from her tombstone in Eutaw Cemetery), m. John M. Smith (b.Sept.20,1843, d. Jan.7, 1925), and they had, in addition to 4 children who died in infancy: (1) Julius F. Smith, d.s.p.; (2) Joshua Franklin Smith, b. June 11, 1868, d. Feb. 17, 1938, m. Caroline Woolf (1878-1960); (3) Mattie Jane Smith, d.s.p. 1933; (4) Lena Smith, b. Oct.15, 1876, d.s.p. July 10, 1901.

4.   George J. Dees, b.1847, shown in the family only in 1850 and probably died young.

5.   A son, b.1849-50, unnamed in 1850, but apparently identical with"J.J.Dees"b.1848 (1860), John Dees b.1849 (1870), and a John Dees b.1851, shown in Choctaw County in 1880, with wife Mattie b.1855, and a son Oliver b. 1879.

6.   Charles E. Dees, b.1852 (Census of 1860) or 1854 (Census of 1870).

7.   Nancy J. Dees, b. 1855-56.

In addition to the above, there was another "W.J.Dees" b. 1850, shown in the family in 1860, but he does not appear again.

Gaddy Dees #110, son of Benjamin Dees #20, appears only twice in the records, the first time in 1810 when, with a wife and 2 children, he received a Georgia passport to move to Alabama,and the second time in the list of Benjamin Dees's heirs, 1821-31, which shows "Gaddy Dees's heirs" to have a child's part of the estate. Gaddy Dees was almost certainly the father of Willoughby Joseph Dees, who appears in Union Parish, La., in 1840, and was living in Ouachita Parish, La. in 1850, and of John B. Dees, who also appears in Union Parish in 1840 and 1850. Mr.Douglas Dees of Elfrida, Arizona, wrote years ago that his father was Willoughby Gaddy Dees, b.1841 in Union Parish, La., and that his grandfather was named Willoughby Joseph Dees. Two sons of Gaddy Dees #110, then, seem to have been:

110a.   John B. Dees, who appears in Union Parish La. in 1840, living alone near Willoughby J. Dees and was living there in 1850, b.1813 in Alabama, with wife Ellen b. 1808 in Georgia, and children: Louisa b.1845, Mary b. 1847, and Martha b. 1849. A fuller account of John B. Dees's family, sent in by a correspondent, states that he was born Jan.11, 1811 in Alabama or Mississippi, and died Jan.16, 1891 in Wilson County, Texas. His wife was, according to this later record, Elizabeth Collins, b. Nov.10, 1807, d.Oct.29,1887 (perhaps her full name was Ellen Elizabeth). Ellen or Elizabeth had been previously married to L.Hendricks, and had a daughter, Harriet Elizabeth Hendricks, by her first marriage. John B. Dees's children were:

1.   Louisa J. Dees, b.Sept.26,1844, d. Feb.18, 1877, m. Sept.12, 1870 Hugh Carr and had issue: May who m. Robert Sells, Lauren who m. Mary Fatherlee, and John who m. Fanny Watkins.

2.   Martha Ann Dees, b. March 2, 1846, d.Sept. 23, 1929, m. Jan.13,1868 James E. Sutton and had issue: John W. Sutton, b. June 21, 1871, d.Sept. 30, 1934; James Joseph Sutton, b. Feb.26,1873, d. May 16, 1953; Robert B. Sutton; a son who m. a Valtine; Lula Mae Sutton who m. a Ballinger; and Walter W. Sutton.

3.   Mary Charlotte Dees, b. July 30, 1848, d. March 19, 1923, m. Abednego Hyatt and had: Annabelle Hyatt who m. Whetstone Randolph; Mamie Lou Hyatt who m. Edward Lorenz; and Jess McCoy Hyatt, b. Nov.7, 1888, d.June 23, 1954, m. Bessie Flowers.
    John B. Dees #110a, his wife, and all his children, are buried in Harmony Baptist Church Cemetery, Karnes County, Texas.

110b.   Willoughby Joseph Dees, son of Gaddy Dees #110, was born 1813-14 (Census) in Alabama, and died in Karnes County, Texas, where he accompanied his brother, John B.Dees above. Willoughby J. Dees was shown in Union Parish, La., in 1840 with

himself and wife, b. 1810-20, a daughter b.1830-
35, and a daughter b. 1835-40. By 1850 he had
moved to Ouachita Parish, La., where he is shown
(incorrectly) in the Census as Willoughby H.Dees
b. 1813-14 in Mississippi, with wife Elizabeth
b. 1811 in Louisiana, and children as given below. Willoughby's wife died young, and her children were reared with those of his brother,John
B. Dees, in Texas. The children were:
1. Virginia Dees, b.1834 (Census).
2. J. Washington Dees, b.1835 (Census).
3. Malvina E. Dees, b. 1839 (Census).
4. Willoughby Gaddy Dees, b. 1841, father of
    Mr. Douglas Dees of Elmira, Arizona, shown
    in the Census, 1870, of DeWitt County,Texas,
    with wife Bethania, b.1851, and children,
    Ann Elizabeth, b. 1867, and Joseph b.1869.
    the following children of Willoughby Joseph
    Dees are shown in the Ouachita Parish,La.,
    Census of 1850, as well as by a descendant
    of John B. Dees #110a, Mrs.Mamie Lou Lorenz
    of Nixon, Texas.
5. Jacob J. Dees. 6. Alfred B. Dees. 7. Oph-
elia L. Dees, m. George Strickland. 8. Calhoun
Dees, m. Clara A. Strickland.

    Zion Dees #113, son of Benjamin Dees #20, b.
1790-94, served in 1814-15 in South Carolina in
the War of 1812 (Adjutant-General's Office in
Washington, #384). This shows that some of Benjamin Dees's family did not move to Alabama with
George Dees #104 and Gaddy Dees #110 until about
1815. He married Sarah Sleaton, Aug.27,1819 in
Clarke County, Alabama, and nothing further is
known of him.

                    ****

Descendants of Mark Dees #21 (James, Emanuel)

    What little is known of Mark Dees is shown in
H.S.F. Vol.XVI, p.189. He was probably born ca
1745-6, and seems to have died in Anson Co.,N.C.
prior to 1790. Probably Nancy Dees, the only
Dees shown in Anson County in 1790, with one
daughter in her family, was Mark Dees's widow.
The following men may have been sons of Mark Dees:

114. Mark Dees. 115. John Dees. 116. Jesse
Dees. 117. Daniel Dees. 118. Stephen Dees. The
only reason to think these men were sons of Mark
Dees #21 is that they do not fit into the genealogy elsewhere, that the name Mark was prominent
in the families of Mark #114, John #115, and
Jesse #116, and that Daniel #117 and Stephen
#118 appear only in Anson County, N.C. in 1800
and 1810, while the other sons of James Dees #6
and their children appear in Richmond and Robeson Counties, N.C., and in Marion County, S.C.
It would now appear that Mark Dees #21 was older
than his brother Benjamin #20, and born ca 1745-
1746, as the indications are that several of
Mark's probable sons above were born prior to
1770. The following is known of these sons:

Mark Dees #114 seems to have moved to Marion
County, Miss., at an early date, with his pre-
sumed brother John Dees #115. The records about
him are very scanty. As a middle aged or elderly
man apparently, this Mark Dees made a deed of
gift to his daughters Ann and Civil Dees, Nov.
13, 1812 (Marion Co., Miss. Orphans Court Record
Book "A", pp.3 and 4). This Mark Dees's son was
probably a Mark Dees, apparently a young man,
shown by the records of Marion County to have
been stabbed in a fight May 1,1812, in the neighboring Parish of St.Tammany in Louisiana, by
Edmund D. Hunt, and Mark died of the wounds May
8, 1812. Mark Dees #114 seems to have died before 1816, for the Territorial Census of that
year shows only the family of his brother, John
#115. Mark #114, then, seems to have had three
children: Mark #114a, Ann #114b, and Civil #114c.

John Dees #115, son of Mark Dees #21, moved to
Mississippi in 1800 and seems to have died there
in Perry County, Miss. after 1830. John Dees testified that he moved to Washington County, Mississippi Territory, in 1800 (Territorial Papers
of the U.S., Vol.5, p.669). The Territorial Census of 1816 shows him in Marion County, Miss.,
with a family consisting of 1 male and 1 female
over 21, and 3 males and 2 females under 21. On
Dec.13, 1816 John Dease signed a petition of the
inhabitants of Jackson Co., Miss., stating that
he settled in Jackson County while it was still

part of West Florida, and asking for proper title
to his lands (Territorial Papers of the U.S.,
Vol.6, p.736ff). In the Census of 1820, John
Dease is shown in Jackson County, Miss. with a
family consisting of 1 male b. before 1775 (himself), 1 female b. 1775-94 (his wife apparently),
2 sons b.1794-1804 (one of them b. 1802-4), 1
son b. 1804-10, and 1 son and 1 daughter b.1810-
20. He had apparently moved to Perry Co., Miss.
by 1830, when the Census shows him as born 1760-
1770 (probably ca 1770 is the right date), with
his wife, b.1770-80, a daughter b. 1800-10, and
a son b. 1810-15. His probable son, Oliver Dees
was living in Rankin Co., Miss. in 1830 with a
family consisting of 2 males b.1800-1810 (the
second male being probably his brother Edward),
a female b. 1800-10 (probably his wife), a female b. 1804-10, and a female b. 1810-20. 1830
is the last year in which John Dees #115 appears
in the records. Three of his probable sons, all
born in Mississippi, were:

115a. Oliver C. Dees, b.1807 (Census) who
appears in 1830 in Rankin County, Miss., above,
but was in Jasper County, Miss., in 1840 and
1850. One person who reported the Census of 1850
in Jasper County for Oliver Dees and his brother
Edward gave every one in both families as born
in Alabama, another that they were all born in
Mississippi, which is probably correct, as Oliver was living in Mississippi from 1830-50, and
Edward from 1840-50. The fact that both brothers were born in Mississippi at early dates
points very strongly to John Dees #115 as being
their father, for he seems to have been the only
Dees living in Mississippi prior to 1820, except
his brother Mark above, who seems to have died
before 1816. The 1850 Census of Jasper County,
Miss., shows "O.C.Dease", with the birth-date
above, his wife Elizabeth b. 1808, and children:
Edward b. 1832; Bridget b.1835; Nancy b.1837;
Thomas b. 1839; Rachel b. 1843; George b. 1845;
and Charles Dease b. 1847.

Edward Dease #115b, son of John Dease #115,
was born 1812 (Census) and died in Monroe County,
Miss., in 1860. He married (1) Margaret _____,
b. 1820, and m. (2) in Wilcox Co., Ala., Nov.8,

1853 Lucinda Stephens. His will, probated in
Monroe Co., July 9, 1860 by his brother, O.C.
Dease, and others, states that 4 negroes who belonged to his first wife were to be divided
among his children by her: Bridget Cooper, Margaret C. Byan (Bryan?), Mary Ann Dease, James P.
Dease, Oliver Dease, Charley P. Dease, and Edward
J. Dease; and his wife Lucinda to be guardian of
his children, Sarah Elizabeth, Gillie J.,Thomas
H., and Martha L. Dease until they were 21 (Monroe Co., Miss. W.Bk.1, p.29). The children by
the first wife, as shown by the 1850 Census of
Jasper Co., Miss. (where the family also appears
in 1840), were: (1) Bridget Dease, b. 1837, m.
a Cooper by 1860; (2) Margaret Dease, b. 1839,
m. a Bryan by 1860; (3) Mary Ann Dease, b.1841,
unmarried in 1860; (4) James P. Dease, b.1844;
(5) Oliver S. Dease, b.1846; and (6) Charles
P. Dease, b.1848. The children by the second
wife, Lucinda, as shown by the will, were: (7)
Sarah Elizabeth Dease; (8) Gillie J. Dease; (9)
Thomas H. Dease; and (10) Martha L. Dease.

115c. Elzy Dees, probably son of John Dease
#115, as he is shown as born 1815 in Mississippi
in the 1860 Census of Washington Parish, La., is
shown in that Census with wife Sarah, b.1829 in
Louisiana, and 2 children born in La., (1) Bail-
ey B. Dees, b.1855, and (2) James D. Dees b.1857.

Jesse Dees #116, probably son of Mark Dees #21,
was almost certainly identical with a Jesse Dees
shown in Franklin County, Ala., in the Census of
1820, with a family consisting of 1 male and 2
females over 21, 2 males and 3 females under 21,
but had moved to Lowndes County, Miss., by the
Census of 1830, with his probable son Mark Dees.
Jesse is shown as born 1770 or earlier, with
possibly a second wife, b. 1790 or later, a girl
and a boy b. 1810-20, and a boy born 1820-30.
Mark Dees is shown in the same Census, he and
his wife being born 1790-1810, and with 3 sons
and 3 daughters b. 1820-30. Nothing further is
known of Jesse Dees and his other children, but
the son Mark moved to Tippah Co., Miss., and
left numerous descendants.

Mark Dees #116a, son of Jesse Dees #116, was born in North Carolina in 1798, according to the 1850 Census of Tippah County, Miss., where Mark was living with his wife Lydia, b.1805 in Kentucky, 3 married sons, and 7 younger children. The following were his children, all born in Mississippi, and dates of birth from the 1850 Census:

1.   Lorenzo D. Dees, b.1817, with wife Mary b. 1819. If Lorenzo D. was born in 1817, he was probably too old to have been Mark's son, and may have been a younger brother. However, another version of the Census gives Lorenzo's birth as 1826 and his wife's as 1829.

2.   Jesse T. Dees, b.1823, with wife Nancy F., born 1829 in Alabama, and sons Mark b.1848 and John b.1850 (6 months old). Jesse's family will be shown more fully later.

3.   Isabella Dees, b. 1825.

4.   Caroline Dees, b.1826, m. Thomas Cheves,and they were the grandparents of G.D.Humphrey, former President of the University of Wyoming.

5.   George Dees, b.1828, with wife Marsha, b. 1832 in Tennessee, and daughter Mary J.Dees, b. 1849 (8 months old) in the 1850 Census.

6.   Polly Dees, b.1830.

7.   Nancy Dees, b.1833.

8.   Mark Dees, b. 1839. His full name was probably Mark Anthony Dees, who was a Confederate soldier from Mississippi, and is stated to have been born Feb.10, 1837 at Columbia, Miss., died March 4, 1926 at Chalybeate, Miss., and married May 1867 Rebecca Jane Brooks.

9.   Betsy Dees, b.1840. 10. Missouri Dees,b.1845.

A fuller account of the family of Jesse T.Dees above, son of Mark #116a, has been sent in by descendants, differing somewhat and probably more correct than the Census records above. According to them, Jesse Dees was born in 1821 and died March 11, 1905 near Wolfe City, Texas. He m. about 1847 Mary Yokum (b.1828 in Franklin Co., Ala., d. April 11, 1898 in Hunt Co., Texas), daughter of John and Mary (Young) Yokum. They had 9 children, all born in Tippah Co., Miss.: (1) Mark b.1848, m. Jennie Hibbert; (2) George b. 1850; (3) John Marion, b. Jan.19,1852, d. Jan.5, 1895 near Wolfe City, Texas, m. Nov.29, 1876 in Milam Co., Texas, Mary Tennessee Merchant (b.April 9,1859 in Bell Co., Texas, d. April 26, 1951), daughter of David Prince Merchant, and had 5 children given below; (4) Bill b.1854, d. June 8, 1908, m. Sept.10,1877 Jennie Oleman; (5) Frank, b.1856, d.Dec.29, 1906, m. Elizabeth Townson; (6) Jeff, b.April 11, 1858, d. Feb.1, 1946, m. Oct.24, 1880 Alice Merchant; (7) Bob, b. March 11, 1860, d. Nov.16, 1925,m. Jan.6, 1887 Nannie Merchant; (8) Nancy, b.1862, d. July 20, 1911, m. Dec.20, 1878 Jim Barker; (9) Lettie b.1868, d. April 28,1907, m. Carrol Webb.

The children of John Marion Dees above were: (1) Mary Leatha, b. June 20,1878, d. June 13, 1944, m. Aug.15,1895 Ed McClellan; (2) David Frank, b. Dec.4, 1881, m. Jan.15,1908 Maude Corgal and had: Gaynell Dees who m. Willie Wynn, Moselle Dees who m. Argyle Apple, Frances Dees who m. Loy S. Pyeatt, and a son who died at birth; (3) James Robert, b. Feb.2, 1883, m. Mar. 15, 1907 Lucy Gregory; (4) Alma Leona, b. Jan. 6, 1888, m. Sept.9, 1906 James W. Watson and had: Flora Alene Watson who m. a Partner, James Ray Watson who m. Jennie Cargal, and John Herbert Watson; (5) Daniel Luke, b. Feb.19, 1893, d.Jan. 19, 1924, m. Feb.4, 1912 Eddie Hackenworth.

Daniel Dees #117, probable son of Mark Dees #21, appears only once in the records, when he is shown with a large family in Anson County, N.C. in the Census of 1810. He and his wife are shown as born before 1765 (which is probably too early for their births), with a family consisting of 1 female born 1765-84, 1 male and 1 female b. 1784-1794, 2 males and 1 female born 1790-1800, 1 male and 2 females born 1800-1810. The descendants of Daniel Dees #117 are quite uncertain, but he may have been the husband of a Nancy Dees, b.1760-70,

shown in Lancaster Co., S.C., adjoining Anson
Co., N.C., in the Census of 1830 with a family
consisting (besides herself) of 1 female born
1810-15, 2 males and 1 female born 1820-25, and
1 male and 1 female born 1825-30. Nancy was obviously a widow, and her age would agree with
the wife of Daniel Dees. The same Nancy Dees
apparently shows up in the adjoining county of
Chesterfield, S.C. in 1850, in the following
family, all born in South Carolina except Nancy:
Elizabeth b.1805, Riley b.1826, Perry b.1828,
William McC. b.1837, Sanford b. 1840, and Nancy
b.1772 in North Carolina. Apparently Nancy Dees
was living in this year with her daughter-in-law,
widow of a son of Nancy, name unknown. If the
identification of Nancy Dees as the widow of
Daniel #118 is correct, the following Deeses in
Lancaster Co., S.C. and in Chesterfield Co.,S.C.
otherwise unidentified, belonged to Daniel
Dees's family:

(1) Robert Dees, b.1794-1804, with wife the
same age, and a son b. 1810-20, shown in Lancaster Co., S.C. in 1820.

(2) Sampson Dees and wife, both b. 1794-1804,
with a son b. 1810-20, also shown in Lancaster
County in the Census of 1820.

(3) E.Dees, b. 1815 in South Carolina, shown
in the 1850 Census of Lancaster County, S.C .
with wife M. Dees, b.1818 in S.C., and children,
all born in South Carolina and all females:
M.Dees, b.1838, L.Dees, b.1840, D.Dees, b.1842,
M.Dees, b.1844, C.Dees, b. 1846, R.Dees, b.1848,
and H. Dees, b.1849. It is unfortunate that only
initials are used in this family.

(4) L. Dees, b. 1800 in South Carolina, shown
in the 1850 Census of Lancaster County, S.C.
with wife, P. Dees b. 1810 in S.C., and children
all born in S.C.: T.Dees, b.1830 (female); H.Dees
b.1832 (male); E.Dees b.1834 (female); J.Dees b.
1836 (male); B.Dees b. 1838 (male); J.Dees b.
1840 (male); J.Dees b. 1842 (male); L.Dees b.1844
(male); and F.Dees b. 1845 (male). Again, the
use of initials only is unfortunate.

(5) H. Dees, b. 1823 in S.C., is shown in Lancaster County in 1850 with wife S.A.Dees, b. 1825 in S.C., a son A.Dees b.1846, and a son L.A.Dees b. March 1850. This man seems identical with a Hial Dees, shown in Lancaster County in 1860 as born 1830, with wife, S.A.Dees b. 1830, and children: Anderson Dees b. 1847, John Dees b. 1849, and Patsy Dees b. 1854.

(6) The 1860 Census of Lancaster County shows John Dees, b.1820 in S.C., obviously a brother of Hial, with wife Margaret b. 1830 in S.C., and children: Tirzah b. 1851 in S.C., Martha b. 1853 in Florida, Irwin b. 1855 in Florida, Hial b.1857 in Florida, and Elizabeth b. 1859 in S.C.

(7) In addition to the family of Elizabeth Dees, b.1805 above, in whose family the aged Nancy Dees, b. 1772, appears, the Census of 1850 for Chesterfield County, S.C. shows the following family, who may have been descended from Daniel Dees #118: Mark Dees b. 1822, Rebecca Dees b.1802, John A. Thweatt b.1831, Peter I. Thweatt b.1834, and Benjamin F. Thweatt b.1844, all born in S.C. This same family is shown apparently in 1860 as M.Dees b.1824, Reulen (?) Dees b.1810, and Benjamin Thweatt b.1846.

Stephen Dees #118, probable son of Mark Dees #21, was born 1760-70 according to the 1840 Census of Anson County, N.C., and seems to have died 1840-50 in that county. He appears in the Census returns of Anson County from 1800 through 1840, except for 1810, when for some reason he does not appear. In 1800 he is shown with three sons b. 1790-1800; in 1820 with a daughter born 1794-1804, 3 sons and a daughter b. 1810-20.The year 1830 does not show Stephen Dees himself, but he appears to be the man b. 1760-70 in the family of his apparent son, Samuel Dees (b.1800-1810) in that year. Others in Stephen's family in Anson County in 1830 were Mary Dees, probably widow of one of Stephen's sons, b.1800-1810, with a son and a daughter b. 1825-30; and James Dees b. 1790-1800, with a wife and 5 children. The year 1840 shows, in addition to Stephen Dees, and his probable children Samuel, James, and Mary Dees, a William Dees, b. 1810-20, with wife

b. 1810-20, and children, 1 son b. 1830-35, and 1 daughter b. 1835-40. William does not appear again in 1850, though the others do, except for Stephen himself. The probable children of Stephen Dees #118, so far as known, were then:

118a.   James Dees, b. 1795, shown in 1850 in Anson County with wife Alice b. 1800, and children, all born in North Carolina: (1) Elizabeth, b.1825; (2) Robert, b.1834.   In James's family in 1850 were also a probable son-in-law and daughter, Wilson Henry b.1823, Belinda Henry b. 1828, and children: Rachel Henry b. 1847 and John Henry b. 1849-50 (8 months old). In addition, the family included a Caroline Henry, born 1832, probably a sister of Wilson Henry.

118b.   Samuel Dees, b. 1805, shown in Anson County in 1850 as overseer for Mary Dees, probably his widowed sister-in-law, with wife Sarah b.1815, and children, all born in North Carolina: (1) Martha b. 1831; (2) William B. b.1832; (3) Sarah J., b.1841; (4) Nancy b. 1843; (5) James H. b. 1845; and (6) Zachariah b.1848.

118c.   A son who died prior to 1830 and was the husband of Mary Dees, shown in 1830 and 1840. This Mary Dees is shown in the 1850 Census as born in 1810, with her probable brother-in-law Samuel Dees, living in the family as overseer, with his family above. Mary's own children are uncertain.

118d.   William Dees, shown previously as living in Anson County, b. 1810-20, in the Census of 1840, but apparently died before 1850. His widow was probably Emeline Dees, shown in 1850 as born in 1810, with children, Margaret b. 1840, and Horra Dees (male) b. 1848.

118e.   Thomas Dees, b. 1815, shown in the Census of 1850 in Anson County, living in the household of Margaret Streator. Margaret may have been a relative of the Stephen Dees family, for an Ellen Dees, with no age given, was living in Anson County in 1850 in the family of Thomas and Mary Streator.

Descendants of William Dees #22 (James, Emanuel)

William Dees #22 and his family are treated
briefly in H.S.F., Vol.XVI, pp.189-90. He seems
to have been born about 1750 and died in Richmond County, N.C., 1810-20, the year 1810 being
his last appearance in the Census there. The name
of his wife is unknown, but she seems to have
been still living in 1810. The Census of 1800
shows that both William and his wife were born
before 1755. The 1790 Census of Richmond County,
N.C. shows William with 4 sons and a daughter b.
1774-90; the 1800 Census shows an additional son
and daughter b. 1790-1800. The daughter b.before
1790 does not appear in William's family in 1800
and had probably died, for descendants knew only
of 5 sons, Shadrack, William, Stephen, Levi and
John, and one daughter, Polly or Mary. The sons
moved from Richmond County to Robeson Co., N.C.
after their father's death, and finally the families of Shadrack, William and Stephen moved to
Richmond County, Ga., where they are still fairly
numerous in and near Augusta, Georgia. Dr.Thomas
C. Deas of Wynnewood, Pa., is a descendant of the
family, and he knew of a family conclave in Augusta in 1926 connected with an estate left in
Texas by a son of Shadrack Dees, in which notes
were made which he consulted. The family knew
that the 5 brothers above came from Robeson Co.,
N.C. with their sister Polly, and Dr.Deas gave
the writer considerable information about the
family, though they knew nothing of the sons
John and Levi except their names. However, all 5
of the sons are shown in Richmond and Robeson
counties, N.C. and they seem unquestionably to
have been the sons of William Dees #22, as follows: 119. Shadrack Dees. 120. William Dees.
121. Stephen Dees. 122. Levi Dees. 123. John
Dees. 124. Polly Dees. The Augusta family
spells the name Deas now, but the records of
North Carolina show it as Dees.

Shadrack Dees #119, son of William Dees #22,
was probably born 1775-80, as his age is given
as b. 1770-80 in the Census of Robeson Co.,N.C.
in 1810, with a wife b. before 1784, a male b.
1784-94 (probably a brother) and 1 son and 2

daughters b. 1800-10. The 1820 Census shows him in Robeson Co., N.C. with the above children, plus 3 sons b. 1810-20. His wife does not appear in 1820 and seems to have died. The year 1830 shows him still a widower in Robeson Co., with the 2 daughters b. 1800-10, 1 son b. 1810-15, and 1 son b. 1815-20. The Augusta, Georgia, Deases remembered only 3 children of Shadrack Dees: 119a, William Dees who went to Texas and died wealthy about 1926; 119b, James Dees who died near Macon, Georgia, and a daughter, 119c, Eliza, who died young. According to the Augusta Deases, Shadrack's wife was named Betsy Moore. He probably died in Robeson Co., N.C. after 1840.

William Dees #119a, son of Shadrack Dees #119, may be identical with a William Dees, b.1813, with wife May I. Dees b.1814, he and his wife and all his children being born in North Carolina, who was living in Russell County, Ala., in 1860, the children being: (1) Mary A.L. Dees b. 1841; (2) Eli W. Dees b. 1846; (3) Nelson A. Dees, b. 1848; (4) William E. Dees b.1850; (5) Nancy W. Dees b.1852; and (6) Rufus G. Dees b.1854.

James Deas #119b, son of Shadrack Dees #119, may be identical with a James Dees b. 1813 in North Carolina, shown in Crawford Co., Georgia in 1850 with wife "E.Dees", b.1822 in Ga., and children, all born in Georgia: (1) N.Deas (f.) b.1845; (2) M.Deas (f.) b.1846; (3) S.Deas (f.) b.1848; and (4) W.T.Deas (m.) b.1849.

Professor James E. Deese of the Department of Psychology, Johns Hopkins University, and his cousin, Miss Sarah L. Deese of Graceville, Fla., wrote me a number of years ago that they were grandchildren of a James M. Deese who came from Lumberton, N.C. (which is in Robeson Co.) and settled in Columbia, Alabama. They said that James M. Deese had a number of children, of whom they knew of only three: (1) Thomas D. Deese of Columbia and Dothan, Ala., who m. Jane Johnson and was the father of James E. Deese; (2) John Deese, father of Miss Sarah L. Deese and her brother James Henry Deese, an Annapolis man; and (3) Florence Deese who m. Mr. O'Neal and had 2 children, Maston and Louella O'Neal. This family may be connected with that of James Deas #119b above.

Eliza Deas #119c, a daughter of Shadrack Deas

#119, may be identical with an Eliza Dees b.1810 and shown in the Census of 1850, Robeson County, N.C. in the family of Nancy Stephenson.

Another son of Shadrack Dees #119 may have been a Shadrack Dees who married Rodiah McCullum May 6, 1847 in Onslow Co., N.C., though both were formerly from Robeson County, N.C. (from the "Raleigh Register", May 25, 1847).

William Dees #120, son of William Dees #22, was probably born ca 1782-3 (b.1780-90, Robeson Co., N.C. Census, 1830 and 1840). He is shown with his family in Robeson County 1820-40,though his family in these Censuses does not correspond too well with the numerous children attributed to him by the Augusta, Georgia, Deases, and in fact, shown in the family of his wife, Catherine Deas, in Richmond County, Ga. in the Census of 1850. The Census records of Robeson County show only a son and 2 daughters, b.1810-20, a daughter b. 1820-25, and a son b. 1825-30. The Census of 1840 shows him with only 2 sons, no wife or female children. The only way this can be reconciled with the Georgia records and the tradition among the Augusta Deases, is that William Deas moved to Georgia about 1835, but left sons in Robeson County, and returned there for a short time in 1840. Confirming this is the fact that the 1850 Census for Richmond Co., Ga. shows William's son, Murphy Dees as b. 1837 in Georgia. William #120 must have died between 1840 and 1850 for the Census of 1850 shows his wife and younger children living with William's brother, Stephen Deas. The Augusta Deases state that William's wife was Marian Catherine McMurphey, and that they had 8 daughters and only 1 son. Apparently the Augusta people did not know anything of the older sons indicated in the Census of Robeson County. According to the Census of 1850, when Catherine Deas was living in the family of her brother-in-law, Stephen Deas, she was born in 1795 in North Carolina. The children, all except Murphy, the youngest, were all born in N.C. and were as follows (from both Dr.Thomas C.Deas and the 1850 Census of Richmond Co., Ga.):

120a. Mary Deas, m. Stephen Shaw. 120b.Eliza Deas, m. William Deas, a cousin. 120c. Ann Deas

b.1824, never married. 120d. Jennet Deas, b.1826
never married. 120e. Harriet Deas, b.1828, m.
John Trader. 120f. Catherine Deas b. 1830, m.
Robert Spiers. 120g. Christian Deas b. 1832,m.
Adam Parish. 120h. Elizabeth Deas (Betsy) b.
1834, m. Wesley Alexander Deas, son of her first
cousin, Alexander (Sandy) Deas, of whom later.
120i. Murphy Deas, b.1837 in Georgia, never
married.

Stephen Deas #121, son of William Dees #22,
was born in 1785 (1850 Census of Richmond Co.,
Ga.), and died some time after 1850, probably in
Richmond Co., Ga. He is shown there in the Census of 1820 with a son b. 1810-20. The year 1830
shows him in Robeson Co., N.C. with 3 daughters
b. 1820-25 and 2 daughters b. 1825-30. Stephen
Deas was the ancestor of Dr.Thomas C.Deas of
Wynnewood, Pa., who handed in so much information
about the descendants of William Dees #22.
    In 1850 Stephen Deas's sister-in-law Catherine
Deas was living with him, along with her children. Dr. Thomas E. Deas says that Stephen Deas
married Marian Moore, and had only two children:
121a. Eli Wesley Deas. 121b. Andrew Jackson Deas,
whose wife was named Catherine Margaret, but Dr.
Deas had no further information about him.

Eli Wesley Deas #121a, son of Stephen Deas
#121, was born July 22, 1815 in Richmond or Robe-
son County, N.C. and died Oct.22, 1867 at Augusta,
Ga. He married about 1845 Susan A. Lamb (b.Sept.
9, 1818, d.June 8, 1894 at Augusta, Ga.). They
were still living in Robeson Co., N.C. in 1850
and later years. According to Dr.Deas, Eli Deas
started with a number of other people to go to
Texas after the War Between the States, but he
became ill in Augusta from a war wound, and died
there as above, his family remaining in Augusta.
Dr. Deas gave the following children of Eli Wesley Deas and his wife: (1) John Deas b. ca 1846
of whom nothing further is known. (2) Matilda
Deas, b. May 28, 1848. (3) Marian Catherine
Deas, b. Feb.16,1852, d. Dec.18, 1897. (4) Nathaniel A. Deas b. May 18,1855, d.Aug.28,1905. (5)
Evander C. Deas, b. July 5,1856, d. Feb.8, 1932.
(6) William Dockery Deas, Dr. Deas's grandfather,
b. April 22, 1859, d. Jan.3, 1936. (7) Oren Deas,

b. April 10, 1862, d. Jan.18, 1932.

Levi Dees #122, son of William Dees #22, appears for the first and only time in the North Carolina records in the Census of 1820 for Richmond County, and seems to have moved away, perhaps to Illinois. The indications are that he was probably identical with a Levi Dees, b. 1790, whose family and posterity were sent in by Mrs. Nellie Burns Sparks of Idaho, several years ago. Mrs. Sparks stated that Levi Dees was born about 1790 in Tennessee, died 1864, m. Mary Vineyard (1796-1823, d. in Illinois), the daughter of Daniel Vineyard, a German immigrant and that they had the following children, all born in Madison Co., Illinois: 122a. Polly b. 1815, d.1834; 122b. Elizabeth b.1816, d.1855; 122c. Nancy b. 1819, d.1842; 122d. William Cox Dees b. Dec.11,1821; 122e. Andrew Dees b.1823. That Levi Dees was born in Tennessee seems to be a mistake, and that all the children were b. in Madison Co., Illinois also seems to be wrong for the 1820 Census of Richmond County, N.C. shows him with 3 daughters b. 1810-20, which corresponds exactly to the three elder daughters above,mentioned by Mrs. Sparks.

William Cox Dees, #122d, son of Levi Dees #122, was born in Madison Co., Illinois, Dec.11, 1821, and died in Utah after 1850. He married in Christian Co., Kentucky, Martha Clifford (b.Oct. 3, 1814, d. Oct.21, 1897), and they had the following children: (1) Susan Dees b. 1836 in Christian Co., Ky. (2) Levi Cox Dees, b.Mar.3, 1842 in Madison Co., Ill. (3) Elizabeth Dees, b. 1844 in Madison Co., Ill. (4) Nancy Adaline Dees, b. 1846 in Holt Co., Mo., married Charles Wright. (5) John Franklin Dees, b. Jan.15,1847 in Holt Co., Ill., see later. (6) Newton Dees, b. Aug.1849 on the journey from Indian Territory to Utah, m. Jerusha Clifford.

John Franklin Dees, son of William Cox Dees #122d, was born Jan.15, 1847 and died Dec.8,1919 at Weston, Idaho. He married June 15, 1873 Margaret Clifford (b. May 7, 1857, d.1929), the daughter of Leander Holmes Clifford, and had issue: (1) Ada Margaret, b. Feb.25, 1874 at Wes-

ton, Idaho, d. Sept.30, 1903, m. Nov.22, 1892
Hyram Jensen; (2) Mary Elvira, b. Nov.15, 1875,
d. Nov.14, 1925, m. Jan.27,1898 Thomas Phillips;
(3) William, b. Nov.25, 1877 in Utah, d. June 10,
1897; (4) George Edgar, b. 1879 at Dayton, Ohio,
m. Lenora Hulett; (5) John b. 1881 in Idaho, d.
in infancy; (6) Alice, b. Oct.22, 1855 at Weston,
Idaho, m. May 4, 1904 Erving Crockett.

John Dees #123, son of William Dees #22, was
probably born ca 1792-3. He appears only once in
the North Carolina records, in the 1830 Census of
Robeson Co., which shows him as born 1790-1800,
with, presumably, a wife, a little older than
himself, b. 1780-90, a female b. 1800-10, a female b. 1810-15, and a son and a daughter born
1825-30. Nothing further is known of John Dees
#123.

The following scattered Deeses in the 1850
Census of Robeson County, N.C., may have belonged to the family of John Dees #123, or at least
to some of the sons of William Dees #22:

1.   Elizabeth Dees b. 1825, and Julia Dees b.
      1832, living together.
2.   Penney Dees b. 1822, with a son Angus Dees
      b. 1847, living in the family of Peter
      McLaughlin.
3.   Catherine Dees, b.1827, in the family of
      Flora McCommerce.
4.   Miranda Dees, shown twice, once as b. 1832
      in the family of Rufus and Celia Waddill,
      and once as b. 1833 in the family of John
      and Nancy Smith.

Polly or Mary Dees #124, daughter of William
Dees #22, had a son Alexander (Sandy) Dees,shown
in the 1850 Census of Richmond County, Ga. as b.
1819 in North Carolina, with wife Nancy b.1816
in Ga., and children, all born in Georgia:
(1) William I. Dees b. 1839; (2) Wesley Alex.
Dees, b. 1841, m. Elizabeth (Betsy) Dees, daughter of his great-uncle, William Dees #120;   (3)
Emma M. Dees, b.1842; (4) Robert C. Dees, b.1843.
In addition to the children, there were shown in
Alexander Dees's family in 1850 John McCullers,
b.1841 in Georgia, and Elizabeth Netherland, b.

1805 in Georgia, perhaps his wife's mother.

****

Descendants of James Dees #23 (James,Emanuel)

As mentioned in H.S.F. XVI, p.189, the posterity of James Dees #23 is very uncertain, and
some of the South Carolina Deeses attributed to
the family of Daniel Dees #117, son of Mark Dees
#21, may have belonged to the family of James
Dees #23.

James Dees #23 seems to have been living in
the family of his father, James #6, in the 1790
Census of Richmond Co., N.C., and the 5 males b.
before 1774 in that year probably were James #6
and his sons: James #23, John #25, Moses #26,
and Samuel #27. The two younger males, b.1774-
90, in the family in 1790 were probably the
elder sons of James Dees #23, who was probably
b. ca 1756-7, certainly after 1755 and before
1765, as shown by the Censuses of 1800 and 1810.
The family of James Dees #23, as shown in the
1800 Census of Richmond Co., N.C.,consisted of
himself, b. 1755-74, a female given as b. before
1755 (though this is doubtful), who may have
been his wife, a little older than he; a male
and a female b. 1774-84, 2 sons b. 1784-90, and
3 sons b. 1790-1800. James #23 had moved to
Anson Co., N.C. by 1810, where the Census shows
him as born before 1765, his wife b. 1765-84
(this may have been a second wife, if the 1800
Census is correct and his wife shown there was
b. before 1755), a son and a daughter b. 1784-
1794, 2 sons and 2 daughters b. 1794-1800, and
a son and a daughter b. 1800-10. James disappears after 1810, and probably died before
1820, when the Anson Co., N.C. Census shows Elizabeth Dees (probably his second wife) with a
daughter b. 1794-1804, a son b. 1802-4, a son
and a daughter b. 1804-10, and a son b. 1810-20.
The following were perhaps sons of James Dees'
first wife: 125. Jeremiah Dees. 126. Alexander
Dees. 127. A son, b. 1790-1800, probably the
deceased husband of an Alcy Dees, b.1790-1800,
shown in the Anson Co., N.C. Census of 1830, with
a son and a daughter b. 1825-30. Children of the
second marriage were perhaps: 128. Mark Dees.

129. James Dees. 130. Gabriel Dees, shown in
the 1840 Census of Chesterfield Co., S.C. with
himself and wife, b. 1810-20, and no children.
What is known of Jeremiah, Alexander, Mark and
James Dees is as follows:

Jeremiah Dees #125, perhaps son of James #23,
is shown living in Lauderdale Co., Miss., b.1782
in North Carolina with wife Sarah, b. 1792 in
North Carolina, and no children shown. This couple was the only Dees family in Lauderdale Co.,
Miss., at the time, and nothing further is known
at present of Jeremiah.

Alexander Dees #126, probably son of James
#23, is shown living in Jefferson Co., Alabama,
in 1830, born 1770-80, with wife born 1780-90
and 3 sons, one b. 1810-15, and 2 b. 1815-20.
He is shown again there in 1840, with himself
and wife with the same birth-dates as in 1830,
a son in the family b. 1810-20, and nearby,Rich-
ard Dees, almost certainly a son just married,
both he and his wife being born 1810-20. The
eldest son, Alexander, was married and living in
Chambers Co., Ala. in 1840. The third son James
does not appear with his family until 1850, when
he and his brother Richard are both shown in
Jefferson Co., Ala. Alexander Dees seems to
have died 1840-50 in Jefferson County. What is
known of the three sons is as follows:

Alexander Dees #126a, son of Alexander Dees
#126, was born in 1815 in North Carolina, ac-
cording to the 1850 Census of Hempstead Co.,
Arkansas. He married Elizabeth Franklin, Jan.14
1840 in Chambers Co., Alabama, and she was b.
1823 in Georgia according to the 1850 Census of
Hempstead Co., Ark. Their children were (from
this Census): (1) Mary H., b. 1840 in Alabama;
(2) Helen A., b. 1844 in Alabama; and (3)Emily
H. Dees b. 1849 in Mississippi.

James Dees #126b, son of Alexander Dees #126,
was born 1816 (Census of 1850) or 1812 (1860).
He married Sally (Sarah) Hamaker, April 20,1843
in Jefferson Co., Alabama. She was born 1821
(Census of 1850) or 1824 (1860) in Alabama.James
Dees and his family are shown both 1850 and 1860

in Jefferson County, Alabama. The 1860 Census
shows him as born in South Carolina, which is a
mistake and should be North Carolina. James Dees
moved to Tuscaloosa Co., Ala. after 1860, where
he died in 1869. On April 24,1869 James E.Dees
was appointed administrator of his father, James
Dees decd. (Tuscaloosa Co.Orphans Court Bk.#10,
p.170). The children of James Dees #126b. (from
the 1850 and 1860 Censuses) were: (1) Nancy A.
Dees, b. 1844 (the 1860 Census says 1842, but
this is impossible); (2) John A.Dees b. 1845
(Census of 1850) or 1844 (1860); (3) David F.
Dees, b. 1847 (Census of 1850) or 1846 (1860);
(4) Thomas J. Dees (called Jefferson Dees in
1860), b. Dec.16, 1848, d. in Tuscaloosa Co.,
Ala., May 2, 1916 (from his tombstone in Grants
Creek Baptist Church cemetery, Tuscaloosa Co.);
his wife was probably Frances M. Deese, b. Mar.
13,1843, d.Feb.9, 1936 (from the same cemetery)
and two of his children were probably the following (from the same cemetery): James S.Deese,
b. Nov.1877, d. Oct.1928, and W.A.Deese, b.Jan.
1880, d. April 1913; (5) James E. Dees b. 1850;
(6) Sarah E. Dees, b.1852; (7) Eliza J. Dees b.
1854; Eliza Dees Rosser, b. April 1854, d.Jan.
1912, is buried in the same cemetery above; she
married E.B.Rosser Jan.4, 1879 in Tuscaloosa,
Alabama; (8) Martha Dees b. 1856; and (9) Mary
Dees b. 1858.

Richard Dees #126c, son of Alexander Dees
#126, was born 1820 in North Carolina (Census of
1850) or 1825 (1860). He married Arasmus Tucker
Jan.2, 1844 in Jefferson County, Alabama. The
Jefferson County Census of 1850 shows her as
"Rosby Dees b.1832 in Georgia"; that of 1860
shows her as Rosanna C. Dees b. 1830 in Georgia.
Richard and his wife had the following children
shown in the 1850 and 1860 Censuses: (1) James
A. Dees b.1845; (2) Martha E. Dees b. 1847 (Cen-
sus of 1850) or 1848 (1860); (3) Nancy Dees, b.
1851; (4) Askady Dees (f.) b. 1856; and (5)
Rebecca M. Dees b. 1859.

Mark Dees #128, son of James Dees #23 (probably), was living in Chesterfield County, S.C.
in 1840 (b.1800-10), with a female, presumably
his wife, b. 1810-20. She must have died before

1850, with no children, for Mark Dees, b. 1800
in North Carolina, was living in the family of
James Dees #129 in Chesterfield County, S.C. in
1850. The Chesterfield Co. Census of 1860 shows
Mark b. 1810, with wife Sarah b.1830, and children: (1) Thomas b.1853, Elizabeth b. 1856, and
Robert b. ca 1860 (6 months old). This was probably the same Mark Dees as the Censuses of 1840
and 1850, though his age as given in 1860 is
much too young.

James Dees #129, probably son of James Dees
#23, b. 1801 in South Carolina (perhaps an error
for North Carolina, but this is not certain, as
the Deeses moved about a good deal), is shown in
Chesterfield Co., S.C. in 1840, 1850, and 1860.
The 1840 Census shows him as born 1800-10, with
wife b. 1810-20, and 2 girls b. 1835-40 (not
shown in 1850). The Census of 1850 shows James
Dees b. 1801 with wife Mary b. 1816, and children: Charity Dees b. 1846, and Mary J. Dees b.
1848. The same family is apparently shown in
1860 as James Dees b. 1810, Jane Dees b. 1830,
John Dees b. 1849 (this probably should be 1850
as John does not appear in the 1850 Census),
Susan E. Dees b. 1851, and R.C.Dees (m.) b.1853.
If this is the same James Dees as the one shown
in 1850, and it seems likely, he had married a
second wife and had a new family in 1860.

****

Family of Gabriel Dees #24 (James, Emanuel)

Very little is still known of Gabriel Dees
#24. He is shown in Richmond Co., N.C. in the
Census of 1790 as a single man, living alone,
but married soon afterwards, and in 1800 is shown
as b. prior to 1774, with wife b. prior to 1774,
a female b. 1784-90, and apparently 3 sons and a
daughter b. 1790-1800. After this, Gabriel Dees
disappears and perhaps moved away.

****

Descendants of John Dees #25 (James, Emanuel)

John Dees #25 was probably the youngest son of

James Dees #6, and born ca 1770, as his birth is
shown as 1770-80 in the Census of 1830, and as
1760-70 in that of 1840. He was apparently still
living in his father's family in 1790, but was
granted land in Richmond County, N.C. in 1792.
He shows up next in Marion Co., S.C. in 1810,
having apparently followed his elder brother Arthur Dees #19, there, and continues to be shown
in Marion County through the Census of 1840, apparently dying there in 1840-50. His widow was
probably a Mary Dees, b.1780, shown in Marion Co.
in 1850, with a daughter, Ann Dees b. 1815, in
her family. John Dees is shown in 1810 with a
son and a daughter b. 1794-1800, 2 sons and a
daughter b. 1800-10. The year 1820 shows him
with a daughter b. 1810-20, probably Ann Dees b.
1815 (of the 1850 Census). The year 1830 shows
him still with his wife, and the daughter b.1815
1820, and apparently 2 sons, John Dees Jr. and
Nathaniel Dees, as heads of families, both these
men and their wives being b. 1800-10, John having
a daughter b. 1825-30, and Nathaniel having a
daughter b. 1820-25, and a son and a daughter b.
1825-30.   Nathaniel Dees disappears in 1840 and
apparently died or moved away, for only John Dees
Sr. and John Dees Jr. are shown in Marion County
in that year. John Jr. is shown with additional
children, a daughter b. 1830-35 and a son and a
daughter b. 1835-40. An Elizabeth Dees, b.1824,
shown in the family of John and Mary Smith in
1850, may have been a daughter of either John
Jr. or Nathaniel Dees. According to these records
John Dees #25 had at least the following three
children: 131. John Dees Jr. 132. Nathaniel
Dees. 133. Ann Dees, b.1815, unmarried in 1850.

****

Family of Moses Dees #26 (James, Emanuel)

Apparently Moses Dees #26 was born around 1750
as he seems to have had sons b. before 1774. His
name is shown twice in the Census of 1800, once
in Richmond County and once in Robeson County,
but it was probably the same man in both cases.
Richmond County shows Moses Dees with a family
consisting of only 2 males, b. 1755-74. This probably means that Moses #26 still had property in

Richmond County on which two men, perhaps his
sons, were living. He himself seems to be the
Moses Dees, with both himself and wife b. before
1755, a male and a female b. 1755-74, a male b.
1784-90, and a male b. 1790-1800 shown in Robeson Co., N.C. in 1800. Moses #26 seems to disappear after 1800, but it was apparently his son
Moses #134 who appears in Marion Co., S.C., adjacent to Robeson Co., N.C. in 1810 with himself
and wife b. 1765-84, 2 males b. 1794-1800, and
3 females b. 1800-10. Two other sons of Moses
Dees #26 were probably the following, who also
appear in Marion Co., S.C. in 1810: Monas Dees
#135, with himself and wife b. 1765-84, and a
daughter b. 1800-10; and Samuel Dees #136, with
himself and wife b. 1765-84, and 3 daughters b.
1800-10. Nothing further is known of these people at present.

****

Family of Samuel Dees #27 (James, Emanuel)

Samuel Dees #27 appears in Richmond County,
N.C. only in the Census of 1810, with himself
and wife b. before 1765. It is possible that
he was the Samuel Dees shown in Anson County,
N.C. in 1820, head of a family consisting of 1
male b. 1760-70, 1 male b. 1800-10, 1 female
b. 1810-20, and 1 female b. 1825-30, but we have
given reason in the section on Mark Dees #21 to
think that this Samuel Dees of the Anson County
Census of 1810 was Mark's grandson, Samuel Dees,
with his father Stephen Dees shown in his family.
Accordingly, all that we know of Samuel Dees #27
is the 1810 record from Richmond County, N.C.

****

Miscellaneous Deeses of Uncertain Origin

1.   Hinds County, Miss., Census of 1850.
Hugh M. Dees, b.1834, and Benjamin F.Dees, b.
1836, both born in Mississippi, were in the family of Stephen J. Moore, b. 1812 in South Carolina, and his wife Margaret Moore, b. 1811 in

S.C. The Moores had younger children: John T. born 1844, Margaret b. 1846, Hannah b. 1847, and a Caroline Moore b. 1833 in the family.

2.   The following men may have been sons of John Dees, son of Joel Dees (b.1766) #51, and grandson of Jacob Dees #11. All these men appear in Henry County, Alabama: (a) John L.Dees b. 1835, living in the family of Joel Dees #51 in 1850; (b) Jason Dees b. 1839, shown in John Dees's family in 1860; (c) James Dees b. 1840 and shown living alone in 1860; and (d) Joel Dees b. 1843, shown in the family of John and Washington Lowe in 1860. These men may have been sons of John Dees (b.1815) by a first marriage.

3.   St.Helena Parish, Louisiana, Census of 1860: William H. Dees, b. 1832 in North Carolina, Sarah J. Dees b. 1843 in Louisiana, and Mary R. Dees, b. 1849 in Louisiana.

4.   Michael Deese (or perhaps Dare), shown in the 1820 Census of Jasper County, Georgia, as born 1775-94, with wife born 1794-1804, and two sons and two daughters born 1810-20.

5.   Lawrence County, Mississippi, Census of 1850: Susan Dees born 1831 and Lucy Dees born 1833, both born in Mississippi, in the family of A.A. and Eliza Shepherd.

6.   Attala County, Mississippi, Census of 1850: Julian Dees (female), born 1831 in Georgia, in the family of Quentin Henderson.

7.   Claiborne County, Mississippi, Census of 1850: Eveline S. Dees, b. 1815 in Mississippi, in the family of Ann L. Abrams.

8.   Hancock County, Mississippi, Census of 1850: William Deese, b. 1826 in Alabama, Eliza Deese born 1825 in Mississippi, and Jackson Deese born 1827 in Mississippi.

9.   Nalciso Dees and Gordon Dees both received land grants in Texas in 1838, Nalciso's land being in McLennan County, and Gordon's in Camp County.

10.   Harriet Dees, born 1836 in South Carolina, shown in the family of Benjamin and Ann Hainey in Chesterfield County, S.C. in 1860.

11.   Whitfield County, Georgia, Census of 1860: Marion F. Dees, b.1831 in Georgia, Elizabeth Dees born 1830 in N.C., and the following children, all born in Georgia: James W. Dees, b. 1853, Marinda B. Dees, b.1845, and William E. Dees b. 1847.

12.   DeKalb County, Georgia, Census of 1850: James Dees b. 1803, State unknown, Rachel Dees b. 1799 in Georgia, and children, all born in Georgia: Mary b. 1834, Charity b. 1836, Cynthia b. 1840, and David b. 1843.

****

Contributed by:

Dr. Benjamin C. Holtzclaw
11 Ampthill Road
Richmond, Virginia

HAYNES

of

SOUTHSIDE VIRGINIA

According to Elsdon C. Smith's <u>Dictionary of American Family Names</u>, p.90, HAYNES denotes a "keeper of hedges or fences; a dweller near the hedged enclosure". It is thought that the names Hagan, Hagen, Haine, Haines, Hayne, etc. are variations of the name as it appeared in Domesday Book. Possibly the name is of Saxon origin, claimed by some to mean "height" or "pinnacle". The name in all its variations is found in early British records and may refer to a family well established in Devonshire at the time of the Norman invasion. In its various forms, the name is found in different parts of Britain at an early date. Several coats-of-arms have been listed but are omitted here, due to their relative unimportance to present generations of Americans.

Haynes immigrants came early to the colonies, especially to New England, New York, New Jersey, Virginia and the Carolinas. John Haynes of Essex came with the Rev.Thomas Hooker in the "Griffin" in 1635, settling in Cambridge. He was followed by Samuel in 1635, James in 1637, another John in 1640 - all to New England. Benjamin Haynes came early to Long Island by way of Lynn, Massachusetts. Shortly before 1700, John Haynes appears, the progenitor of a prominent South Carolina family who dropped the final "s" from the name.

This chapter deals with <u>Henry Haynes</u> (1704-1784), <u>William Haynes</u> (1727-1806), and <u>Richard Haynes</u> (1763-1850), and descendants.

It has been impossible to prove the identity of the father of Henry Haynes, therefore one can only suggest the possibilities and point out the fact that there were sixty known Haynes emigrants from England to Virginia between 1620 and 1700; probably twice that number actually came. Among them were George Haynes, with a grant of land in Charles City County in 1654; Richard with a grant in 1642, taken out by Samuel Abbott (county not given); Henry, Master of the "Robert", ordered committed by the General Assembly in 1658, until he paid a levy of two shillings; Richard, appointed Public Executioner, York County, 1677; and William, of King and Queen Quit Rent Rolls of the early 1700's. Any one of these could have been the progenitor of this Haynes family in America; or it could have been some other of the name, who came first to one of the other colonies.

Through extensive research of Virginia county records, followed by intensive study, many descendants of HENRY HAYNES whose will was probated in Henry County, Dec.23, 1784, of WILLIAM HAYNES whose will was probated in Bedford County, June 25, 1781, and of JASPER HAYNES whose will was probated in Culpeper Co. Jan.21, 1782, have reached the conclusion that these three men were brothers, although no specific document has been found to date supporting this theory. In spite of the fact that the name Haynes is often mis-spelled in early records, the correct spelling of this family's name is found to be fairly consistant in Virginia court documents.

If indeed these three men were of the same family, or even two of them, there may have been other brothers. For example, the George Haines whose land bordered on the 151 acres sold by Thomas Moorman to HENRY HAYNES in Orange County in 1745 (of which later) may have been a brother of Henry. In St.Paul's Parish, Hanover County, Stephen Hanes owned land until 1796, after which date his name does not appear in the land or personal property tax books; he may have been the Stephen Haynes who moved to Knox County, Tennessee. Then there was a Richard Haynes mentioned in Prince Edward County records of 1750 (<u>Order Bk.1, p.145</u>), which was within the same decade that Henry Haynes and his son William are known to have lived there; in fact, the Richard Haynes of this chapter was born there in 1763. The name of John Haynes has been found in many of the areas where the other names appear, so this name might be added to the list of possible brothers. The reason for the emphasis on these few among many with the surname of Haynes is the repetition of the same given names among known descendants, and their proximity at varying periods throughout the eighteenth century.

The name of the father of HENRY HAYNES is unknown, as has been stated. It may have been William Haynes, whose estate was administered in Lunenburg County in 1748, and whose marriage is recorded in New Kent County, 1704, possibly a second marriage. There was also Richard Haynes, whose name was recorded in an old Hanover County Order Book as living in St. Paul's Parish in 1739. A third possibility is the William Haynes of Essex County, whose estate papers were filed by his wife Elizabeth in 1743-44. Other possibilities could be cited (without proof) including Thomas and Charles Haynes, who were living in Gloucester County, Virginia, in 1690, from which King and Queen was formed.

A complete genealogy of the family of HENRY HAYNES, his son WILLIAM, and his grandson RICHARD has been impossible to compile for several reasons. Firstly, few members of the family remained after 1800 in the area now known as Franklin County, Virginia. They migrated many times in many directions, thus losing contact with the few who remained in southside Virginia, near the small settlement of Penhook. Also, there were apparently unrelated Haynes families in the area, for example the Drury Haynes, thus making it impossible to classify all early documented facts

with specific family groups, to which may be
added the complications caused by the repetition
of given names. It was therefore decided to
follow one line from HENRY HAYNES, 1701-1784,
and to give the known descendants of Richard
Haynes, 1763-1850.

Note: Some Descendants of Henry Haynes, b.1701,
was privately printed in 1965 by Julia Clare
Simmons, Houston, Texas, and is now out of print.
Copies were given to the Virginia State Library,
Houston State Library, and the library of Jackson, Mississippi. It has also been filmed by
the Southwestern Genealogical Library of El Paso,
Texas (Reel 16: 156). This book shows some of
the descendants of Henry Haynes's son John, born
1731; also the families of Phelps Haynes (b.1770)
and his son James Phelps Haynes (b.1797); the
family of John Andrew Haynes; and includes some
collateral descendants of Henry Haynes (1701-84).

****

HENRY HAYNES,   1701-1784

At the session of court held the 23rd day
of December, 1784, in Henry County, Virginia, the
last will and testament of Henry Haynes, decd.,
dated 5th March, 1784, was exhibited by Parmenas
and Henry Haynes, executors. The will mentions
sons William and John, daughter Dinah English,
grandson Henry English, sons Henry and George,
daughters Mary and Ann Greer, granddaughter Mary
Ann Greer, and appoints sons Parmenas and Henry
to be executors. Securities: Rentfrow (?) and
William Greer. Witnesses were Phillip Realey,
John Clarkson and Joseph Clarkson, the last-named
signing by (x) his mark.
The birth and death records of Henry Haynes
are from the Bible of his son Parmenas Haynes,
once in the possession of a descendant, Miss Ella
May Thornton, State Librarian in the State Cap-
itol, Atlanta, Georgia, 1942. According to this
record, Henry Haynes was born Dec.24, 1701 and
died Dec.2, 1784. Henry's wife Mary died May 2,

1782, aged 81.

Exact birth dates of the children of Henry Haynes are not known, except for Parmenas #7. However, the ages of William #1, Henry #4, and George #5 appear on their Oaths of Allegiance and prove the year of birth.

Children of Henry Haynes and his wife Mary:

1. William Haynes, born 1727 in King and Queen or Spotsylvania County, Virginia, of whom later.

2. John Haynes, born 1731 in Spotsylvania Co., Virginia, died ca 1802 in Greene County, Georgia, (Will Bk.E, pp.167-173 shows inventory and appraisal of personal estate), married 1752 Sarah Phelps, born 1732 in Goochland County, Virginia, the daughter of Col. John Phelps and wife Mary (according to several descendants); she died 1785 in Wilkes County, Georgia. John Haynes was granted land for service in the French and Indian Wars; in Meade's Old Churches and Families of Virginia, Vol.2, p.13, he was recorded as a vestryman in Antrim Parish. On June 17, 1753, he purchased land from his father-in-law, John Phelps, in Lunenburg County, Virginia. John's father, Henry Haynes, witnessed the deed (D.Bk.3, p.281). John also was associated with his brother William in land transactions ca 1750. John Haynes and his wife Sarah, Aquilla Greer and wife Elizabeth, sold 660 acres on the east side of Staunton River to Henry Woodcock for £250 on Nov.20,1783 (Bedford Co. Book 7, p.292).

A photocopy of "The Inventory and Appraisement of the Personal Estate of John Haynes decd.", found in Will Bk.E, Greene County, Georgia, pp.167-173, was made available to this compiler by Julia C. Simmons. It is an interesting document because of the many names of local residents which are mentioned. The first appraisement (no date given) was made by James Park, Jesse Clay, and Peter Brook; the second return, dated Sept.7, 1802, was unsigned. Sales beginning in the same month and continuing through the year indicate a sizable sum involved, covering negroes, household items, books, tools, farm implements, grain and live stock. The notes from purchasers accepted by the administrators, Thos. and Henry Haynes, represented a large amount of the total.

Children of John and Sarah (Phelps) Haynes, all born in Bedford County, Virginia (Ref: Old Bible Records and Land Lotteries, published by the Georgia Chapters of the DAR in 1932, Vol.4, p.143; not all these items are in agreement).

(1) Jane Haynes, born Sept.2, 1753.
(2) Mary Haynes, born Sept.1, 1755.
(3) Millie Haynes, born March 4, 1758.
(4) John Haynes Jr., born Oct.15, 1762, died after 1810 in Virginia, married (1) in 1781 Martha Walker (?). The two eldest children may have been by this marriage:
(a) William, who married a Miss Combs.
(b) Martha, who married James Powell.

John Haynes married (2) Nancy Shields (b. before 1775, d. in Tennessee) in Nottoway County, Virginia. Children of the second marriage:

(c) Nancy, born 1799 in Georgia, m. James Motley in Morgan County, Georgia, 1817.
(d) John Haynes III, born Dec.20,1800 in Georgia, died in Sugar Valley, Georgia, March 4, 1879, married 1825 Ann M. Simmons,(born in Ga. May 20, 1808, the daughter of John King Simmons. She died in Sugar Valley Dec.20, 1879).
(e) Smith Haynes, born 1803.
(f) Samuel Haynes, born 1806,married a Miss Dean. (The U.S. Census of 1840 lists Smith and Samuel as aged 36 and 40 respectively.)
(g) Carrie Haynes, born 1808, married

in Georgia John Reeves.
- (h) Elizabeth Ann Haynes, born 1809, thought to have married William Pearson.
- (i) James M. Haynes, born June 26, 1811, died 1867, married 1829 Luranna Mooty Floyd (born March 3, 1807, d.1880).

- (5) Lucy Ann Haynes, married Oscar Lowe (no dates given).
- (6) Thomas Haynes, born May 9, 1765,owned land in Greene County, Georgia.
- (7) Henry Haynes, born Nov.9, 1767,married Rebecca Tatum ca 1794 in Wilkes Co.,Ga.
- (8) Phelps Haynes, born July 4, 1770, died 1850, married Lucy Hurt in Greene Co., Georgia. (Phillip appears as his given name in Old Bible Records, op.cit.).

3. Diana (or Dinah) Haynes, daughter of Henry Haynes and wife Mary) was born ca 1733 in Caroline County, Virginia, married Stephen English and lived in Bedford County, Va. Stephen's will, probated March 24, 1783, mentions the following sons:

- (1) Henry English, born ca 1763, died in Greene County, Georgia 1820. He marr. (1) Betsy Haynes, daughter of Henry Haynes Jr., July 22, 1784 (Hinshaw's Encyclopedia of Quaker Genealogy,Vol.6, p. 912); she died Aug.29, 1806 and Henry English m. (2) May 10, 1809 Nancy Middleton.
- (2) Stephen English Jr., died 1869, marr. Elizabeth Dudley Jan.3, 1781 (Franklin Co. Marriage Records). They probably had a daughter Sally Ann who m. Benjamin Musgrove Dec.7, 1842 (Hinshaw, op.cit. p.966), and a son Robert.
- (3) William English, born 1760, died July 4, 1815 (Bedford County, Virginia W.B. 14, p.182). Married Adria Dudley who later married William Kemp (see Pension Record W 7970; Wulfeck, Early Va.

74

(4) Parmenas English, b.1764, died May 23, 1826 in Oglethorpe County, Georgia, m. (1) Sarah, daughter of Henry Haynes Jr., April 1,1784 (Hinshaw, op.cit. p.912); he married (2) Nancy Starkey (DAR Patriot Index p.222, and Oglethorpe County, Ga., W.Bk.D, p.8 . Sarah Hudson is given in the DAR Patriot Index as the first wife; this may be an error, or she may have been another wife).

(5) James English, died 1827, married Ann Robinson (Robertson), daughter of George and Lucy Robertson, March 17, 1794 (Hinshaw, op.cit. p.912). They lived in Franklin County, Virginia.

(6) George Lewis English, died 1830, possibly in Columbia, Missouri. He marr. (1) Ann Smith, daughter of John Smith Aug.14, 1790 (Hinshaw, p.912); he m. (2) Nancy Haynes (?)

(7) Charles Frederick English, died 1804, married (1) Jane B. Robertson, dau. of George and Lucy Robertson, Oct.16,1792 and they lived in Bedford County, Va. Jane married as her second husband William McGlasson, son of Matthew McGlasson, Feb.21, 1806 (Hinshaw,p.955).

The above data may not be complete, and so far no names of daughters have been found. Stephen English Sr. is said to have been the son of John and Mary English of Hanover County, Virginia. Stephen English Jr.'s sisters and brothers may have been Elinor, Ann, Mary, Lucy, John, Charles, and also an older son not named in Hanover Co. Will Book "C" 1727, presumably named William. Two of the sons may have gone first to Lincoln Co., Kentucky, where English Station was established. The names of the sons of Stephen and Diana English, given above, are in order as named in the will of 1783.

4. Henry Haynes Jr., son of Henry Haynes and wife Mary, was born 1735 in Caroline Co.,

Virginia (?); he married Sarah Greer (?)
and his will was probated in 1810 in Greene
County, Georgia, with Henry English, Parmenas English, and William Greer exectrs.
(W.Bk.3, p.92, 1806-16.) Named in the will
were his son Parmenas Haynes and his five
daughters, Sally English, Nancy, Delilah,
and Mary Greer, and Jane Hudson, also Henry
English Sr. and his (Henry English's) eight
children: Henry Jr., Stephen, Lucy, Sally,
Dinah, Nancy, Jane, and Polly English.
Henry Haynes named Lewis Autry in his will
but the relationship was not shown. The
wife of Henry Haynes also shared in his
estate but her name was not given.
Possibly a search of records in both Oglethorpe and Greene Counties, Georgia would
reveal further relationships of those named.
Henry English Sr. may have been both a
nephew and son-in-law of Henry Haynes Jr.;
Henry English's eight children were undoubtedly grandchildren of Henry Haynes Jr.
Dinah (her X mark) English, one of the
five witnesses of the will, was possibly
the sister of Henry Haynes Jr., in the
event that she went to Georgia with two of
her sons; or she may have been his granddaughter. There are records in Bedford Co.
Virginia showing that Henry English marr.
Betsy Haynes July 22, 1784, and that Parmenas English marr. Sarah Haynes April 1,
1784. If these were daughters of Henry
Haynes Jr., then Betsy was probably not
living in 1810.

5. George Haynes, son of Henry Haynes and
wife Mary, was born in Caroline County,
Virginia; he married Lucy Ann (Phelps?).
He gave a deed for the 200 acres left him
by his father to Barnabas Arthur, Aug.30,
1787, on Bull Creek in Franklin County,Va.
(D.Bk.1, p.254). This land adjoined Robert Powell's on the south side of Pigg
River, now Franklin County, Virginia, the
area in which several Haynes families
lived near the present Pittsylvania Co.
line. George Haynes removed from the
county soon after this date.

6. Mary Haynes, daughter of Henry Haynes and wife Mary, was born 1739 in Caroline Co., Virginia, and married _____ Greer. The husband's given name may have been David. It is not known whether the granddaughter Mary Ann Greer, mentioned in the will of Henry Haynes, was the daughter of Mary Haynes Greer or of Ann Haynes Greer, shown later.

7. Parmenas Haynes, son of Henry Haynes and wife Mary, was born July 1, 1742 in Orange County, Virginia, and died March 1, 1813 in Oglethorpe County, Georgia, near Athens. He married (1) Elizabeth Baber (died Nov. 29, 1779) on Dec.15, 1767, daughter of Robert Baber; he married (2) Delia Greer, daughter of Aquilla Greer, on Dec.2,1781. Children of the first marriage:

   (1) Nancy Haynes, born Dec.10, 1768, m.(2) Jesse Eley. Possibly her first husband was James Shackleford of Bedford Co., Virginia.
   (2) Robert Haynes, born Nov.2, 1770. He m. Lucy Phelps Sept.27, 1794.
   (3) Richard Haynes, born March 5, 1773. He married Abi Ragon, daughter of Jonathan, July 4, 1800 in Oglethorpe Co., Georgia.

   Children of the second marriage:

   (4) Parmenas Haynes Jr., b. March 11,1783, d.1849, married Jane, daughter of John and Susannah Phelps (b.Feb.1789, d.Nov. 2, 1844) on April 30, 1807. Children:
       (a) Polly Eliza Haynes, b.May 27,1808
       (b) John Phelps Haynes, b.Jan.4,1812
       (c) Delia Ann Haynes, b.June 22,1815
       (d) William Glenn Haynes, b.May 1,1818
       (e) Lucy Phelps Haynes, b.Jan.15,1821
       (f) Robert Henry Haynes, b.Feb.17,1823
       (g) Sarah Jane Haynes, b.June 21,1825
       (h) Richard Parmenas Jasper Haynes, b. Sept.3, 1827
   (5) Sally Haynes, b.Nov.7, 1785, d. 1860, married Woody Jackson Sept.3, 1807.
   (6) Delia Haynes, b. Feb.10, 1788, married

William Greer, March 24, 1808.

(7) Polly Haynes, b. Dec.2, 1794, married James (or John) Thorington, Apr.7,1812.

(8) Jasper Haynes, b. Nov.3, 1797, m.Lucy Slaten 1820.

(9) Henry Haynes, b. July 8, 1800, d. Oct.16, 1825.

8.   Ann Haynes, daughter of Henry Haynes and wife Mary, was born May 2, 1744 in Orange County (?) Virginia, and died in Lowndes County, Mississippi in 1832. She married (1) Asa Lowe, and (2) Lt. James Greer who was born 1744, died 1825 (see DAR Patriot Index, p. 286, under Grier); they were married in Bedford County, Virginia, April 28, 1767, with Parmenas Haynes as surety (Hinshaw 6: 924). Ann and James Greer moved to Georgia, and a son, Henry Greer, b. 1769, married Susannah Tillery (b.1777), Henry died in Lowndes County, Mississippi.

Note: The above data were taken from the Bible record of Miss Ella May Thornton, whose father, Eugene Hascal Thornton married Emma Neal, Atlanta, Georgia, Oct.12,1883, and was the grandson of Nancy Haynes and her second husband Jesse Eley. Many other names of descendants appear in the same records.

*****

In considering deed records, the genesis of Virginia counties should be kept in mind, and the fact that changes in boundary lines often altered the county of residence in name only. This applies to the following counties in regard to the movements of Henry Haynes and his children: King and Queen was formed from New Kent in 1691; Hanover from New Kent in 1720-21; Caroline from Essex, King and Queen, and King William in 1727-28, King William having been taken from King and Queen in 1701-02; Spotsylvania from Essex, King and Queen and King William in 1720-21; Orange from Spotsylvania in 1734; Louisa from Hanover in 1742; Albemarle from Louisa and Goochland in 1744; Culpeper from Orange 1748-49; Madison from Culpeper 1792-93; Lunenburg from Brunswick 1746; Prince Edward from Amelia 1753-54 (Amelia having been taken from Brunswick and Prince George in 1734);

78

Bedford from Albemarle and Lunenburg 1753-54; Halifax from Lunenburg 1752; Pittsylvania from Halifax 1766-67; Henry from Pittsylvania 1776-77; and Franklin from Bedford and Henry 1785-86. The boundaries of Patrick County were also affected during this later period, but so far no pertinent Haynes data have been reported from this county.

1728   Pat.Bk.14, p.92, Sept.28, 1728.
(Consideration not stated)
George the Second .... doth "give and grant Henry Haynes of King and Queen County, Va., one certain tract or parcel of land containing 370 ac. lying and being on the branches of South River in St.George's Parish in the County of Spotssilvania beginning at Hickery, standing on Mr.Bayler's line - on hill dividing Robert Stublefield's line to William Pruet's line". Metes and bounds given. (Land Office Records are available in the Archives Division, Virginia State Library, Richmond, Virginia.)

1731   Crozier's Spotsylvania Co. Records, 1955, D.Bk.B, p.118:
March 25, 1731, Henry Haines of Spotsylvania Co., planter, to Thomas Hubard, same county, planter, for 1000 lbs. tobacco - 1720 ac. St.George's Parish, Spotsylvania Co., part of patent granted said Haines Sept.1728, on branches of South River, adjoining land of Robert Stubblefield, Robert Bayler, and William Pruett. Wit: William Waller, John Talbert, John Nalle. Mary, wife of Henry Haines, acknowledged her dower. (Note: Acreage does not agree with patent of 1728; this should be checked with county deed books. See also Crozier, p.132, for sale of 100 acres.)

1732   Caroline County, Virginia. Campbell's Colonial Caroline, p.352:
Henry Haynes reported as serving twice on jury during period 1732-45.

1734   Crozier's Spotsylvania Co. Records, D.Bk.C,
p.134:
On July 27, 1734, Henry Haynes with William
Waller and John Stubblefield witnessed deed
of John (his X mark) Smith, St.George's Parish, to his grandson John Tyre, for 100 ac.

1734   Crozier, op.cit. p.136:
Henry Haynes of Caroline Co., planter, to
Thomas Dillard of Spotsylvania Co., on
branches of Mattapony, part of patent
granted Haynes, Sept.28,1728. Wit: Roger
Quarles, John Stubblefield, John Dickenson.
Nov.5, 1734, Mary, wife of Henry Haines,
acknowledged dower etc., of St.Margarett's
Parish, Caroline Co. Metes and bounds
given. John Smith's line also mentioned in
original record.

1737   Caroline County, Va. Campbell's Colonial
Caroline, p.361:
Henry Haynes and John Smith were appointed
constables.

1738   Caroline Co., Va. Campbell op.cit. p.435:
Henry Haynes together with William Durrett,
John Smith and others, charged with violat-
ing laws governing worship; fined 5 sh. or
50 lbs of tobacco.

1739   Crozier, op.cit. p.147:
On May 1, 1739, John (his X mark) Smith of
St.George's Parish, Spotsylvania Co.,
planter, to Thomas Dillard of same parish
and county, planter, 1200 lbs. of tobacco
and 3 bls. Indian corn; 200 ac. in St.
George's Parish, Spotsylvania Co. - part
of patent granted said Smith Sept.28,1728
joining lands of John Tyre, Ralph Williams,
Thomas Hubbard, William Pruet, and near adjoining lands of Thomas Carr, Gent., decd.
and John Robinson, Esq., now Humphrey Bell's
..... Wit: Robert Holloway, Mary (her X
mark) Asmon. Margaret, wife of John Smith,
acknowledged dower ...... (Note: Although
Henry Haynes's name is not mentioned, this
record is important because of the land

description and the fact that Smith's patent was granted on the same date as Haynes'
Sept.28, 1728. See also Crozier, pp.180,
188, for deeds involving original land
grant to Henry Haynes.

1739 Patent Book 18, p.262:
"Whereas, by one patent under the great
seal of the Colony and Dominion of Virginia
bearing date of 23rd day of July, 1722,
there was granted unto Edward Ripping,
Richard Hickinson, Ralph Gough, 10,000 ac.
of land in Spotsylvania Co., now in Orange
and Hanover Counties on the south side of
the Rapid Anne (Rapidan) on condition of
cultivating and improving it - and whereas
they failed to make cultivation and Samuel
Cobbs made humble suit to our Lt.Governor
and Commander-in-Chief of our said Colony
and Dominion and hath obtained a grant for
the same and hath relinquished all of his
right and interest in 400 ac.,part of the
said tract, unto Henry Haynes. Therefore,
in consideration of 40 sh. we grant unto
Henry Haines the said 400 ac. of land lying and being in Orange County, this 26th
day of May, 1739." Metes and bounds follow. (Land adjoined lands of John Red,
William Keaton, and Richard Winston.)

1739 Patent Bk.18, p.304:
Jasper Haynes, in consideration of 25 s.,
was granted 250 ac. of land in Hanover Co.,
Va. on the branches of Pritties' Creek,
beginning at Thomas Moorman's corner.
June 29, 1739. (This land was later in
Louisa County.)

1739 Crozier, op.cit. p.148:
On Oct.1, 1739, John Talbert of St.George's
Parish, Spotsylvania Co., planter, to Thos.
Hubbard, 100 ac. same parish and county,
part of patent granted Henry Haines Sept.28
1728, by him conveyed to Thomas Hubbard,
and by said Hubbard to said Talbert May 7,
1734, now conveyed back to Hubbard. Wit:
Edmund Waller, John Waller, Margaret, wife

of John Talbert.

1741   Orange County, Va. <u>D.Bk.6</u>, p.301:
Henry Haynes of Caroline County, of the
one part to Benjamin Winn of the other part
5 sh. Tract of land containing 400 ac. lying and being in Orange County - which said
land was granted to Henry Haynes by patent
bearing date 26th day of March. (Note: this
should have been dated May 26, 1739.) This
deed bears date of Nov.25, 1741. Wit:
Henry Reid, Joseph Bloodworth, Robert
Martin.

1742   Orange County, Va. <u>Order Book 34</u>, 1743-46.
(Exact date not available.) Record of suit,
Henry Haynes vs David Cave. Zachary Lewis
attorney for Haynes (p.368); George and
Stephen Smith securities for defendant.Case
dismissed (p.480).

1742   Orange County, Va. <u>Deed Bk.7</u>, 1742-43.
(Exact date of deed not available.) John
Powell of Caroline County bought land from
William and Ann Phillips. (This deed is mentioned here in support of the belief that
the wife of Henry Haynes's son, William b.
1727, may have married Sarah Powell, who
could have been a daughter of John Powell.
The latter may also have been the father
of Ambrose Powell, who left a will in Augusta Co., Va. in 1783 mentioning his sister
(?) Sarah Haynes, and children Dicey and
Stephen. This John Powell of Orange County
was not a son of Benjamin Powell whose will
in <u>Orange Co. W.Bk.3</u>, p.506, mentions William Lewis, Salley, Honorious, Betsy Riddell
and Franky in 1800, although he could have
been a brother.

1743   <u>Pat.Bk.20</u>, p.473:
In consideration of 40 sh.,400 ac. of land
in Orange Co., Va. granted to Henry Haynes
on March 3, 1743. Description includes
William Keaton's, John Red's, and Richard
Winston's lines. (This patent may be for
an additional 400 ac. or it may be a con-
firmation of the grant to him bearing the

date of May 26, 1739.

1745   Louisa County, Va. <u>D.Bk.A,</u> pp.192-3.
On June 20,1745, Thomas Moorman of the
county of Louisa sold to Henry Haynes of
Oring (Orange) County 151 ac. in aforesaid
county adjoining Mr. George Haines on
county line (and?) Richard Durrett. Consideration, Ŀ17. Wit: Benjamin Henslee,James
Goodall. Recorded June 25, 1745. (See deed
to Jasper Haynes who bought land in Hanover
County in 1739, adjoining Thomas Moorman.
The Moorman family was prominent in the
early Quaker annals of Virginia, having been
associated with Cedar Creek in Hanover Co.,
and later with South River and Goose Creek
Meetings in Bedford County. In the latter
county, there appears to be a close connection between the Moorman family and that
of William Haynes (d.1781), believed to
have been a brother of Henry and Jasper,
possibly also of Richard, Stephen and
George Haynes.)

1746   Louisa County, Va. <u>Deed Bk.A</u>, pp.248-9:
On Sept.23, 1746, Henry Haynes of the Par-
ish of St.Thomas, County of Orange, sold to
Benjamin Henson of the Parish of Frederick-
sville, county of Louisa, 150 ac. in Louisa
County, bounded by lines of Mr.George Haines
Orange County line and the line of Mr.Thom-
as, lines on both sides ye mane (sic) road
and is called and known by name of Darrel
(Durrett's) Ordinary. Consideration Ŀ25.
Mary, wife of Henry, relinquished dower.
Henry signed deed in own handwriting.

1749   Ibid, pp.350-1:
On June 26, 1749, John <u>Dowell</u> (is this the
John Powell of Orange County? See deed dated
ca.1742) of the Parish of Fredericksville,
County of Louisa, to Henry Haynes of same
place 400 ac. in county of Louisa, adjoin-
ing William Craddock. Consideration Ŀ70.
Metes and bounds given. Signed by John (X)
Dowell. Recorded June 27,1749. Mary, wife
of John, relinquished dower. (Woods' <u>Albe-</u>
<u>marle</u> County, p.181, states that John Dow-

ell had a "pioneer patent" of 400 ac. on
Priddy's Creek, and that he died during the
Revolutionary War; that he had sons John
(d.1791), William (d.1795), Thomas (d.1815)
and Ambrose (d.?). Could the Ambrose Powell
who died in 1783 in Augusta County, Virginia, have been Ambrose Dowell? In any event
these 400 ac. were probably in Hanover Co.
in 1738 - see deed to Jasper Haynes of 250
ac. on Priddy's Creek - and later in Louisa
County. This acreage may have adjoined
Dowell's other land in Albemarle County,
where Woods stated the former owned 1,000
ac. between 1738 and 1759. This question
of the names <u>Dowell</u> and/or <u>Powell</u> is raised
herein with the specific hope that further
facts will aid in the identification of
the wife of William, eldest son of Henry
Haynes, d.1784. In this connection, it
should also be noted that an Ambrose Powell, son of Robert Powell, was a ward in
1773, with Robert Powell Jr. his guardian
(Campbell's <u>Caroline County</u>, p?). The land
of a Robert Powell adjoined Haynes's land
on Pigg River in Franklin County, Virginia.
Ambrose Powell, the ward of Robert Powell
Jr. in 1773, may have been the Ambrose Powell who d. 1783 in Augusta Co., Va., and
both may have been brothers of the wife of
William Haynes (1727-1806) who is said to
have been Sarah Powell.

1751 Louisa Co., Va. <u>Deed Bk. D</u>, pp.22-24:
On Nov.5, 1751, Jasper Haynes of the county
of Caroline, to John Dowell of the county
of Louisa and Parish of Fredericksville,
for ₤27 current money, (Note: Acreage not
available; probably the deed was for the
250 acres acquired by Jasper in 1739 by
patent, the land then being in Hanover Co.)
"Beginning at Thomas Mo<u>re</u>man's corner Two
white oak saplins and running thence north
Sixty-five degrees West at Ninety-eight a
branch, in all one hundred and fifty three
poles to a pine and hickory bush in Gough
and Kickason Line thence along their line
North Sec Thirty-seven Degrees East three
Hundred and ten Poles to a White Oak in

84

Orange Co. line thence along that line
south Sixtyfive degrees East One hundred
and ten poles to Thomas Moreman's Corner
two pines in the said County line thence
along Moreman's line South Twenty poles
Nine degrees West Three hundred and three
poles to the beginning. Signed: Jasper
Haynes (but no wife signed). Wit: John
Hurt, William Haynes, John Haynes. (Note:
Who was John Haynes? Was he a son of Henry
(d.1784)? And was William also Henry's
son? Jasper Haynes who d. ca 1782 did have
a son William, possibly his youngest child
b.1763, who could not have witnessed the
1751 deed. Jasper Haynes had no son John;
his will was probated in Culpeper County
Jan.21, 1782. Witnesses were Humphrey
Sparks, Alexander Waugh, and William Phillips. Was this the William Phillips with
wife Ann who sold land in Orange County to
John Powell in 1742-3, and was he related
to the Joseph Phillips mentioned in the
deed from Henry Haynes to the latter in
1752?)

1752   Louisa County, Va. Deed Bk.A, p.512:
        Deed dated Oct.21, 1752. Henery Haynes of
        county of Louisa to Richard Durrett of said
        Co. 400 ac. of land in Louisa Co. on branch-
        es of Pritey's Creek on the uper (sic) side
        of Chestnut Mountain, adjoining William
        Craddocks.Metes and bounds given. Signed by
        Henry and Mary Haynes. Wit: Hugh Boyle,
        William P. Taylor (his X mark), Sarah U.
        Taylor. (Thus, both Henry and Jasper Haynes
        had land on Pritey's Creek; see deed dated
        1739.)

1752   Orange Co. Va. Deed Bk.12, p.88:(Month and
        day not available)
        In 1752 Henry Haynes and wife Mary of Louisa
        County on the one part and Joseph Philips of
        the other part, of said county, for and in
        consideration of £120 current money of Va.
        to him on hand, paid by same Joseph Philips
        for a certain tract of land lying in Orange
        County and bounded as followeth: To wit:
        Beginning at corner of William Heaton's

fence (?) to John Red's line on the brow
of a small valley then along said Heaton's
line N.E. 313 poles to 2 corner pines
thence 12 poles above said Red's corner
thence along his line S.E. 299 poles to
the beginning. Signed by Henry and Mary
Haynes. Wit: Richard Winslow, John Harrison, Tully Choin (Chinn?).

1753   Pittsylvania Co., Va. <u>Record Book, 1739-</u>
        <u>1770</u>, p.180:
        On March 23, 1753 Henry Haynes acquired
        400 ac. beginning at the mouth of Bull
        Run Creek, thence down Blackwater River.
        Also 400 ac. in the Fork of said Bull Creek
        "being surveyed for Robert Walton". (Al-
        though this county was not formed until
        1766-7, land surveys for this area are
        available in the county.)

1753   Lunenburg Co., Va. <u>Deed Bk.3</u>, p.281:
        June 17, 1753. Henry Haynes witnessed a
        deed to land purchased by John Haynes. The
        land was in that part of Lunenburg which
        became Bedford in 1753-54. (It was sold by
        John Haynes Nov.23, 1762. <u>Bedford Co.D.B.2</u>,
        p.108.)

1753   Pittsylvania Co., Va. <u>Record Bk. 1737-70</u>,
        p. 189.
        On July 6, 1753 Henry Haynes acquired 400
        ac. beginning at Robert Walton's upper
        line on Bull Run, thence up both sides of
        said Run. Also 400 ac. beginning at Ran-
        dolph's lower lines on Staunton River,
        thence down to Smith's Mountain. (During
        this same year William Haynes acquired 900
        ac. of land in this county and John Haynes
        of Lunenburg County acquired 400 ac. on the
        Blackwater and Bull Run. John and William
        were sons of Henry Haynes; it is possible
        but not probable that the Henry above was
        the son of Henry and Mary Haynes, rather
        than the father, who died in 1784. How-
        ever,it is not likely that Henry Jr., b.
        ca 1735, would have acquired 1600 acres by
        the age of eighteen. Furthermore, personal
        examination of the records did not offer

proof that the William Haynes of this 1753 record was the William Haynes who died 1781.)

1754   Bedford County, Va. <u>County Order Bk.1A</u>;5: July 22, 1754. "On the petition of John Henslee and Others for a Road from the Island ford on Staunton River by the mouth of Black Water River to the Road at the Meadows of Goose Creek which is granted and Henry Haynes is appointed Surveyor thereof ....." In the presence of: William Callaway, Zachariah Isbel, Thomas Pullin, and Edmond Mainon. (Note the name of Benjamin Henslee in 1745 deed.) On the same day, on the motion of William Mead who was granted Letters of Administration on the Estate of John Mead decd., he together with Henry Haynes, his security, entered into and acknowledged bond ..... It was ordered that Henry Haynes, Stephen English, William Verdeman and John Richardson, or any three of them, appraise in current money the slaves (if any) and Personal Estate of John Mead. (Evidently Henry Haynes lived in Bedford County for a few years, then moved to Prince Edward, then back to the land he entered in Pittsylvania Co.,which came to be known as Henry County at the time of his death, but which may have been what is known today as Franklin County, Virginia. Henry Haynes definitely owned land in Bedford County on Craddock's Creek at the time of his death as he willed it to his son Parmenas.)

1756   Pittsylvania Co., Va. <u>Record Bk. 1737-70</u>, p.240:
On June 24, 1756 Henry Haynes entered 400 acres on Cedar Creek, joining John Good's on both forks. Also 400 ac. on the East Ford of Bull Run, adjoining David Wilson. (These land entries could possibly have been made by Henry Haynes Jr. who was b. 1735. They bear the same date as the 400 ac. entered by William Haynes on Ruddy's Creek, recorded in Pittsylvania County.)

1758   Bedford County, Va. Survey Bk.1.
On March 19, 1758, 254 ac. were surveyed
for Henry Haynes on Enoch's Creek on the
west fork of Goose Creek. It is not
known what became of this tract.

1758   Patent Bk.33, p.438:
In consideration of 15 sh. Henry Haynes
was granted on June 2, 1758, 150 ac. on
Blackwater River against the mouth of
Bull Creek. (This transaction did not
give Henry's residence. This land was in
Bedford County; in 1759 it was deeded to
Samuel Smith.)

1758   Prince Edward County, Va. Deed Bk.5, 296:
On Sept.2, 1758 David Murry and Elisabeth
his wife, of same county, in consideration
of ₤50, deeded to Henry Haynes of same
county "that tract lying and being in the
county of Prince Edward on the South
branches of Appomattox River, containing
by estimation 218 ac. more or less, being
part of a tract of land containing 2970 ac.
granted Edward Nix, late of said county,by
patent July 10, 1745, and by him .....
sold to David Murry ... and bounded ....
to John Pleasant's line." Wit: Peter Lee,
Isaac Staples, William Haynes (son of Henry
Haynes, d.1784). In considering the residence of Henry Haynes during the period
1754-1763, when he appears to have spent
time in both Bedford and Prince Edward
Counties, a possible explanation lies in
the notes found under "South River Monthly
Meeting, Bedford Co., Va." in Hinshaw's
Encyclopedia of Quaker Genealogy, Vol.6,
pp.291-2: "... in this same year the
western counties were completely demoraliz-
ed by an Indian outbreak which drove many
in great fear from the mountain region back
to the older settlements ..." Under "Goose
Creek Monthly Meeting, Bedford Co., Va.",
ibid, pp.347-8: ".... there they reached
the mountain barriers in extreme western
Bedford County. There the more daring
spirits had gone through the passes to
claim the fertile river bottoms of the Roan-

oke (or Staunton River, as it was once
called). But with the start of the French
and Indian Wars, and the panic of 1755-56,
the settlers poured back through the gorges,
fleeing before the Indians for their very
lives. In one week it is said that more
than 300 inhabitants of the 'up country'
and the extreme western part of the county
poured through Bedford City ...."

1759   <u>Vestry Book, St.Patrick's Parish</u>, 1755-74,
Prince Edward County, Virginia:
Date of entry, Sept.1759.
In obedience to the written (within?) order
now the subscriptions have peaciably (sic)
and quickly processioned all the patent
land in our presen<u>ts</u>: present, Robert Jenn-
ings, Elkanah Jenings, William Hill,James
Walker, Manasseth McField, Joel Watkins,
James Matthews, William Thurman, Richard
Wooldrage, Benjamin Witt, John May, Richard
Bennett, John Wright, John Pleasant, Alex-
ander Meidrey, Henry Dikes, Jacob Winfrey,
<u>Henry Haynes</u>, David Henry, David Wright.
Signed by Robert Williamson, Elkanah Jenings
and Richard Shermin, Processioners.

1759   Bedford County, Va. (Exact ref.unavailable)
<u>Mortgage Bond</u>:
Henry Haynes of Prince Edward Co. Planter,
to Samuel Smith, a Planter of Hallifax Co.,
a bond of Ł60 and as security agreed to
deed to him 150 ac. of land lying on Blackwater River, on both sides of river near
mouth of same in Bedford and Hallifax Cos.
(See previous deed for same acreage patented in 1758.)

1759   Bedford County, Va. <u>Deed Bk.1</u>, p.202:
On March 26, 1759 Henry Haynes of Prince
Edward County,Va. sold to Samuel Smith of
Halifax County, Va. the above 150 ac. of
land. Wit: George Walton, John Haynes and
William Haynes. (Note: George Walton marr.
Mary Leftwich, daughter of Col.William
Leftwich and Elizabeth Haynes, daughter of
William Haynes of Bedford Co. (d.1781) who

was probably the brother of Henry Haynes
who died 1784.)

1760   Patent Bk.33, p.717:
        On March 3, 1760 Henry Haynes patented 100
        acres of land in Bedford Co., Va. on the
        north side of Staunton River, at the foot
        of Smith's Mountain. (Staunton now known
        as Roanoke River. This acreage probably
        adjoined land patented earlier in Pittsyl-
        vania Co. in 1753, as shown previously. At
        the present time this land may be in Frank-
        lin County, Virginia; Smith's Mountain is
        within a few miles of Penhook, Va., the
        small village north of Pigg River, where
        William Haynes (1727-1806) lived at the
        time of his death.)

1760   Bedford Co., Va. Deed Bk.1, p.316:
        On Nov.24, 1760, George Walton of the Co.
        of Lunenburg sold to Henry Haynes of Bed-
        ford Co. for £20, 125 ac. of land lying
        on the north side of the river Staunton.
        Signed by George Walton. No witnesses.
        (Henry Haynes, son of William 1710-1781,
        was born ca 1745. He could not have been
        the grantee, although Henry Haynes Jr., b.
        1735, could have been the purchaser.)

1762   Bedford Co., Va. Deed Bk.2, p.40:
        On Feb.27, 1762 Henry Haynes of Prince
        Edward County sold to Stephen English of
        the Parish of Russell, Bedford County, for
        £30, 100 acres of land lying on the north
        side of River Staunton, in Bedford County,
        granted to Henry Haynes by patent bearing
        date of March 3, 1761. John Haynes and
        Talbot C. Scrugg witnesses. (Note: This
        date should be March 3, 1760, see patent
        above. This Henry Haynes could not have
        been the son of William Haynes of Bedford
        County who died 1781. It is possible that
        he could have been Henry Jr., b.1735, but
        this is not probable. Stephen English was
        a son-in-law of Henry Haynes who d. 1784.)

1763   Prince Edward Co., Va. (Note: this deed is
        definitely on record in Prince Edward Co.,

but letter from county official failed to give exact reference.)
On Oct.17, 1763 Henry Haynes and Mary his wife, of Bedford County, in consideration of Ł50, sold to Robert Routledge of Prince Edward County 218 ac. of land on Appomattox River. (Richard Haynes, grandson of Henry and Mary Haynes, was born in Prince Edward County, Va. on Sept.19, of this same year. It is possible that Richard's father, William Haynes, 1727-1806, left soon after for the Penhook area which eventually became Franklin County, Va. in 1785-6 - a short distance from the west line of Pittsylvania County, Virginia.)

1764 Journal of the House of Burgesses, 1758-61: Under date of Nov.30, 1764 (Col.) John Phelps petitioned that four soldiers be allowed their pay and included the name of Henry Haynes.

1766 Journal of the House of Burgesses 1766-69: Under date of Dec.7, 1766 Col. Phelps petitioned that these same four soldiers of a Ranging Company in 1763 be reimbursed. (This may have been Henry Haynes Jr., son of Henry Haynes d.1784, since it is unlikely that the father would have been on the frontier at the age of 62, patriotic though he was.)

1767 Clements, M.C., History of Pittsylvania Co. Virginia, Appendix, p.276: First list of tithables, Pittsylvania Co., 1767; list taken by George Jefferson in "Cambden" Parish: John Smith and Henry Hains (together). (It is possible that Henry Haynes was living across the line in Bedford Co., Va. at this time, which, if so, would have relieved him of paying taxes in another county where he owned land. However, he may actually have been living in that part of Pittsylvania which became Henry Co. in 1776, and which became, shortly after his death, Franklin Co., Va. It is significant to note this association of the names Smith and Haynes.)

1768   Bedford Co., Va. <u>Deed Bk.3</u>, p.153:
       On May 24, 1768 Henry Haynes purchased 315
       acres of land lying on both sides of Crad-
       dock's Creek in Bedford Co. from John Tal-
       bot. (It appears that Henry Haynes kept
       this tract, which was willed to his son
       Parmenas in 1784; it was sold by Parmenas
       Haynes to William Trueman and recorded in
       Bedford County <u>Deed Bk.8</u>, p.65.)

1769   Bedford County, Va. (Exact ref. lacking):
       On March 20, 1769 Henry Haynes sold 125 ac.
       of land lying north side of Staunton River
       to Henry Hatcher. (This is probably the
       tract purchased in 1760 from George Walton.)

1771   Pittsylvania Co., Va. <u>Court Record Book,
       1767-1772</u>, p.293:
       At the June term of Court, 1771, there is
       this entry: "Deed from Benjamin McCraw to
       Henry Haynes was proved by the Oaths of two
       of subscribing witnesses thereto ....
       ordered to be certified." (Note: Deed
       searched for in deed books but could not
       be found.)

1772   Pittsylvania <u>Court Record Bk. 1772-1775</u>,
       p.34:
       At the August term of Court, 27th day,Henry
       Haynes asked permission to build a grist
       mill on both sides of Bull Run. (It is not
       known whether this was Henry Haynes Sr.,
       aged 71 at the time, or Henry Haynes Jr.)

This concludes the land records pertaining to
HENRY HAYNES, all of which indicate that he was
a rover, restless, and imbued with the pioneer-
ing spirit to move to the frontier where land
was cheaper. There are no deeds on record for
him in Henry County, Virginia, although there
is one for his son John, dated April 1779 (<u>Deed
Book 1</u>, p.210) who purchased land from John
Smith for £400.   Other records which follow
include the name of HENRY HAYNES:

1775   Pittsylvania Co., Va. <u>List of Tithables</u>
        <u>1767-1785</u>, pp.122 and 149 (abstracted by
        George Shelton).
        Henry Haynes Sr. 5 tithes, negroes Sam,
        Book(er), Chloe, and Violet. Henry Haynes,
        2 tithes, negro Tobe. (Both father and son
        were included in the 1776 list, also George
        Haynes. This was the year Henry Co., Va.
        was taken from Pittsylvania County.)

1777   Henry Co., Va. <u>Court Minutes</u>, Book 1, p?
        Henry Haynes and three of his sons took the
        Oath of Allegiance in Henry Co., Va. on
        Sept.13, 1777. On that day their ages were
        recorded as follows: Henry aged 76, William
        aged 50, Henry aged 42, and George aged 40.
        (Note: These records were examined in 1955.
        It is possible that both John and Parmenas
        Haynes were on military duty in 1777; it is
        known that both of them were in service.
        The names are also found in Hill's <u>History</u>
        <u>of Henry County, Va</u>., pp.305-7; the orig-
        inal county record was reported missing in
        1963. See also <u>Virginia Mag. of History and</u>
        <u>Biography</u>, 1st.series, 9: 139-140.)

1782   In a Commissioner's Book, #3, found in the
        Court House in Henry Co., Va. in 1955 by
        the compiler, were the following entries
        for Henry Haynes:
         Certificates for 185 lbs. of beef from
        Com. of Henry Co. furnished to Gen.Greene's
        Army sick in Hospital at Henry Court House,
        p.9; for 300 lbs. of beef for same purpose,
        p.10; 275 lbs. of beef, p? for ___ bushels
        of corn and 12 bundles of fodder, p.12.

        These certificates were probably all issued
        at Session of Court held March 1, 1782. Re-
        cord of certificates also appear in Court
        Minutes, Bk.2, pp.167,169. In the Commiss-
        ioner's Bk.3, p.142, Sept.13, 1783, there
        was the record that Henry Haynes Sr. was
        allowed £3.16s.4d. for beef furnished to
        the Continental Line. Likewise his sons
        Henry Jr. and William were also on the list
        as well as James and John Majors, with

allowances for services. (Note: <u>Majors</u> is
a significant name in Richard Haynes's
family; see later.)

1785   On pages 103-4 of the first <u>Will Book of
Henry County, Va</u>. 1777-1799, is shown the
inventory of the estate of Henry Haynes,
dated Jan.10, 1785, returned by the apprai-
sers William Swanson, Philip Realy, and
David Clarkson.
Items: 7 grown negroes and children; 4
horses; 2 head cattle; 8 old hoes; cooper's
tools; 3 roap hooks; 1 Dutch oven; 1 saddle
and bridle; 1 trunk; 1 pan; 1 pr. fire
tongs; 1 pr.sty<u>ll</u>ards; 1 gun; 5 water vess-
els; earthen ware; p<u>ut</u>er knives and forks;
1 hymn book; 1 chest; 5 chairs; cotton;
iron wedges; 1 cow & calf; 2 cow hides; 1
bed; 1 spinning wheel; 1 bell; s<u>c</u>illet;
tallow; beeswax; leather; salt; w<u>oo</u>llen
wheel; 1 grindstone; 1 bag; 1 bedstead;
...... amounting to Ł493.7s.3d. with date
of inventory given as Dec.8, 1784. Items
mentioned in final accounting but not in
inventory were: jug of honey, 1800 lbs. of
tobacco, 52 lbs. of corn, and "pork sold
before appraised".

1785   On page 105, same reference, appears the
list of items sold and the purchasers on
Jan.16, 1785:
Parmenas Haynes bought cotton, black bag,
stillards, cross cut saw, compass, grub-
bing hoe, and ½bu. salt; William Swanson
bought hammer, cooper's ax, wheel, hooks,
Dutch oven, hoes, tallow, and 1 pc.<u>moxer</u>;
Henry Haynes Jr. bought 2 axes, pan,tongs,
ax handles, trunk, 2 yards cloth, saddle
and bridle, honey, ½ bu? and 1 rifle gun;
Robert Cowan bought 1 handsaw, 2 cow hides
etc.; George Haynes bought 1 adz, drawing
knife, 2 wedges, box, iron, 2 dishes,etc.
Other purchasers were: David Clarkson,
Jeremiah Maxey, William Birdict (Benedict?)
Henry English, Philip Realy, Stephen Law,
John Haynes, Capt. Benjamin Green, and
Stephen Hail. The proceeds were slightly
over Ł67, to which was added 5s. from

94

Henry Jr. for a barrel of corn, and Ł2.10s.
in cash from Parmenas, making a total of
Ł70.5s.11d. The debts allowed were for
travelling expenses to court, "gaziting"
estate, debts including one to Henry Jr.,
Ł47 for 2 coffins, and "William Haynes a/c",
all amounting to Ł65.1s.1d. which, on Sept.
18, 1785, left a balance of Ł2 plus. However, at the final settlement on Sept.22,
the final figure shown was the Ł70.5s.11d.
shown above.

****

MAJORS:

Because of the association of the Haynes
and Majors families, some facts about the Majors
appear here, rather than in the biography of
Richard Haynes who married Margaret Majors,
thought to have been a daughter of Thomas Majors.
A tentative list of the children of Thomas and
Sarah Majors, compiled by Dr. Troy E. Majors,
formerly of Knoxville, Tennessee, where he was
associated with the University of Tennessee, presently living in Wichita, Kansas, is shown later.
Thomas Majors is first shown in Washington
County, Virginia when he bought land in 1792
(D.Bk.1, 278), and he and his wife Sarah sold
153 ac. for Ł100 to Ezekiel Ranbaugh on the south
fork of the Holston River, Aug.12, 1795 (op.cit.
p.423). His son Absalom married Elizabeth Smith
on Sept.9, 1795 (Marriage Register 4, p.311).
After this date the family is found in Jefferson
Co., Tennessee, in the neighbourhood of Cheek's
Cross Roads, where Richard Haynes lived in 1805.
Various records for the Majors family are available in Jefferson County prior to 1810, after
which date many of them are found in Rhea County,
Tennessee.
In 1808 Thomas Majors received a letter of
"dismission" from the Bent Creek Baptist Church;
his wife Sarah was evidently not living at this
time. Thomas was living in the household of his
son Abner Majors, in Rhea Co., Tenn. in 1830
(Census, p.391). His sons Abner, Thomas Jr.,Peter,
John, Elias, Absalom, and Jesse were in this

county before 1830; three of them left there in 1829.

The will of Thomas Majors was recorded Aug. 6, 1832, with son Abner as Executor. The will book is missing so there is no way of securing a list of the heirs, to prove or disprove that Margaret Majors Haynes was his daughter. The 1830 Census indicates that Thomas was 90-100 years of age. His approximate birth date would have been 1740, and so he could have been the father of Margaret, wife of Richard Haynes. Other Majors records are available but will not be noted here except for the marriage of a Richard Haynes and Catherine Majors in Rhea County on Feb.28,1829, and the 1830 Census which lists an Absalom Majors in Fayette County, Indiana (which adjoins Union Co., Ind.); Absalom settled later in Cass County, Missouri.

Following is the tentative list of the children of Thomas Majors,(born ca 1735, died Aug.1832 in Rhea County, Tennessee; burial place not known) and wife Sarah _____. Residence of Thomas Majors ca 1735-1786, not known; ca 1786--1791, Washington County, North Carolina/Tenn.; 1792-1795 South Fork of Holston River, near Abingdon, Washington Co., Va.; 1796-1814, Cheek's Cross Roads and near Witts Foundry, Jefferson Co., Tenn.; and 1815-1832 Camp Creek, Rhea Co., Tenn.

1. Margaret Majors, born ca 1761, probably in Virginia, died April 5, 1826, Union Co., Indiana. She married ca 1782 Richard Haynes who was born Sept.19,1763 in Prince Edward Co., Va., and died Feb.2, 1850 in Union Co. Indiana, the son of William Haynes.

2. Absalom Majors, b. 1770 in Virginia, died probably in Cass County, Missouri, where he was living in 1850. He married Sept.9,1795 in Washington Co., Va., Elizabeth Smith.

3. Abner Majors, born ca 1770 in Va. (probably twin of Absalom), died probably in Rhea Co. Tenn., where he was living in 1840. He m. July 23, 1797 in Jefferson Co., Tenn., Rachel Roddye (Bk.1, p.230) who was born ca 1770 in Pittsylvania Co., Va., the daughter of James Roddye and wife Lydia (Russell).

4. Peter Majors, born ca 1773, possibly in North Carolina, died Nov.23, 1844 in Rhea County, Tennessee, burial place not known. He married May 24, 1797 in Jefferson Co., Tenn., (Bk.1, p.219) Mary (Polly) Wright (born 1780 in N.C.), daughter of James and Lucy Wright. Peter Majors died probably in Bledsoe County, Tenn., where he was living in 1850.

5. Mary (Polly) Majors, born ca 1775, married Oct.23, 1799 in Jefferson Co., Tenn. (Bk.1, p.300) Jeremiah Riddle.

6. John Majors, born ca 1777, married Feb.2, 1799 in Jefferson Co., Tenn. (Bk.1, p.277) Keziah Duncan.

7. Elias Majors, born ca 1780, died 1847 in Cedar County, Missouri. He married Oct.15, 1802 in Jefferson County, Tenn. (Bk.1,410) Margaret Floyd, daughter of William Floyd.

8. Nancy Majors, born ca 1783, died ca 1827, Giles County, Tenn. She married May 12, 1806 in Jefferson County Asa McGee.

9. William Majors, born ca 1785. He married Feb.13, 1807 in Jefferson Co., Tenn. Rachel McGee, probably daughter of James McGee.

10. Dicey Majors, born ca 1787 in Washington Co., N.C./Tenn. She married May 6,1812 in Jefferson Co., Tenn. James Doherty.

11. Isaac Majors, born 1790, Washington Co., N.C./Tenn., died possibly Carrol or White County, Arkansas. He m. ca 1812 in Giles County, Tennessee, Mary _____.

****

WILLIAM HAYNES, 1727-1806

WILLIAM HAYNES was the eldest son of Henry Haynes, 1701-1784, and his wife Mary. He was born either in King and Queen County, Virginia - the residence of his parents prior to their land grant dated Sept.28, 1728 - or in Spotsylvania County, Virginia, where the land was entered. It is unlikely, however, that the parents were living in St.George's Parish, Spotsylvania a year or so before the date of their land grant.

William Haynes was probably living with his parents in 1745 when his father, Henry Haynes, then of Orange County, Virginia,bought land in Louisa County, Va., adjoining "Mr.George Haines" Possibly at the age of 19 he first secured land in Pittsylvania County, Va., unless the grant in 1746 involved the William Haynes who died 1781 in Bedford County, Va., rather than William Haynes born 1727, probably a nephew of the other William. However, a careful analysis of the land holdings of the former, in order to determine the identity of the two William Haynes in question, was made by Senator Hopkins, a descendant of William who d. 1781, and as noted previously, there is no proof that this William was involved in the Pittsylvania land grants.

William Haynes was married probably about 1750. The marriage may have taken place in Louisa County, Virginia, where his father was living until 1752, when he sold land in Orange County; or it may have taken place in a county further south although no record has been found. Prince Edward County was taken from Amelia in 1753-54, and, in 1763, it is known that William Haynes lived in Prince Edward as his son Richard was born there in that year. It is probable that William lived there on land owned by his father, purchased in 1758 and sold in 1763 during the month following Richard's birth. Records a few years later indicate that William Haynes lived in Pittsylvania County, Virginia until the area in which he lived became part of Henry County in 1776-77 where he is on record as having taken the Oath of Allegiance. At the time of his death, his land holdings were in Franklin Co., Va. which had been

taken from Bedford and Henry in 1785-6. A record
of land transactions and other items, copied for
the most part from original sources, is listed
chronologically below:

Note: It has been mentioned previously that the
changes in boundary lines have made it difficult
to locate various land grants of this period.
Note also that there was a Haymes family in Pittsylvania County, and a Drury Haynes family in
Franklin County, Virginia, apparently unrelated
to our "Pigg River Haynes" family.

1746   Pittsylvania Co., Va. Record Bk. 1737-1770,
        p.30:
        On Sept.19, 1746, William Haynes was enter-
        ed for 100 acres on Staunton River, begin-
        ning on Russel's lower line. (See comment
        above regarding determination of identity
        of this William Haynes, as well as in some
        of the deeds listed below.)

1754   Pittsylvania Co., Va. op.cit. p.203:
        On Jan.30, 1754 William Haynes was entered
        for 400 acres on Jonathan Creek, joining
        John Richardson's lines.

1756   Pittsylvania Co., Va. op.cit. p.240:
        On June 24, 1756 William Haynes was enter-
        ed for 400 acres on Ruddy's Creek, joining
        Walton's line. (Three years previously
        Henry Haynes was granted land beginning at
        Robert Walton's line; in the same year
        (1753) John Haynes of Lunenburg Co., be-
        lieved to have been William Haynes's young-
        er brother, was entered for 400 acres on
        Blackwater River. Their entries in the same
        source as above, pp.188 and 189 respective-
        ly.

1758   Crozier's Virginia Colonial Militia, 1651-
        1776:
        In Sept.1758, a William Haynes is listed as
        a member of the Militia of Amelia Co., Va.
        (p.65)- roster taken from Hening's Statutes
        at Large. Since Amelia borders Prince Ed-
        ward County, this could be William Haynes

whose son Richard was born in the latter county in 1763. The names of George, John and William Haynes appear as members of the Bedford County Militia (ibid, p.68) - in fact, the name of William Haynes appears twice. On p.74, a John Haynes also appears as a member of Lunenburg Militia. In 1742, a William Hains is listed as a member of Company 3, Augusta Co. Militia (p.92). If this last-named is William Haynes b. 1727, he would have been 15 years of age at the time, approximately the same age as his son Richard when the latter enlisted in the Revolutionary War.

1760   Patent Bk.33, p.715:
On March 3, 1760, in consideration of 55s. William Haynes was granted 514 acres in Bedford County, Va. "beginning at John Haynes's Corner Oak, running to a Corner Beech on Craddock's Creek .... said land lying on both sides of Craddock's Creek a north branch of Staunton River". (This land is now in Bedford County, probably near the land owned by William Haynes in what is now Franklin County, Va.)

1763   Bedford County, Va. Deed Bk.2, p.193:
On May 24, 1763 William Haynes sold the above tract of land to Barnabas Arthur for Ł100. Ben Howard, Justice of the Peace in Bedford County, certified that he examined William Haynes's wife, who waived her dower rights, but he did not give her name.

1765   Patent Bk.36, p.793:
On July 26, 1763, in consideration of 25s. William Haynes was granted 251 acres in Bedford County lying on the south side of Staunton River, beginning at the mouth of a branch on the river, thence up the branch as it meanders, to a creek on the river and down the same as it meanders to the beginning.

1766   <u>Patent Bk.36</u>, p.1019:
On Sept.6, 1766, in consideration of 26s., William Haynes was entered for 243 ac. in Halifax County, Va. on both sides of Bull Run Creek. (This land is now in Franklin Co., Va.)

1767   Pittsylvania Co., Va. <u>List of Tithables 1767-1785</u>, p.5:
William <u>Hayes</u> is listed with 2 tithables. (Since his name appears on the same page with Robert Crump Sr., Robert Crump Jr., and Peter Renfroe, it can be assumed that this is William <u>Haynes</u>.) On p.50, in the list taken by William Witcher in 1770, William Haynes is listed with 3 tithables and a negro Sam, and three years later, with 2 tithables. On the list taken by John Donaldson ca 1775, William Haynes is listed with only 1 tithable, on p.138.

1768   Pittsylvania Co., Va. <u>Deed Bk.1</u>, p.524:
On Nov.25, 1768, William Haynes sold 243 acres to William Swanson for Ł30, along both sides of Bull Run Creek, acquired by patent Sept.<u>22</u>, 1766. (Note slightly different date of patent above.)

1769   <u>Patent Book 38</u>, p.591:
On April 6, 1769, in consideration of 30s. William Haynes was entered for 300 acres in Bedford County, Va. on both sides of Pittman's Creek.

1769   Pittsylvania Co., Va. <u>Record Bk. 1737-1770</u>, p.457:
On Aug.25, 1769 William Haynes was granted 400 acres on a branch of Town Fork adjoining Mullings' line on the lower side, thence along ......

1770   Bedford County, Va. <u>Deed Bk.3,</u> 460:
On July 24, 1770 William Haynes, in consideration of Ł40, sold 251 acres lying on the south side of Staunton River to Thomas Loving. His wife did not join in the deed.

1770   Bedford County, Va. <u>Deed Bk.3</u>, pp.457-8:
On July 24, 1770 William Haynes of Pittsvl-
vania Co. sold to Henry Haynes and Aquilla
Greer, both of Bedford County, 150 acres
each, "said land lying and being on both
sides of Pittman's Creek, the same being the
300 acres granted me by Patent bearing date
April 6, 1769." (This land was probably in
what is now Franklin County, Va. - part of
the acreage which Henry Haynes owned at
the time of his death, 1784, then in Henry
County.)

1772   Pittsylvania Co., Va. <u>Court Minute Bk.2</u>,72:
At a court held in Sept.1772, James and
Robert Donald & Co. (Scotch merchants of
Glasgow) brought suit against William Haynes
son of Henry Haynes, for the sum of Ŀ7.4s.3d.
In the March term, 1773, John Wilkinson &
Co. sued William Haynes for Ŀ3.11s. During
the September term 1773, the same litigants
sued for Ŀ4.13s. (Did William Haynes main-
tain a trading post prior to the Revolution?
This record could not be located in Chatham
for personal examination.)

1777   Pittsylvania Co., Va. <u>Book of Estrays</u>:
On Feb.22, 1777 "We, the subscribers, being
first sworn, have viewed and appraised one
stray hog, taken up by Thomas Black, to 5s.
the said hog is marked with a Snallon (?)
fork in the right ear and a Floruier of
Delews (Fleur de lis?) in the left. Given
under our hands this 22nd day of Feb.1777".
Signed by James Dillard, William Devin and
William Haynes before William Witcher.
<u>Note</u>: Although William Haynes took the
Oath of Allegiance during the same year in
Henry County, Va., the fact that his land
was so near the Pittsylvania County line,
as well as that of other persons contained
in this court item, indicates that this is
the William Haynes, 1727-1806.

1777   Henry County, Va. <u>Court Minutes, Bk.1</u>:
On Sept.13, 1777 William Haynes, along with
his father Henry Haynes, and brothers Henry
and George, took the Oath of Allegiance.

(The age of William Haynes was 50 years,
thus verifying his birth year as 1727. The
original records were missing in the Henry
County Court House in 1964.)

1780   Henry County, Va. <u>Grant Bk.D</u>, p.286:
On Sept.1, 1780 in consideration of Ł1,
William Haynes was granted 193 acres in
Henry County on the north side of Pigg
River, on a branch called Dinner Creek.
(Land now in Franklin County, Va.   There
are also references to his land grants in
Pedigo's <u>History of Henry and Patrick Cos.</u>
p.316.)

1780   Henry Co., Va. <u>Grant Bk.E</u>, p.655:
On Sept.1, 1780, in consideration of 15s.
William Haynes was granted 110 acres lying
and being on the Grassy Fork of Bull Run.
(From 1782-85, William Haynes was listed
in Henry County, with 547 acres; when
Franklin County was formed in 1785-86, he
was listed with 547 acres. These were undoubtedly his three tracts of land in
Henry County, since they totalled 546 ac.,
that is, 243 plus 110 plus 193 acres.)

1782   Henry County, Va. <u>Court Minutes Bk.2</u>, 167:
At a Court held March 1, 1782, William
Haynes was given a certificate for 275 lbs.
of beef furnished for Gen.Greene's Army
sick in hospital at Henry Court House.
Others granted certificates were Aquilla
Greer, Benoni Perryman, William Swanson,
Henry Haynes Sr. and Jr., Robert Bohannon,
Robert Powell and David Witt - all names
of significance in the Haynes family research. James Majors was allowed 20 3/4
lbs. of bacon for use in the hospital,and
John Majors was allowed Ł3.10. for a
rifle gun furnished for use of the Militia
- the latter by John Dillard, a Commissioner - also significant names. In <u>Bk.3</u>, p.10
there is also a record of payment to William Haynes for items provided to Captain
Thomas Smith.

1782   Henry Co., Va.   Commissioner's Record 3,
        p.139:
        In 1782 William Haynes was given allow-
        ances for items furnished to the Contin-
        ental Line, although in May of the pre-
        vious year, food was given to the local
        militia. (On p.146, an allowance was made
        to James Majors. Could Margaret Majors,
        wife of Richard Haynes, have been a relat-
        ive of this Majors family whose descend-
        ants were reported as having gone to
        Georgia?)

1783   Pittsylvania Co., Va.   Court Minute Bk.4,
        p.504:
        At a Court session held during the May
        term, 1783, "We Paton Smith and Jesse
        Heard being chosen by John Sullivant and
        William Haynes to settle a certain matter
        of controversy do award the said John Sul-
        livant Ł3.18s."

1784   Henry County, Va.   Will Bk.1, pp.103-5,
        1777-99:
        William Haynes mentioned first among sons
        of Henry Haynes in his will; a negro boy
        named Willsby was left to him. He was al-
        lowed Ł3.16s. on account by the Clerk of
        the Court in the final settlement of his
        father's estate. (Since William Haynes
        was not an heir to any part of his father's
        land, it is possible that both he and his
        brother John had previously received help
        from their father in land purchases.)

1787   Franklin County, Va.   Wingfield's An Old
        Virginia Court, p.38:
        Reference is made to William Haynes's ap-
        pointment to appraise the estate of John
        Kirby (?) together with John Law Sr. and
        William Graves. At the March term of
        Court, p.57, William Haynes was allowed
        money for acting as a witness; on p.79,
        there is reference to his being on a jury.
        George Haynes and Parmenas Haynes, his
        brothers, were summoned to Court to show
        why they did not list property for taxes
        (p.76). Earlier in 1786, p.21, there is

reference to James Majors who, with others,
was appointed to view a road from the
County Road leading to Henry County Court
House - "the nearest and best way to David
Stewart's". (This is further proof that
the James Majors family of Henry County,Va.
in 1782 was in Franklin County after its
formation.)

1787 Pittsylvania County, Va. <u>Marriage Register 1767-1862</u>, p.9:
On June 19, 1787 William Haynes was surety
on the marriage license bond of Diana
Haynes to John James. (It is not known why
this marriage license was not secured in
his daughter's county of residence which,
at the time, was Franklin; John James did
live in Pittsylvania County, and they resided there after their marriage.)

1788 Franklin County, Va. <u>Deed Bk.2</u>, p.44:
On Oct.18, 1788 John Bolton of Amelia Co.,
Robert, James and Matthew Bolton and Robert
Perryman, of Franklin Co., legatees of Rob-
ert Bolton, in consideration of ₤20, con-
veyed to William Haynes of Franklin County
100 acres more or less on the north side of
Pigg River in Franklin County.

1791 Franklin Co., Va. <u>Deed Bk.2</u>, p.279:
On April 2, 1791 John Muse in consideration
of ₤45, conveyed _____ acres to William
Haynes. (The searcher reported that the
number of acres was not given, but that
Muse was listed in land books at Richmond,
Va., approximately with 71 acres on the
west side of Owens Creek at this time. His
wife was Lucy.)

1792 Franklin County, Va. <u>Marriage Bk.1</u>, p.976:
On July 23, 1792 William Haynes was surety
on the marriage bond of George Crump and
Dyce Haynes.

1792 Franklin Co., Va. <u>Order Book</u>, 1789-179?
At the October Term of Court, 1792 "William Haynes is appointed surveyor of a road

from the head of Bull Run to the end of
Smith Mountain in the place of William
Greer of the list filed to be his gang."
(A map indicating the location of Staun-
ton and Pigg River, Bull Run and Dinner
Creek, in relation to Smith Mountain and
the Franklin, Bedford and Pittsylvania
County lines would be of great help in
locating some of the tracts mentioned
herein.)

1793   Franklin County, Va. Order Bk. 1793-1799,
        p.13:
        In this source there is a record of a suit
        brought by the Walker administrators again-
        st Haynes. It is not clear whether it is
        William Haynes who is involved, or his son
        Henry, who was married to Susanna Walker
        in 1789, and possibly to Luiza Walker in
        1790. Robert Powell was also a defendant.
        There is more in regard to this suit in
        the same source, pp.24, and 409; on p.183
        there is an item stating that the suit of
        the Commonwealth against Haynes had been
        dismissed. On Aug.7, 1793 Henry and Steph-
        en Haynes were on the jury list (p.12). On
        p.418 there is record of a motion made to
        exempt 3 negroes of Burwell Law from pay-
        ment of county and parish levies in future,
        "also the property of William Haynes the
        same".

1799   Franklin Co., Va. Deed Bk.3, p.714:
        On July 18, 1799, William, Daniel, Burwell
        and David Law conveyed to William Haynes,
        in consideration of ₤100, 100 acres on
        Dinner Creek. Witnessed by Stephen Haynes,
        Haynes Morgan, William Brooks, and John
        Ironley.

1799   Patent Bk.41, p.293:
        On June 5, 1799 William Haynes was entered
        for 119 acres on Denner Creek (Franklin
        County?) by the Commonwealth of Virginia.

1803   Franklin Co., Va. Deed Bk.4, p.522:
        On Sept.26, 1803 William Haynes conveyed
        100 acres of land on Dinner Creek to George

Crump for 20s. Wit: Tarrell Brown, James
(X) Blackley, Burwell (X) Law. Land was
on Law's Road. George Crump was the son-
in-law of William Haynes.

1803   Franklin Co., Va. <u>Deed Bk.4</u>, p.586:
On Oct.18, 1803 William Haynes deeded 100
acres more or less on Grassy Fork of Bull
Run to Henry Haynes for 30s. Wit: Tarrell
Brown, Burwell (X) Law, Benjamin Hancock.
(Note: This is Henry Haynes, son of William Haynes, but not the same Henry Haynes
who bought 150 acres from Henry Hatcher
for ₺159 on June 7, 1802, recorded in
Franklin Co., Va. <u>Deed Bk.4</u>, p.345; he was
the son of William who d. 1781. The Henry
Haynes who asked permission to build a
grist mill on both sides of Bull Run (Pittsylvania <u>Court Order Bk.2</u>, p.34, Aug.27,
1772) was probably Henry Haynes Jr. who d.
in Greene County, Georgia in 1810, inasmuch
as Henry, son of William Haynes, would not
have been more than 12 years of age in 1772,
or it could have been Henry Haynes Sr. who
died 1784.)

1806   Franklin Co., Va. <u>Deed Bk.13</u>, p.564:
On April 3, 1806, William Haynes, William
Law, and John Perkins deeded 271 acres to
George Crump. (Note: It appears that this
joint deed included the 71 acres purchased
by William Haynes from John Muse in 1791,
and 200 acres of adjoining tracts owned by
Law and Perkins.) This is the last deed
made by William Haynes. When he died he
left three tracts of land - the 547 acre
tract mentioned previously under date of
1780, a 119 acre tract, and a 100 acre
tract, making a total of 766 acres, but
which, when surveyed, amounted to 780
acres.

1806   Franklin County, Va. <u>Deed Bk.5</u>, p.326:
<u>Bill of Sale</u>:
Sept.20, 1806 shows the following entry:

"Know all men by these presents that we
John James and Dinah his wife, Henry Haynes,

Richard Haynes, Stephen Haynes, George
Crump and Dicey Crump his wife, all heirs
and legatees of William Haynes Deceased
hath this day bargained and sold and by
these presents doth bargain and sell deliver and confirm unto Sarah Haynes wife
and Relic(t) of William Haynes deceased
the Property as follows viz: one negro boy
named Frank, one negro girl named Mary,
and one negro child named Moses, one Mare,
one bed and furniture, and household and
kitchen furniture, five head Cattle, sun-
dry hogs, also one negro woman named Bet,
for and in consideration of her part to
the personal property of William Haynes
deceased chosen by her as a child's part
and agreed to by the said John and Dinah
James, Henry Haynes, Richard Haynes, Stephen Haynes, and George and Dicey Crump, to
be her own and entire property to will and
dispose of the same as she pleases and we
the said legatees doth bind ourselves our
heirs and in case there should come any
claim against said estate we will pay our
proportionable part thereof. In witness
whereon we have hereunto set our hands and
seals this 20 day of September in the year
of our Lord 1806."

Signed and acknowledged in the presence of

Lewis Potter Sr.
John (his X mark) Willys
Lewis Potter

Signed by: John and Dinah (X) James
            Henry H. (X) Haynes
            Richard (X) Haynes
            Stephen Haynes
            George Crump and Dicey (X) Crump

At a Court held for Franklin County, April
6, 1807: This Bill of Sale from the legatees of William Haynes to Sarah Haynes was
proved by the oath of Lewis Potter Sr. and
Lewis Potter Jr., two of the witnesses
hereto, and ordered to be recorded. Teste:
James Calloway, Clk. Sarah Haynes's name

appeared on personal property tax lists
until 1813, after which date she was probably not living.

1807   Franklin Co., Va.   Order Bk.,County Court,
       1806-1811, p.147:
       At the August term of court, John Smith,
       Complainant, by his Counsel, brought a suit
       in Chancery against Richard Haynes, George
       Crump, Stephen Haynes, and David Law. The
       last-named three were ordered not to "pay
       away any money or secret(e) or remove any
       property or effects which have been in
       their hands belonging to the defendant
       Richard Haynes who, it appears, from the
       affidavit of the complainant, is not a re-
       sident of this state, but that they return
       the same in their hands subject to the fur-
       ther order of the Court, and that they be
       served with a copy of this order". (Neither
       the cause nor the outcome of this case in
       Chancery is known, since the Chancery Re-
       cord is missing for this period, due to a
       fire in 1870 which destroyed some of the
       Court Records. One can only speculate that
       John Smith may have made a loan to Richard
       Haynes after the death of his father, ac-
       cepting as security the inheritance due to
       Richard. Whatever the outcome, land and tax
       records indicate that Richard received no
       land. It is not known what portions Henry
       Haynes and Diana Haynes received. It is
       possible that Stephen Haynes and George
       Crump made some sort of cash settlement with
       the other three heirs, but if so, it is not
       on record.)

1807   Franklin County,Va. Tax Book:
       The three tracts of land, aggregating 766
       acres, were listed under the name of William
       Haynes in the land books for 1807. The tax
       books of Franklin County for 1808 are miss-
       ing. From 1809 through 1819 the land is
       thus listed: George Crump and Stephen Haynes
       in fee, 780 acres on Pigg River, 20 miles
       east of the Courthouse (Rocky Mount, Va.).

1818   Franklin Co., Va. <u>Deed Bk.8</u>, p.455-6:
       On Dec.3, 1818 Stephen Haynes and Nancy
       his wife executed two deeds to George
       Crump, conveying to him 75 acres on Pigg
       River for $400, and 400 acres on Pigg
       River for $1000. Witnesses to both deeds
       were John James (his brother-in-law),George
       W. Clement, Temple Perkins, and William
       Crump.

1818   Franklin County, Va. <u>Deed Bk.10</u>, p.39:
       On Dec.3, 1818 George Crump (Dicey, his
       wife, did not join in the deed so evidently
       she was not living at that time) in consid-
       eration of $1,400 conveyed to Stephen
       Haynes 265 acres on Pigg River. Witnesses
       were the same as the deed on the same date
       from Haynes to Crump. One can only guess
       by what process of law George Crump and
       Stephen Haynes acquired full title to the
       lands left by William Haynes. Undoubtedly
       it was an amicable settlement, as indicated
       by the following letter from Stephen Haynes
       to his brother Richard, (copied from the
       original):

                          Franklin, Oct.14,1833

Dear Brother,

Through the mercies of providence myself and family are yet in the land of the living, and are
enjoying tolerable good health, hopeing that you
and family are all well. I received your letter
of the 5th June which informed me that you was
well, which gave me pleasure to hear from you,
and also you informed me that you wish me to procure all the evidince that I could, relative to
your enlistment and service in the revolutionary
war, I have don so and have proven by the affidavids of Daniel and Burwell Law, that you enlisted under Capt.Henry Conaway in the Regular
Service and serve as much as two years and up-
wards but the time of your enlistment and ridgment and Battalion not recolected, I have given
the affidavids into the hands of Nathaniel H.
Claibourn our repersentive to Congress to carry
with him to Congress who will do all that he can

for you, and who nows the men that deposed and
the magistret who they deposed under and Clerk
who has sertified that he is acting Justice of
the piece, it will be necessary for you to make
your repesentive to Congress your power of att-
erny to act for you and make him acquainted with
all the circumstances of this letter who can see
Claibourn our member to Congress who will assist
him to procure your pension, if you recollect the
time of your enlistment and ridgment and Battalion that you was attach to you had better inform
your Congressman as he may find your name enroll-
ed in the War Department and if your name can be
found their it will answer every purpose, I now
of no man living that was with you in service
but Major Samuel Cochrain who is now living in
Sumner County Tennessee. Your relations in the
cuntry are generally well as fare as I no, my
son Lewis Haynes is dead, he died last August, no
more at present but remain your loving Brother
till death Richard Haynes

                            Stephen Haynes

                    ****

WILLIAM HAYNES left the following heirs, according to the Bill of Sale on record in Franklin
County, Virginia, in 1806:

1.   Diana (or Dinah) Haynes, born ca 1758, d.
      1844. Since her name appears first among
      those who signed the Bill of Sale on Sept.
      20, 1806(as previously shown), it is as-
      sumed that she was the eldest child. She
      married John James on June 19, 1787 (Marr-
      iage Register 1767-1862: 9, Pittsylvania
      Co., Va.) with William Haynes as surety.
      John James died intestate in 1813, leaving
      a large amount of personal property in-
      cluding 17 slaves. John Muse, William
      Witcher, Charles Powell, George Crump, and
      Bristow Gilbert were appointed appraisers
      on Feb.15, 1813 (Accounts Current, Book 5,
      p.48). On April 4, 1837 (Pittsylvania Co.
      Deed Bk.40, p.437) Diana James deeded two
      negro girls to her son John James, the in-

crease of a woman Meriah whom she purchased
with "my own money", and one-third part of
all personal property to her daughter Dicey
Hatchett of Sangamon, Illinois; and same
to her daughter Frances Witcher of Pittsylvania County. Three grandsons also received
legacies: William H. James, Spencer James,
and John J. Witcher. Diana reserved a life
estate in the property. On May 27, 1837
(Deed Bk.42, p.400) Harrison Hatchett and
wife, in consideration of $140, deeded John
James Jr. "their right and interest in 128
acres, it being the dower right and interest of Diana James in the estate of John
James, decd.". On Jan.1, 1845 the inventory and appraisement of Diana James's estate were recorded (Will Bk.9, p.429). On
March 28, 1846 (Deed Bk.50, p.57) Frances
Witcher for $120 deeded her one-third of
the dower land to her brother John James
Jr. Frances Ann James married Armistead
Witcher on March 28, 1834. The names of
only three grandchildren of Diana (Haynes)
James are known.
Note: Since John James, born 1752, is
listed in the D.A.R. Patriot Index, p.365,
it can be assumed that least one of the
descendants of John and his wife Diana
Haynes was a member of the D.A.R. Therefore it should be possible to learn more
of the family of Diana Haynes if, indeed,
the D.A.R. applicant actually had family
information of the maternal line.

2. Henry Haynes, born ca 1760, married (1)
Susanna Walker, Jan.16, 1789 (Marriage
Bonds, Bk.1, 1847, Franklin Co., Va.).
Surety: Robert Boulton, Minister,Thomas
Douglas. Although not recorded in the
above reference, a slip of paper was found
in Oct.1963 among Old Marriage Files, in
the courthouse at Rocky Mount, Va., and on
it this record: "Henry Hanes and Luiza
Walker, married according to law. Signed:
Thomas Douglas, 20th April, 1790." (If
this is a second marriage, Susanna must
have died and Henry Haynes possibly married her sister.) Henry Haynes married Mary

Wheat July 4, 1797 (<u>Marriage Bonds Book 1</u>,
1848); Stephen Haynes was Surety. Mary
Haynes, "daughter of Henry Haynes", married
Benjamin Norris Feb.19, 1807, with Josiah
Wheat as Surety (ibid, 3040). On Feb.2,
1807, Henry and Mar<u>e</u>y his wife deeded to
Anthony Street "the tract of land on which
said Street now lives, on fork of Bull Run,
adjoining lands of Matthew Farmer, the land
where widow Jones now lives, and lands of
John P. Hudson, Phillemon Sutherland ......
containing 110 acres. Consideration $300."
Signed by their marks. Wit: Daniel Brown,
Tarlton Brown, John Hale (<u>Deed Bk.5</u>, 503).
Henry Haynes apparently left Virginia about
this time - a few months after he entered
into the Bill of Sale pertinent to a property settlement with Sarah, wife of his
father, William Haynes. (He may have gone
to Alabama, since his son, John R. Haynes
is reported to have married Martha S. Hancock, daughter of Field Allen Hancock, in
Jackson County, Alabama. Lewis Haynes, son
of Stephen, is also said to have died in
Alabama in 1833.)

3. Richard Haynes, born Sept.19, 1763 in
Prince Edward County, Virginia, and died
1850 in Union County, Indiana, of whom
later.

4. Stephen Haynes, born 1773 in Pittsylvania
Co., Virginia, died 1843. He married Nancy
Oglesby ca 1795 in Franklin County. The
will of Stephen, probated Sept.4, 1843
(<u>W.Bk.5</u>, pp.513-4) in the same county names
Nancy his wife, sons Robert, William O.,
Alfred, Stephen W., and John O.W., and daughters Elizabeth, Julia Ann, also Frances
the widow of Lewis who died 1833, and the
latter's children. Witnesses were John
James, Charles Powell, and William Crump.
His wife was executrix. The inventory of
his estate (ibid, p.543) lists 33 negroes
including four children. The accounting
(ibid, 727-9) indicates a large estate.His
children are listed below in what is be-

lieved to be their order of birth:

(1)   John Oglesby Winston Haynes, born ca
        1798; married (1) Elizabeth Martin,
        May 3, 1821; married (2) Elizabeth
        Anne Keen, March 2, 1840. They had,
        among others, Elizabeth b. 1840;Nan-
        cy O., b.1843; Elisha Keen, b. 1845
        (who m. Pauline Edwards May 23, 1863
        and had a son William); William Dan-
        iel, b.1847 (who m. Fannie K. James
        June 3, 1873); Stephen Lewis, b.1856
        and John Thomas b. 1863. Stephen
        Lewis was still living in the early
        1940's when contact was made by the
        Indiana Haynes descendants with des-
        cendants in Virginia.

(2)   Robert D. Haynes, born ca 1796 (ac-
        cording to U.S.Census for 1850 in
        Franklin County). In 1855 (D.Bk.24,
        p.9) he deeded his brother, John O.W.
        Haynes, 9 slaves and the entire tract
        of land where he lived. In 1854 he
        deeded 10 acres to Sally Horsley,and
        in 1858, 41½ acres to Henry Law or
        Low. He may have died unmarried(D.B.
        23:247, and D.B.25:312 respectively).

(3)   Lewis Haynes, born ca 1800, married
        Frances, daughter of Robert Powell,a
        neighbour, Feb.27,1821. According to
        a letter written by Stephen Haynes to
        his brother Richard, in Indiana,Lewis
        Haynes died in August 1833. His widow
        Frances Haines was listed in the 1850
        Census with Nancy, aged 25; Robert S.
        aged 21; and Ophelia aged 32. There
        were also William M., b.1825, and
        Mary Elizabeth (who m. John W. John-
        son Sept.10, 1844, and had children
        Lewis, Lockey, and Booker). Robert S.
        Haynes married Jemima L. Craghead
        June 30, 1857. In 1853 Patrick A.
        Bassett and Mary E. his wife, of Sauk
        City, Wisconsin, deeded to Paschal
        Powell and William Haynes, son of

Lewis and Frances (Powell) Haynes,
200 acres on Little Bull Run, joining
lands of .... Robert Powell, being
land heretofore held by Sarah Powell
as dower in the estate of William
Powell for $451.66 (Deed Bk.23:136-7).
A deed pertinent to this land follows, and another is found earlier
(D.Bk.16, p.328).

(4)   William O. Haynes, born ca 1802; he
        married Julia Hancock of Alabama ca
        1820. There is no record of him
        available except in his father's will.

(5)   Alfred Haynes, born 1812, died un-
        married. He is listed in the 1850
        Census; appraisement of his estate
        dated Dec.29,1855 (W.Bk.9, p.349).

(6)   Stephen Haynes, b.1814, listed in the
        1850 Census.

(7)   Julia Ann Haynes, b.1816, listed in
        the 1850 Census with her brothers
        Alfred and Stephen; d.s.p.

(8)   Elizabeth Haynes, born ca 1818, m.
        Adam Law Dec.17, 1835. (Their dau.
        Nannie O. married William Hunt.)

Note: Dr. L.C.Haynes and his sister, Florence Haynes Hancock, contributed to the
data gathered by the compiler of this genealogy. They descended from Stephen Haynes
(1773-1843) through his son John O.W.Haynes
and the latter's son William Daniel Haynes.
There were 4 children in this family of
Franklin County, Virginia:

(a)   Lewis Claude Swanson Haynes, M.D.,
        was a physician connected with the
        U.S.Veterans' Administration shortly
        before his death ca 1950 in Mount
        Jackson, Va. His wife was Martha
        Lovelace. No children.

(b)   Elizabeth Haynes, married Page K.
        Gravely. She lived in Rocky Mount,
        N.C., and died 1968. Their daughter
        Elizabeth m. Bruce Lea: children,
        Bruce Jr., Page, Winston, and Haynes.

(c)   Blanche Haynes, married R.N.Younger.
        She is aged 88 (1972); two daughters,
        Elizabeth, who m. Harold Farley of
        Richmond, Va., one dau. Elizabeth who
        was b. 1960; and Mary who m. James
        Todd of Radford, Va.; they have a son
        Stephen James who m. Beverly Hutton,
        and daughter Elizabeth Shelley.

(d)   Florence Haynes, married Hugh Hancock
        and lived in Bluefield, W.Va. She d.
        1966, Hugh Hancock d.1968, and dau.
        Frances d. 1970. Sons: William T.
        who lives (1972) at Bluefield,Haynes
        who lives at Alexandria, La., and
        Hugh who lives at Salem, Va., and has
        daughters, Gail (Mrs.Kenneth Friedman
        of New York City) and Ingrid (Mrs.
        Edward Asher of Arlington, Va., the
        mother of Rhett b.1966 and Zorba b.
        1971).

5.   Dicey (Eurydice?) Haynes, born ca 1775 in
      Pittsylvania County, Va., died before 1831,
      married George Crump July 23, 1792, with
      her father as Surety (Marriage Bk.1, 976).
      George Crump's will was probated Jan.2,1831
      in Franklin Co. (W.Bk.3, 505), and was wit-
      nessed by Temple Perkins, John Potter, and
      Lewis Hancock; executors were John James,
      Stephen Haynes, and William Crump, son of
      George Crump. Other children are mentioned
      in the will but not by name; Dicey, his
      wife, is not mentioned although the will
      was dated Dec.6, 1818, so she may have died
      before that date. The appraisal of real es-
      tate amounted to $7,689, and his twelve
      slaves at $4,732. Among the chn. were:

(1)   William Crump, m. Gilly Law, Oct.2,
        1815.

(2)   Libby R. Crump, m. Benjamin Smith,
      Jan.25, 1823.

(3)   Miriam Crump, m. Capt.George W.
      Brown Feb.6, 1826.

(4)   Dinah H. Crump, m. Stephen Law May 1,
      1826.

(5)   Hannah M. Crump, m. Pleasant E.
      Breedlove Jan.7, 1828.

(6)   Elizabeth Crump, m.John Young Nov.15,
      1828.

(7)   Frances P. Crump, m. Henry P. Smith
      Jan.29, 1831.

(8)   Sarah Crump, m. Thomas Shelton May 8,
      1834.

(9)   Nancy Crump, m. Charles A. Weather-
      ford April 10, 1843.

Note: Since the marriage records fail to
indicate parentage of Sarah and Nancy, they
may have been children of William Crump; on
the other hand, they both joined in the
following deed (D.Bk.14, 316):

In 1834, six heirs, together with their
husbands, joined in conveying 705 acres
Pigg River and Dinner Creek, Franklin Co.,
Va. to William Crump. In this deed the
name of Miriam Brown appears as Missouri;
Elizabeth Young and her husband were of
Giles County, Va. (where family tradition
says that George Crump died). The other
heirs lived in Franklin and Pittsylvania
Counties. The two daughters listed above
who did not join in the deed were Libby
Smith (who may be the same as Elizabeth
who m. (2) John Young), and Frances P.
Smith (who may not have been living three
years after her marriage).

One researcher commented upon the Haynes-
Crump deeds in Franklin Co. as follows:

"It seems as if one deed would have been sufficient. George Crump was not an heir of William Haynes. If his wife were an heir, but dead, then their children would have been among the heirs of William Haynes." This comment was made more than twenty years prior to the discovery of the Bill of Sale dated Sept.20, 1806,which indicates that there must have been some sort of agreement among the heirs of William Haynes, for at this time, Dicey Haynes Crump was living.

The above record of five children completes the family of William Haynes for which there is documentation. There may have been others who were not living and who had no known heirs at the time of William Haynes's death in 1806. Among them may have been:

John Haynes, born ca 1761, who was listed as a tithe with one horse in Franklin County in 1787. He may have gone to Jefferson County,Tenn. where a John Haynes and wife Elizabeth appear in the Minutes of the Bent Creek Baptist Church prior to 1790, and who have not been identified to date. When it is remembered that Richard Haynes bought his first farm in Jefferson Co., Tenn. from Zere McGee of Grainger County in 1806 and that William Majors married Rachel McGee in Jefferson County on March 13, 1807, the following deed becomes of special interest in the Haynes family study: On Feb.1, 1789 James McGee of Hawkins County in North Carolina, sold to John Haynes of the same county 125 acres on Cedar Creek, a branch of Holston River, for Ł25 (Hawkins Co., Tenn. Deed Bk.1, p.15, 1788-1800). Jefferson Co. was created in 1792 from Hawkins and Green Counties. This deed further indicates that there was a John Haynes in the area which later became Jefferson County, Tenn., by 1789; John Haynes was listed as a tithe with one horse in Franklin County, Va., in 1787, but not after this date. So far there has been no proof of the identity of John and Elizabeth Haynes of Jefferson County, Tennessee.

Hannah Haynes, who married Randolph Humph-
phreys in Bedford County, Va., April 29,
1790, was "of age" but has not been identified to date.

Elizabeth Haynes, thought to have been the
wife of Burwell Law, and neighbour of the
William Haynes's families, has also not yet
been identified.

Mornin' Haynes, who married Benoni Perryman of Henry County, Va. Nov.25, 1782,also
not identified.

James Haynes, listed in Henry County, Va.,
1783 with one tithe and 3 horses, not yet
identified.

William Haynes who married Polly Laurence
in Sumner County, Tenn. Jan.1, 1792, and
soon after was killed by Indians, not yet
identified. (Major Samuel Cochrane, mentioned in Stephen Haynes's letter, shown
previously, went to Sumner County.)

In addition to the above, there are many
other conjectural relationships of the William
Haynes family with Powell, Law, Smith, Tyre (or
Tyree), Talbott, Hubbard, Perkins, Greer, Perryman, Bolton, Potter, and other families in the
area. For example, the Potter family name is
found on various legal documents of the Haynes
family; Stephen Potter of Lawrence Co., Indiana
testified that he grew up with Richard Haynes in
Virginia (shown on the latter's pension application # S 32-307) thus leaving one to wonder if
his mother were a sister of Sarah Haynes, wife
of William Haynes of this chapter (1727-1806).
Lewis Potter (Jr.?) lived in Indian Creek Tp.,
Lawrence County, Indiana, after 1830.

One of the main objectives of the careful
search conducted on the Haynes family was to
find proof of the maiden name of the wife of
William Haynes. This has not been accomplished
although hope remains that it will be found in
the records of some collateral family. Various
names have been mentioned, such as Dowell, Win-

ston, and Powell - in fact, descendants of Stephen Haynes, born 1773, feel certain that it was Powell. The best evidence of this exists in the following will on file in Augusta County, Va.:

"In the Name of God Amen, the 31st day of March 1779, I Ambrose Powell of the County of Augusta in Virginia ..... do make my last will .... First it is my desire that my Rifle gun, left with John Offill should be given to Jacob Gilasby, son of John Gilasby, Secondly it is my will and desire that all the rest I possess in this world should be equally divided between all my brothers and sisters except Sarah Haines and her two children, Stephen and Dicey Haines it is my desire that they should possess an equal part with my Brothers and Sisters ..." Signed by his (X) mark. Richard Bohannon was named Executor, and witnesses were: Robert Gaius, John Offill, James Bohannon. The will was probated Aug. 16, 1783.

Note: This will was examined in Augusta County, Virginia, but no supplementary records could be found, such as receipts, which might indicate whether or not Sarah Haynes, wife of William Haynes, were the legatee, and if so, her relationship to Ambrose Powell, who may have been a brother of Robert Powell Jr. of Franklin County. See comments under 1749 entry for HENRY HAYNES, (1701-1784), also first entry for 1782 under WILLIAM HAYNES.

****

RICHARD HAYNES, 1763-1850

The search for the parents of Richard Haynes (1763-1850) and also those of his wife Margaret Major(s) (17?-1826), began many years ago. The fact that he was a Revolutionary soldier had been established not only through family tradition but also because of his tombstone in the Witt

Cemetery, Union County, Indiana, which bears the inscription "A Revolutioner", and a great-grand-daughter proved his line for D.A.R. membership. In 1928 four descendants visited Union County and found the tombstone, which had been placed in an upright position by members of the Benjamin Dubois Chapter of the D.A.R. Stones marking the graves of Richard Haynes's wife and a few of his descendants were lying flat on the ground, some of them broken.

Note: Through all three of these generations (i.e. Henry Haynes 1701-1784, William Haynes 1727-1806, and Richard Haynes 1763-1850) descendants are entitled to recognition for their patriotic service during the Revolutionary War, although Richard is the only one recorded as having had actual military service.

Possibly the first evidence in print of the service of Richard Haynes was the biography of a grandson, Charles N. Wales of Xenia (now Converse, Indiana) Ind., published in the History of Miami County, Indiana, by Brant and Fuller, 1887. His daughter Frances established a supplementary DAR line for Richard Haynes through the General Francis Marion Chapter, of Marion Co., Indiana. This was accomplished through receipt of the service record received from the Bureau of Pensions in 1910; her National number is #84216. At that time the service record revealed only the facts that (1) he served as a Private for two years and six months in the 14th Va. Regiment, Continental Line under Capt.Henry Conway and Col.Charles Lewis,and (2) that he had two tours of duty, fourteen weeks in all, in the Militia, officers not named. His place of enlistment was given as Pittsylvania Co. and his date and place of birth as Sept.19,1763 in Prince Edward County, Virginia.

Deed records, taken from the Register of Deeds in Tennessee, indicate that Richard Haynes bought 100 acres of land lying on Flat Creek in Jefferson County, from Zere McGee of Grainger Co. Tenn., on July 26, 1806 (D.Bk.H, p.224). Wit: James McGee and William Cox. This same tract, "on the waters of Nolichucky River", had been bought by Abner Majors from Joseph Dorman in 1798

and sold by the former to McGee two years later.
William Majors, brother of Abner, married Rachel
McGee in Jefferson County Feb.13,1807. Richard
Haynes sold this tract (D.Bk.K, p.114) to James
White on March 28, 1812 for less than he paid
for it. It was in this area that Jane Haynes
was born in 1805; the settlement called Cheek's
Cross Roads - a spot indicated by a historical
marker, on the edge of a town called Russell-
ville, now in Hamblen County and not far from
the lake developed by the Tennessee Valley Auth-
ority through a dam on the Holston River. On the
Matthew Rhea map of 1832, Cheek's Cross Roads
was on the Hawkins and Jefferson County line,and
near the Grainger County, Tenn. line as well.

On March 16, 1816, Richard Hanes (sic) purchased 80 acres of land for $280 from Jacob Wil-
son Jr.; both were of Jefferson County, Tenn.
It was located "on the north side of the knobs
that divide the waters of the French Broad and
the Holston on Cox's Branch" (D.Bk.D). The testators were John McFarland Jr. and Richard Haines
Jr. This land may have been in a district known
as the McFarland Settlement; the compiler has a
county map showing the location. On March 8,1819
(D.Bk.P, p.68) Richard Haynes Sr. deeded this
land to James Hurst "including the plantation
wherein James Hurst now lives". In the description, a ridge of iron ore is mentioned, which perhaps supplied the iron for Witt's Foundry, another traditional family spot. This land transaction probably occurred about the time of Richard's decision to leave Tennessee.

An item of interest found in Jefferson Co.,
Tenn., appeared in Court Minutes, Bk.6, 1812-18;
Henry Justice died in 1815 at Richard Haynes's
house, and his will was given to Richard and
William Haynes by voice (noncupative), who, in
turn, reported it to the court and signed for the
deceased. A record of 100 acres of land surveyed
for Richard Hynes on Dec.26, 1809, is recorded in
Roane County, Tennessee. Where the family of
Richard Haynes lived in 1820 is not known; the
Census records for Jefferson County are not available and the name is not found in the Indiana list
for that year. Tradition has it that he came to

Indiana in 1821.

The Roster of Soldiers and Patriots of the
American Revolution Buried in Indiana, compiled
by the Indiana D.A.R. in 1938, includes the service record of Richard Haynes (p.182), together
with brief and incomplete family data.

Through the Jeffersonville, Indiana land
office a grant of 160 acres was made to a Richard Haynes on March 23, 1829, for Cert.#2252,
purchased Sept.27,1817 (D.Bk.3, p.180). This
land, SE ¼ Sec.11, Tp.2 N, Range 1E, lies in
Northwest Tp., Orange Co., Ind. on Lick Creek.
The sale of this land has not yet been traced.
A land entry was also made at the land office
in Brookville in 1821, this item being found in
the State Auditor's office in Indianapolis: 80
ac. lying in the W.½ of the NW Quarter of Sec.
28, Tp.18, Range 12E (Tract Bk.2). Apparently
this land was in either Randolph or Wayne Co.,
Ind., and considerably north of Union County,so
it may have belonged to Richard Haynes Jr.

There are deeds in Union County covering
land transactions for Alfred Haynes and Jefferson Haynes, long believed to have been closely
related to Richard Haynes Sr.; and recently
Jefferson Haynes has been proven to be a grandson.
The Bible record of Richard Haynes Jr.(of
whom later), son of Richard Haynes, was located
in the home of a descendant living in Grant Co.,
Indiana, which led to a search of the records of
Henry Co., Indiana. It was learned through a biography of David Haynes that the family lived in
Wayne County between 1821 and 1832. After coming
to Henry County, members of this branch lived in
Blue River, Prairie, and Stony Creek Townships.
In the same county there was a "Jimtown" where a
grandson, James Doherty was reported to have
lived, but his name was not found in the county
records nor was it in Boone County, where there
also is a Jamestown. One of Richard Jr.'s sons
was a school teacher; another was postmaster at
Dan Webster (formerly Hillsboro), Indiana.

Tradition also gathered about the "Alf" Haynes who had lived in Union County. On Sept. 27, 1827 the marriage was recorded of Alfred Haynes and Mary Leeper(s); they lived in Tazewell County, Illinois at the time a deed for the sale of their land was made in Union County in 1829 (D.Bk.C, 234). In the Tazewell County Census p.159, line 10, an Alfred Haynes is shown aged 20-30, wife 20-30, and one male under five.

A "Jeff" Haynes reportedly died of cholera near Oldenburg, Ripley County, Ind., ca 1849; records show that (Thomas) Jefferson Haynes married Cynthia Wheeler in Union Co. in 1833 (Bk.B, 1826-38, p.261, married by Moses Jeffries, Baptist minister), and his land in that county was sold to Charles Daniels in 1845 (D.Bk.8, p.274), land which had been purchased from William Shoemaker in Township 12, Sec.36, north of Range 5W. This land was further described as 80 acres in the W ½ of the SE Quarter. The farm could not have been far from where Richard Haynes lived with his son-in-law, James Wales, in 1830; the latter named a son Charles Nutter Wales, and Charles Nutter's name appears on the deed of "Jeff" Haynes as a witness. When Richard Haynes' estate was admitted to probate Aug.7, 1850, his son-in-law James Wales petitioned the Court to declare his estate insolvent after the personal property was appraised at $104, the chief item of value being one grey horse listed at $50 - the horse which had taken him over the state in his wanderings between 1830 and 1850. A notice appeared in the American for August, 1850, stating that the estate was insolvent. There is therefore no probate record listing his children. However, a descendant, Mrs. Maude Maibach of Oxford, Ohio, supplied the names of the orphan children of "Jeff" Haynes, who scattered from Cincinnati,O., to Xenia, Miami Co.,Indiana, after the death of the parents. She reported that there were no records available, since the contents of the house were burned after the parents' deaths; her father had died in the Masonic Home in Franklin, Ind.; she also knew that her grandfather was Jefferson Haynes and that he was related to Richard Haynes Sr., but could offer no proof. The eventual discovery of Jefferson's parentage would seem to ex-

plain the close kinship felt by Jane Haynes Wales'
descendants for those of "Jeff" Haynes's family
whom they knew.

The first real "break through" in the search
for the names of Richard Haynes's parents was the
letter of Stephen Haynes regarding the pension
application of his brother Richard, as previously
shown. Correspondence with Dr. Marshall Wingfield
of Memphis, Tennessee, author of Marriage Bonds
of Franklin Co., Va.,1786-1858, led to the
suggestion that Dr. L.P.Haynes (previously mentioned) who was at the time connected with the
Veterans' Bureau in Texas, might be able to help
as his boyhood home had been on the Haynes's
farms near Penhook, in Franklin Co., Virginia, as
previously shown. Dr.Haynes knew that Stephen's
father was William Haynes and that his wife was
said to have been Sarah Powell, because of a con-
tinuous kinship with Powell descendants for generations.

After this correspondence with Dr.Haynes
began, the interest of State Senator Walter Hopkins of Richmond, Virginia (now deceased) was
aroused, and he included the Haynes family research as an extension of the work he had done in
the Bedford County records, Virginia. With con-
tributions from a number of descendants, he engaged persons to search the court records of Pittsylvania and Franklin Counties, and integrated
his own data from Bedford County with the results,
as well as with the voluminous amount of material
found in the Virginia State Library and Archives,
and other items from various sources. These data
were summarized earlier in this chapter, relating
to Henry Haynes, 1701-1784, and William Haynes,
1727-1806.

The search continues for the family data
of Margaret Major(s), wife of RICHARD HAYNES.
Some time ago, correspondence with Miss Penelope
Allen of Chattanooga, Tennessee, told of Majors
records in Tennessee and of their connection with
Roddye, Cheek, and other familiar names. The
Minute Book of the Bent Creek Baptist Church,1785-
1844, located in Hawkins County, Tenn., has been
examined in Knoxville; it contained both Haynes

and Majors items, especially the intriguing fact that Mary Majors was excommunicated (p.2) for raising a stick and trying to beet Jesse Cheek without provocation, and made his horse throw him, and for three other reasons! Thomas Majors was one among many dismissed from the church to another location. Brother Majors received his letter on Saturday, March 2, 1808 (p.60). He is known to have gone to Rhea County, Tenn., where he died a few years later, leaving a will, but failed to name his children in it. Some of the facts briefly noted in the family data of Henry Haynes, 1788-1865, son of RICHARD HAYNES, who also went to Rhea County along with other Jefferson County families, indicate that Thomas Majors was the father of Margaret.

The following data were found in the Pension Files in the National Archives:

In the Plea for a Pension under the Act of 1832, entered at the Union County, Indiana, Court on the first Monday in Sept.1832, RICHARD HAYNES stated that, when he enlisted, he marched to Albemarle Courthouse, Virginia, thence to Fredericksburg, Alexandria, Baltimore, Philadelphia, Bound Brook, Morristown, Head of the Elk, White Marsh, Valley Forge, across the Delaware, Monmouth, White Plains, West Point, and back to Bound Brook. This means that he was with the Army of General Washington during two terrible winters of cold and starvation. He stated that he was in the battles of Monmouth and White Horse. At Bound Brook he received a furlough to go home to Virginia, where he became ill. In the meantime his regiment had marched to Charleston and was captured by the British; therefore he did not receive his discharge papers. Since he enlisted Feb.8, 1777, this return to Virginia and subsequent illness must have taken place in the fall of 1779. Since he related that he served two short tours in the Militia - about ten weeks in all - against the Tories and the Cherokee Indians this latter service must have been in the period of 1780-81, or perhaps even later.

Richard Haynes stated that his father's family Bible record showing his birth date, which

is the same as the one given on his service record, had been left at home. When asked where he
was living when called into service, Richard ans-
wered that it was in a county now called Franklin
in Virginia. Since this place was evidently Penhook, referred to previously as being near or on
the county line between Pittsylvania and Franklin
Counties, it would seem to explain why his place
of residence appears as Pittsylvania in his service record. Franklin County was not formed from
Bedford, Henry and Patrick Counties until 1785-6,
so it is possible that the line between Pittsylvania and Henry was not clearly marked when Richard enlisted in 1777. He said that he continued
to reside in Virginia for ten to eleven years,
after which he moved to Tennessee. Since his son
William, as indicated in the 1850 census of Jefferson County, was born in Virginia in 1786, Richard was probably married immediately after the
war. His daughter, Susan Skeen, said she was born
in Virginia in 1795, while his son Richard Jr.
gave North Carolina as his birthplace in 1798.

The tax list for 1787-8 of Washington Co.,
Tenn. shows Richard Hains as #187, Thomas Majors
as #184, and William Runnels as #186. The three
families had later connections in Rhea Co.,Tenn.
It is possible that the family of Richard Haynes
remained in southwest Virginia while he was push-
ing into the Tennessee area which was claimed by
North Carolina. The actual move of the family to
Jefferson Co., Tenn. possibly followed the settlement of the Thomas Majors family in the county,
before 1800. Richard then said that he had spent
the last ten to eleven years in Indiana. There is
the testimony of Stephen Potter of Lawrence Co.,
Indiana in the pension file, made under oath on
Oct.26, 1833, that he and Richard enlisted in
1777 for a term of three years.

On Oct.31, 1836, a Richard Haynes married
Nancy Ritchey in Lawrence County (Bk.1, p.29).It
is not know whether this was Richard Haynes 1763-
1850; he was at Potter's home in 1833. There was
a James C. Skeen, born Tennessee 1798, living in
Indian Creek Township, who may have been a brother of Moses Skeen (Census, #890).

Information available at this time to the compiler, regarding the children of Richard Haynes, appears below. Although there is no proof of the exact dates of birth of seven of the ten children listed, their names appear in what is believed to be the correct order: the names were supplied by Mrs.Arthur Hollingsworth, a descendant, to whom the list was given by her father, a grandson of Richard Haynes:

1. Richard Haynes, born Sept.19, 1763 in Prince Edward Co., Ind., m. Margaret Majors, b? d. 1826. Children:

    2. Jerry Haynes, b. ca 1784
    3. William Haynes, b. Sept.19, 1785
    4. Henry H. Haynes, b. June 4, 1788
    5. Thomas Haynes, b. ca 1790
    6. Sarah Haynes, b. ca 1792
    7. Susan Haynes, b. 1795
    8. Richard Haynes, b. May 20, 1798
    9. Crockett Haynes, b. ca 1799
    10. Mary Haynes, b. 1802
    11. Jane Haynes, b. April 22, 1805

2. Jerry Haynes, born ca 1784 in Virginia (?) married Nancy Cheek in Jefferson County, Tenn. Sept.21, 1804 (Bk.1, p.514). Nothing further is known of them. If Nancy were a daughter of Jesse Cheek, an early settler of Jefferson County, it is possible that Jerry and Nancy could be found, if it could be learned where Jesse Cheek went after he left Jefferson County, Tennessee.

Note: One of the many unsolved Haynes puzzles relates to Mary Ann Haynes, aged 18, and Alfred Haynes aged 13, shown in the household (#1209 Jefferson Co.Census,Tenn.1850) of Lemuel Carmichael Sr., aged 66, and his wife Louisa, aged 43. John Haynes (household #1208) and William Haynes (#1210) were also sons of Louisa, previously married to a Haynes, as proved in the will of Lemuel Carmichael found in Sevier County, Tenn. (W.Bk.1, 1849-97, pp.96-8) wherein they are named as stepsons. Mrs. R.P. Russell of

Birmingham, Ala., who descends from Alfred and his wife Tabitha Murry, may eventually be able to link her Haynes family to one of the sons of Richard (1763-1850) since practically all other Haynes families of East Tennessee have been ruled out after extensive searching.

3.   William Haynes, born Sept.19, 1785 in Va., died ca 1870 in Jefferson County, Tenn. He married Elizabeth Cox, daughter of William and Rachel Cox, Jan.28, 1805 in Jefferson Co. (Bk.1, p.598). Elizabeth Cox (Betsy) was born in North Carolina Nov.19, 1788 (Bible record). In the 1830 census they are shown with 2 males under 5, 1 male 5-10, 1 male 15-20, 2 females 5-10, 2 females 10-15, 1 female 15-20. It is possible that some of the children were not living at home in 1830. The 1840 census, p.291, Northern District, shows 10 in the family, living beside Moses Skeen and his family of 12.
The youngest son, Rufus, is responsible for the following Bible record, supplemented by some county records and by correspondence: Anna, b. Dec.6, 1805, m. William Austin Mar. 21, 1821 and moved to Johnson Co., Missouri near her parents; Rachel, b.March 7,1808; Margaret, b. Dec.1, 1810, m. Robert King May 19, 1830; Sarah b. Jan.13,1813, m.John F.Wester March 14, 1830 and moved to Johnson Co., Missouri in August 1843; Elizabeth b. Dec.1, 1814; Susan b. March 1, 1817, m. George Petty Jan.1, 1838; Thele, b. May 7, 1819; Clary, b. Jan.21, 1822; Jane, b.Jan. 21,1822 (twin), m. James Haynes and moved to Johnson Co.; William C. b. Aug.18,1824, m. Eleanor McCuistian April 14, 1852 and moved to Colorado?; Richard b.Feb.5,1827, m. Martha Satterfield and remained in Jefferson Co.; John Hodges, b. July 22, 1829; Rufus, b. March 13, 1833; Wealthy Adeline, b. July 16, 1836, m. Calvin Butler Oct.3, 1857.
The Bible bearing the names and birth dates of the above fourteen children in now in the possession of Barbara Greer(Mrs.C.T.)

who descends from Anna Haynes Austin
through their daughter Margaret, b. Oct.13
1827; she m. Solomon Starr in Jefferson Co.
April 7, 1847. Both died in Stephenville,
Texas, he in 1804 and she in 1812. Their
son Joseph Lee Starr, b.July 31,1850, m.
in Cass County, Missouri, July 17, 1873
Mary Esther Gerry, b. Sept.8, 1851 in
Scranton, Pa. Both d. in Los Angeles,Cal.,
she in 1914 and he in 1918. Their daughter
Stella Mary, b.Sept.24, 1880, m. Andrew H.
Doig Sr., b. Sept.2, 1874 in Monmouth,Ill.,
on June 12, 1901. Their youngest child,
Barbara, b. May 24, 1917 in Huntington
Park, Cal.,m. Clarence Thompson Greer, b.
Nov.10, 1915 in Overly, N.Dakota, m. May
21, 1938. They have 4 chn: Brian, Jane,
Dennis and Eileen Greer.

Although several of the children of William
Haynes (1785-1870) remained in the area of their
birth, it is possible that others followed the
Austins to Missouri.
On Oct.3, 1818 Joshua Dellis sold 60 acres
to William Hanes for $600 "part of tract granted
to Robert McFarland by the State of N.C., being
a part of Mill Creek, east side, running from
McFarland's line west to where it joins the meeting house". Wit: William Cox Sr. and Jr.(D.Bk.0).
On Jan.2, 1818 Joshua Dellis sold him an additional 30 acres for $20 ($200?). No estate administration was found for William Haynes, whose ad-
dress in the 1860's was Talbott's Station, Jefferson County, Tennessee.

4.   Henry H. Haynes, born June 4, 1788 in Va.,
        died Aug.13,1865 in Clinton Co., Indiana.
        Buried in Hopewell Cemetery, Clinton Co.
        He married Lucinda Neal in Roane Co.,Tenn.
        Aug.23, 1808, with Abner Majors as bonds-
        man (Marriage Bond Bk.1). Lucinda died Jan.
        7, 1842, buried Hopewell Cemetery. The
        parents of Lucinda are unknown at present,
        but she may be related to the Benjamin Neal
        who was Constable in Pittsylvania Co., Va.
        (List of Tithables and Miscellaneous Lists
        1767-1785, p.24), or to the Benjamin Neal
        who was guardian of Polly, Betsy, and Dor-

cas Cox of Jefferson Co., Tenn whose account was
settled in 1813; or she may have been a daughter
or sister of Matthew Neal of Rhea Co., Tenn. who
sold 70 acres on Camp Creek to Abner Majors,Apr.
14,1815 (D.Bk. A-D, p.405). This deed was witnessed by Jesse Roddye and Thomas Majors. There
was also a James Neal in Rhea County in 1818,
where he was listed as a juror. In Rhea County
on Nov.24, 1817, Richard Waterhouse sold to Henry
Haynes 95 acres on Camp Creek (D.Bk.E, p.159).
This land was sold by Henry Haynes on Oct.1,1818
(D.Bk.3, p.153).

Henry Haynes is shown in the 1830 Census of
Rhea Co., Tenn.(p.391) as: 1 male 40-50, with 2
males 5-10, 2 males under 5, 1 female 30-40, 1
female 15-20, 2 females 10-15, 1 female 5-10,
living near the Majors and Roddye families. A
Thomas Majors aged 35 and Elias Majors aged 38
were living in Bledsoe Co., Tenn. (next to Rhea
County) in 1850. Also in the Census #494 was
William Nail, born in Georgia, aged 64; #505 was
Thomas Nail,born in Georgia, aged 60; #525 was
Newton Nail, born in Tennessee, aged 34; and
#801 was John Nail, aged 66, born in Georgia.
There were also Swafford family ties in Bledsoe
County in 1850.

Note: In Bounty Land Warrant 12923-80-55,
1812, found in the National Archives, it is shown
that Henry Haynes's application for Bounty Land
was granted for service as a 2nd.Lt. under Capt.
James Berry and Major Thomas C. Clark, East Tenn.
Militia, in the War with the Creek Indians. Henry
(often referred to as Harry) was drafted in Rhea
County, Tenn., Jan.1, 1814 and honorably discharged May 12, 1814. He was engaged in the Battle of Horseshoe Bend, and for this service was
entitled to bounty land of 60 + 80 acres,located
in Clinton County, Indiana. (See Warrants 14273
and 72929.)

Henry H. Haynes left Rhea Co., Tenn. soon
after 1830. In 1834 "Henry Haynes of Union Co.,
Ind." patented 80 acres of land through the Craw-
fordsville, Ind., land office; certificate 21813.
The description of the land indicated that it was
in Clinton Co., Ind. This same description is
found in Clinton Co. dated Sept.16,1835 (D.Book
19, p.28).

Henry Haines is shown in the 1840 Census of Clinton County (p.718) as: 1 male 50-60, with 2 males 15-20, 2 males 10-15, 1 male 5-10, and 1 female 50-60.

Henry H. Haynes administered the estate of a William Y. Haynes in Clinton County; he gave bond April 17, 1847, and in <u>Probate O.Bk.2</u>, p. 213, Henry H. Haynes was appointed administrator. The estate was settled in the April term of Court 1854 (Box 104, File 11, 1848). Debts amounted to $55.62; estate sale. $74.93. Henry H. Haynes asked for the remainder, indicating that William was unmarried (<u>Bk.A 1</u>, p.229, 1853-58).

On Feb.12,1855 Henry H. Haynes purchased from Hueston and Jane Davis 50 acres, the North end of West ½ of Sec.16, Tp.22, Range 2 E (<u>D.Bk. 17</u>, p.393), which is land he owned at the time of his death. He sold the 80 acres he entered in 1834 to Daniel Kimbel on Jan.10, 1855 for $1,350 (op.cit.300). This deed was also signed by his second wife Elizabeth (d.June 30, 1860, aged 58 yrs.10 mths.5 days; buried Laymon Cemetery, Clinton Co., Indiana) whom he probably married between 1849 and 1860. He is not found in the 1850 census, unless he is the Henry Haines shown in the household of Margaret Petre in 1850, aged 25 with an error in age. It is also possible that this was Henry Jr., son of Henry and Lucinda, living with his aunt.

On Oct.28, 1857 Henry H. Haynes purchased from Thomas Oliphant for $200 the North ½ of Lot 68 in Michigantown (<u>D.Bk.20</u>, pp.262-4). He sold this lot on Jan.2, 1866 to F.A.Gue (<u>D.Bk.28</u>, p. 191). Catherine Haynes joined with him in this deed. Henry H. Haynes married his 3rd wife,Catherine Berry, Jan.9, 1862 in Clinton County. However, Henry is shown in the 1860 census for Clinton County, Johnson Tp. (#139) as aged 72, born in Va., with Elizabeth, aged 56, born in Pa.

Henry Haynes died Aug.13, 1865. On Sept.6, 1865 Catherine Haynes of Clinton County gave a quit claim deed to James M. Haynes and Robert N. Haynes, her share of 50 acres in Sec.16, Tp.22, Range 2 E, purchased from Hueston and Jane Davis in 1855 (<u>D.Bk.27</u>, p.532). Catherine Haynes married David Airhart, Sept.14, 1871 (Marriage Book C-5, p.166).

Based on what is known of the family, in addition to the number of children indicated in the 1830 and 1840 census records, a tentative list of the children of Henry H. Haynes and Lucinda Neal are given as follows:

17 Richard T. Haynes, b. ca 1809, bur. Hopewell Cemetery, Clinton Co., Ind.
18 William Y. Haynes, b.ca 1811, d.1847.
19 Margaret Haynes, b. July 8, 1812.
20 Thomas Jefferson Haynes, b. ca 1814.
21 Elizabeth Haynes, b. ca 1817.
22 John T. Haynes, b. ca 1820.
23 Robert N. Haynes, b. ca 1823.
24 Henry Haynes Jr. b. 1825.
25 James M. Haynes, b.June 22,1826 or 28.

5. Thomas Haynes, born ca 1790 in Virginia, married Sally Cheek in Jefferson County, Tenn. June 6, 1811(Bk.1, p.598). She was probably the sister of Nancy Cheek, wife of Jerry Haynes. No record of Thomas Haynes exists and he is said to have been "lost in Missouri". It is quite possible that he was the eldest son of Richard Haynes (1763-1850) rather than the fourth child as previously indicated. He could have been the father of Alfred Haynes who married Mary Leeper in Union County, Ind., Sept.27,1827 (Marriage Bk.1, p.43), and of Richard Haynes who married Catherine Majors in Rhea Co., Tenn. on Feb.28, 1829.

6. Sarah Haynes, born ca 1792 in Virginia, married Oct.4, 1818 William Doherty Sr. in Jefferson Co., Tenn. (Marriage Bk.1, 1379). William may have been the son or grandson of Joseph Doherty whose will in Jefferson County, Tenn. was made on March 12, 1802, naming sons William and Joseph (W.Bk.1,31). No record of this family is available, though they are said to have moved to Ill. The William Doherty aged 22 at the time of the 1850 census of Jefferson County, Tenn.

may have been their son; he is shown with wife Caroline and daughter Martha Jane. A Jim Doherty, nephew of Jane Haynes Wales, lived at Jimtown around 1860-70. He has not been located either in the Jimtown area of Boone County or Henry County, Indiana. Dicey Majors married James Doherty, May 6, 1812 in Jefferson County, Tenn. (Bk.1792-1820, p.1038). The relationship of James Doherty to William Doherty is unknown, but Dicey Majors would have been a cousin of Sarah of this record.

7.   Susan Haynes, born 1795 in Virginia according to the 1850 census record of Jefferson County, Tenn., Dist.13. She married Moses Skeen May 22, 1816 (Bk.1, p.1245). He was the son of John Skeen and Catherine White; the latter was living with Moses(aged 84, born in Virginia) in 1850. Moses and Sarah are reported to have had 13 children. Living in their household in 1850 were:

26   Cassada Skeen, aged 25
27   Margaret Skeen, aged 22
28   Martha Skeen, aged 20
29   Morris Skeen (Moses Jr.?) aged 18
30   Dorcas A. Skeen, aged 15
31   Crockitt Skeen, aged 15
32   Clusby Skeen, aged 12
33   Lafayette Skeen, aged 10

Moses Skeen is incorrectly listed as Morris Skeen in the census record. Other Skeen families listed in Dist.13 in 1850 were John A. Skeen aged 28, with wife Jane, and children Henderson and Taylor; James E. Skeen aged 33 with wife Sarah and children Martin, Columbus, Marrisa E., Emeline T., Mary E., and Marcelus. All were born in Tennessee with the exception of Marrisa and Emeline, who were born in Missouri in 1843 and 1845 respectively. There was also a Puty (?) Skeen aged 21, with children Eveline, John and Eliza Jane; she was possibly a widow - her two youngest children were born in Missouri.

8.   Richard Haynes Jr., born May 20, 1798, according to the family Bible record in possession of the compiler. The 1850 census record states North Carolina as his birth state, but this may be an error. In 1814 Richard married Susannah Mendenhall, born June 7, 1793 in N.C., the daughter of Mordecai and Phebe (Cannaday) Mendenhall of Guilford County, N.C., who emigrated to Lost Creek Monthly Meeting, Jefferson Co., Tenn. (Hinshaw's <u>Encyclopedia of Quaker Genealogy</u>, Vol.1, p.1108). It is not understood why Susannah was not dismissed for "marrying out of unity", but at any rate they went to Indiana early in 1818. They lived for about ten years in Wayne County, and in 1831 moved to Henry County, Indiana where there are several land transactions on record for Richard. He was shown in Perry Tp., Wayne County in 1830 (<u>Census 17</u>: 244) with wife, 3 sons and 3 daughters. Records of their children were copied from the Bible record and supplemented by census records and notes taken from local historical sources.

34	William Haynes, born Jan.1, 1818
35	Hannah Haynes, born Nov.15, 1819
36	Davis Haynes, born Nov.7, 1821
37	Louiza Haynes, born Oct.10, 1823
38	Matilda Haynes, born Jan.27, 1826
39	Silas Haynes, born Oct.27, 1828, died July 18, 1833.
40	Susannah Haynes, born Jan.14, 1831
41	Richard Haynes III, born May 14, 1834

It should be pointed out that the Bible record is incomplete; it stops ca 1850. Richard Haynes Sr. was killed at a sawmill near Newcastle in 1852, on Nov.5, aged 54 yrs. 5 mths. 15 days. Susannah d. Aug.13, 1873 aged 80 yrs. 2 mths. 6 days. References to land transactions of Richard Haynes Jr. are available in the following Deed Books of Henry County: H:601; H:18; G:124, and in others, with most of the acreage in Sec.29, 36, 30, 27, and 19 in Prairie, Stony Creek, and Blue River Tps. Abstracts were not made by the compiler, who spent some time in Henry County in 1939.

9.   Crockett Haynes, born ca 1799 in Tennessee (?) and died young, according to family tradition.

10.   Mary Haynes, born 1802 in Jefferson Co., Tenn., married Daniel Petre Jr., Union Co. Indiana Sept.12, 1828 (Bk.B, p.69). She and her husband are shown in the 1850 Census of Clinton County, Indiana (#862). He was listed as a hotel keeper in Michigantown on the old Michigan Road, and the name was spelled Petra. Daniel's age was 49, Mary's 48, both born in Tennessee.
Their children listed in 1850 were:
42   William Petre aged 20
43   George Petre aged 18
44   Mary Petre aged 14
45   Daniel Petre aged 6

Daniel J. Petre sold 120 acres to James Daily in 1851 (D.Bk.13, p.486), and purchased 80 acres from the James Daily estate on Dec.16, 1856 (D.Bk.18, p.334); 40 acres lay in the S.½ of the SE Quarter of Sec.15, Tp.22, Range 1 E. This land was not far from the Henry Haynes's farm ("Polly's" brother) or from that of John Petre, brother of Daniel J. Petre Jr., whose wife Margaret was "Polly's" niece. Daniel Petre Jr. purchased 40 acres from Anthony Emley on Feb.18, 1852 in the W ½ of the SE Quarter of Sec.20, Tp.22, Range 1 E (D.Bk.14, p.134). On Dec.26, 1864 Daniel sold 40 ac. to David Kelly in the S ½ of the SW Quarter of Sec.16, Tp.22, Range 1 E (D.Bk.28, p.115); on Nov.7, 1865, 40 acres to Hiram Wyant in the N ½ of the SW Quarter of Sec. 15, Tp.22, Range 1 E (op.cit. p.151).Since Daniel Petre Jr. and family were not found in the 1870 census of Clinton Co., Ind., they may have gone to Iowa or to Missouri. The records of Union Co., Indiana indicate that Daniel Jr. sold 97 acres to Alexander Chambers on Aug.28, 1835, part of SW¼ of Sec.26, Tp.15 N, Range 3E (D.Bk.F, p.479). Daniel Petre (Sr.?) sold land to Joseph Baldwin May 13, 1836. John Petre sold land to William Beck on the same date, and lots 42,43,and 44 in Dunlapsville, Union Co., Indiana (D.Bk.F, p.5) on Oct.14, 1834. It is possible that the father and two sons left Union Co., Ind., about the same date. There are other Petre marriages recorded in Union County, including one to Pullen and one to Gossett, both southside Virginia names. All of these families may have gone first to LaPorte County, as did John and Margaret Petre before they settled in Clinton County, Indiana.

11. Jane Haynes, born April 22, 1805 in Jefferson County, Tennessee; married July 27,1824 in Union Co., Indiana (Bk.1, p.87) James Wales who was born March 13, 1788 in Sussex or Surrey County, England, son of James and Martha Caffyn Wales. Jane's mother died two years later so it is possible that "Polly", her older sister, kept house for their father, Richard Haynes (1763-1850) until "Polly's" marriage to Daniel Petre Jr. in 1828. At the time of the 1830 census in Union County, Richard Haynes was living with his daughter Jane (Bk.15, p.508).

James Wales came from England in 1818 and walked from Pittsburgh to Butler Co., Ohio, where he probably visited his relative, Richard Caffyn, who had come to this country a few years earlier. James Wales was "of Butler Co., Ohio" when he purchased 80 acres of land in Union County from Isaac Medcalf for $600 on Jan.21, 1822. It was located in the S½ of the SW Quarter of Sec. 33, Tp.12, Range 1 W (D.Bk.A, p.264); he possibly added to this tract later, since he describes the farm of 110 acres "off the east side of NW Quarter of Sec.33, Tp.12, Range 1W" in his will. On Jan.23, 1837 he bought 80 acres of land from John Biggs for $950 in the N½ of the SE Quarter of Sec.29,

Tp.12, Range 1W (<u>D.Bk.G</u>, pp.49-50). Peter
Wales, brother of James, may have accompanied him to America; a Peter Wails is shown
in neighboring Fayette County in the 1830
census. He is said to have gone to the
north part of the state near Goshen; there
is no deed record for him in Elkhart Co.
however. Since James Wales owned land at
one time in LaGrange County, Indiana, Peter
Wales may have gone to this county, which
adjoins Elkhart.

In the Book of Estrays found in the courthouse at Liberty, Ind., there is an entry
concerning "one black horse 3 yrs. old past
15 hands high, spot before hip, spot in
left hip with small white ring round close
to the edge of hoof on the off forefoot"
taken up by James Wales living on Hanna's
Creek. Also "one bay mare with white snip
on her nose, shod before, fifteen and ½
hands high, 4 yrs.old". Aaron Gard and Robert Harvey appraised the first stray at $35
and the second at $40, on Oct.15, 1827.
Disposition of the animals was not recorded
by Lot Gard, J.P.

Pioneer conditions in Indiana during the
early 1800's were the same as those usually
found on the frontier. There were crude,
windowless huts built by the early settlers
which sometimes had only three sides, and
were heated by a fireplace upon which the
cooking was also done. Indian depredations
were a common occurrence even after treat-
ies were signed, and the wilderness was in-
fested by wolves, bears and panthers. The
wild turkeys, deer, and game birds furnished food, badly needed since it often took
three or four days for the return journey
to the mill - a trip made frequently, as
one could carry on horseback only enough
corn to be ground, insufficient for their
needs. Moccasins were used as foot cover-
ings, and coats for the men were made of
deerskins, tanned and with the hair left
on. Spinning wheels were necessary for all
households, as clothing was usually "home-

grown and home-made".
James Wales's death occurred in Union Co.
on Feb.29, 1856. He left a will dated Oct.
26, 1854, probated March 17, 1856, witnessed by John Yaryan, Lewis J. Cline, Welling-
ton Dawson, and E. Burnside. (This will was
written by the father of General Burnside
of Civil War fame.) In it, James Wales
named his wife Jane and all of his children
as legatees. The "homestead farm" was left
to his wife during her lifetime, after
which it was to go to his youngest son Charles Nutter Wales with the provision that
"he pay $600 in three equal annual instal-
ments" to the other heirs. The balance of
his real estate he ordered to be sold at
public auction, the proceeds to be divided
as directed. Charles Nutter Wales was named
executor.
Jane Wales continued to live on the "homestead farm" for many years; the family of
Powell Slade lived with her at one period.
In 1850 her son-in-law Alexander McKillip
and his motherless son Richard lived in the
Wales household. Between 1860 and 1870,and
possibly before, her orphan niece Hester
Ann Haynes lived there. Jane Haynes Wales
died May 31, 1892 at the home of her son,
Lorenzo D. Wales, who was then living on
the "homestead farm" with his family. Jane
became a member of Hanna's Creek Christian
Church in 1824 and she was a faithful member for almost 70 years. During her lifetime, she never ceased to take an interest
in relatives, both in the south and in the
north.

The births and deaths of the James Wales
family are recorded in a Bible given to the
compiler by a granddaughter, Mary Wales
Post:

46   Richard Wales, b.June 9, 1825
47   Martha Wales, b. April 11, 1827
48   Daniel Petre Wales, b.Nov.19,1828
49   James J. Wales, b.June 23, 1831, d.
     Nov.19, 1910. No issue.
50   Margaret Wales, b.Oct.15, 1834, d.Feb.
     14, 1838.

51 Mary Jane Wales, b. Jan.15, 1837
52 Lorenzo Gard Wales
53 Charles Nutter Wales, b.Aug.16, 1845

17. Richard Haynes, born ca 1809 in Rhea or
     Roane County, Tenn. He may be the Richard
     in the Rhea Co. Court Minutes, p.258: ord-
     ered by the court to be appointed overseer
     of road from Piney Bridge on the Valley
     Road to the dividing ridge above Thomas
     Majors, in place of Abraham Wright, and
     to have the same hands the said Wright had,
     Feb.1833; p.306: overseer, Nov.1833; p.331:
     relieved of above Feb.22, 1834. He married
     Catherine Majors, 1829.

18. William Y. Haynes, born ca 1811 in Rhea Co.
     Tenn. Estate administered by father (?) in
     Clinton County, Ind., and settled in 1854.
     Probably unmarried.

19. Margaret Haynes, born July 8, 1812 in Rhea
     Co., Tenn. She died Oct.25, 1853, buried
     Laymon Cemetery, Clinton Co., Indiana.She
     married John Petre, son of Daniel Petre Sr.
     and Margaret Snyder, who came from Tennessee
     to Union County, Ind. Margaret Haynes and
     John Petre were married in Union Co. Sept.
     20, 1832 (Bk.B, p.213)and moved to LaPorte
     County, according to a biographical sketch
     of Daniel Petre, born July 4, 1834 and m.
     Mary Lamberson Aug.15, 1856 (Portrait and
     Biographical Record of Boone and Clinton
     Counties, p.840). This is the source of
     the statement that his mother, Margaret,
     was the daughter of Henry Haynes and Lu-
     cinda Nail (the name is Neal on Roane Co.
     Tenn. records; there were both Neal and
     Nail spellings of the name in Roane ca.
     1810), also that Henry Haynes fought with
     Jackson at the Battle of Horseshoe Bend in
     the War of 1812, repeating an old family
     tradition. The names of Margaret Petre's
     children appear on p.859 of the 1850 cen-
     sus; the father died Aug.15, 1849, aged
     46 yrs.9 mths.5 days, buried Laymon Ceme-
     tery. There is another record of the
     children in her Guardian's Docket (Bk.1,

140

p.65, 1851) of Clinton County, where the
family had moved to in 1838.

54 Mary J. Petre, aged 17. She d. 1855.
55 Daniel Petre, aged 16.
56 John Petre, aged 15.
57 Lucinda Petre, aged 13; she m. Thomas
    B. Lucas Nov.3, 1864 (Bk.C 4: 328).
58 Samuel Petre, aged 11.
59 Henry Petre, aged 8.
60 Sarah Petre, aged 3.

Note: There is a Daniel Petre (soldier) buried
    in Clinton Co., Ind. (Brandon Cemetery)
    who was b. July 4, 1834, d.Oct.23, 1899,
    son of John Petre and Margaret Haynes.With
    him is buried Mary Petre, b. Sept.30,1833,
    aged 68 yrs.11 mths.3 days.
    There is also a tombstone in Brandon Ceme-
    tery for James Petre, b. June 8, 1867, d.
    Sept.4, 1940, probably a son of Daniel and
    Mary Petre. His wife Hannah is buried with
    him, b. June 29, 1865, d. April 5, 1908.
    They married June 23, 1888 (Bk.C:8:381,
    Clinton County). William Petre, b.1905,
    d.1924, may have been their son.

    Margaret Haynes died in 1853 and Nelson
    Purdom was appointed guardian. On Sept.3,
    1859, Daniel, John and Lucinda petitioned
    the Court to partition the farm land, con-
    sisting of 80 acres S SW Sec.16, Tp.22,
    Range 1 E among the six heirs, although the
    three youngest children were still under
    age. Nathaniel Bell was appointed to do
    this (Probate Record A: 227-230). The final
    decree was dated Dec.29, 1859 and the par-
    tition deed recorded (D.Bk.22, p.551). Dan-
    iel had one son James, shown in the 1880
    census, and Daniel Petre, aged 69 and a
    resident of Michigantown, Clinton County,
    is a descendant. He told the compiler in
    Oct. 1963 that some of the Petre descend-
    ants had intermarried with the Landis fam-
    ily and lived in White County, Indiana.

20. Thomas Jefferson Haynes, born ca 1814 in
    Rhea Co., Tenn., married Cynthia Wheeler

in Union Co., Ind., Oct.28, 1833 (Bk.B, p. 261). It is not known where they lived during the first years of their marriage. One son said he was born in Marion County, Indiana. After 1840 (not found in 1840 census) the family purchased from William Shoemaker in Union County 80 acres, the W½ of the SE Quarter of Sec.36, Tp.12 N,Range 5 W, for $250 (D.Bk.7, p.418). In 1845 this land was sold to Charles Daniels. In 1844 "Jeff" Haynes sued Joseph Van Vactor for trespassing. On June 29, 1844 he purchased 58 acres from Thomas Gardner in Sec.20, Tp.11, Range 1 W (D.Bk.K, p.185) and sold it the next year to Van Vactor (op.cit. p.240). This land was in Center Tp. and near relatives. The family moved to Ripley County, Indiana before 1849.

Thomas Jefferson Haynes, his wife Cynthia and daughter Louisa died in the cholera epidemic of 1849, and their death records are shown in the 1850 Ripley County Mortality Record 2: 174. The present owner of the farm thought that they may have been buried beneath a tree in one of their fields, along with household items that could not be burned. From time to time, pieces of china and crockery have been turned up at the spring plowing.

Voluminous notes have been collected on the estate settlement and guardianship records, briefly abstracted as follows:

Three guardians were appointed for the orphaned children: James Wheeler; Benjamin Nutter; Charles W. Hunt.

Ripley County Probate O.Bk.E, pp.35,43,71,77,220, 298, 326.
Thomas W. Sunman was appointed administrator of the estate of Jefferson Haynes on Sept.10, 1849. Inventory and appraisement were filed in the amount of $81.07 (not given in detail), and a bill of sale was filed for personal estate of $111.44 (p.71). Sunman was allowed to rent the farm to raise

assets (p.220).There is a note of petition (p.298) filed by the administrator (the petition does not appear); however, James Wheeler, guardian, filed answer to the petition. The Court, having examined both documents, decided that the land should be sold for the purpose mentioned in the petition. The administrator filed an inventory and appraisement in the amount of $325, and entered additional bond. Administrator ordered to sell at auction lands and tenements, advertising same in the "Ripley Co. Whig", and to make a report at the next term of court.

Probate O.Bk.1, pp.7,8,9,10,40,46,250,251.
Administrator received money from Nathaniel Morris who purchased the land Jan.5,1853. Charles N. Shook was appointed Commissioner to make a deed for land to Nathaniel Morris for 40 acres in the SE Quarter of the NW Quarter of Sec.22, Tp.10 N, Range 12 E. Morris was the highest bidder and paid $335. (This land was east of Batesville in Adams Tp., Ripley Co., Ind., and not far from Oldenburg in Franklin County, where Jasper Newton Haynes thought that his parents were buried. No deed to Jefferson Haynes could be found for this land, nor a land entry from the Government, nor a mortgage on same; nor could a deed of sale to Morris be found in the deed books, although both Grantor and Grantee Deeds under Nathaniel Morris as grantee, the Sheriff of Ripley County as grantor, and Charles Shook, Commissioner, were examined. A William Voegele now owns the land and lives at Route 3, Batesville.)

Sunman showed in his report to the Court: $81.07 personal items; $30.37, the difference between inventory and actual sale; $20 rent of farm; $355 sale of real estate; a total of $486.44. Bills were allowed and amounts of each given, including taxes, administration ($15.40), Rachel Pease for medical service ($17.56), etc. totaling $216.30, leaving a balance of $270.14. The

Court ordered that the heirs were entitled to the difference; Sunman paid $270.14 to the Court and asked to be discharged. All heirs were entitled to one-sixth of $267.98 (possibly publication charges were deducted).

James Wheeler was appointed first guardian of the orphaned children. It is not known what his relationship was to the "Jeff" Haynes family. He could have been a brother of Cynthia Wheeler Haynes, or he could have been a brother-in-law, with Cynthia being a widow when she married Jefferson Haynes. Hinshaw's Encyclopedia of Quaker Genealogy, N.C., Vol.1, p.887, shows Cynthia Wheeler (formerly Hunt) was dismissed Sept.5, 1827 for marrying out of unity. This Cynthia was born June 16, 1807 and was the daughter of Zebulon and Mary Hunt. A Jesse Wheeler was dismissed Sept.6,1827 (op.cit. p.844) who could have been her husband, with the marriage being a civil one and not in accordance with Quaker custom. There were also a James Wheeler and James Wheeler Jr. living in Pittsylvania County, Virginia, near the home of the Haynes family: List of Tithables, Pittsylvania Co., Va. 1767-1785, p.37: James Wheeler and son James Wheeler 2 tithables on Thomas Dillard's list. Same ref: p.24, shows a Benjamin Neal, a Constable in Pittsylvania County; there was also a Benjamin Neal in Jefferson County, Tenn. after 1800. It is possible that James Wheeler Jr. may have come to Union County, Indiana circa 1830.

James Wheeler died in 1851 and Benjamin Nutter was appointed second guardian of the orphaned children of Jefferson Haynes. Benjamin Nutter gave a receipt on July 25, 1855 to Henry T. Shipperd, Clerk, showing he received $267.48 (50¢ deducted for printers fee) the amount coming to heirs named in this Order, viz: Margaret Jane Haynes aged 18, James L. Haynes aged 17, Jasper Newton Haynes aged 13, Martha W. Haynes aged 12, Amanda E. Haynes aged 10,

and Hester Ann Haynes aged 8. Benjamin
Nutter died ca 1857; he failed to pay out
certain bills for the Haynes children and
William Swafford obtained judgment against
his estate. In the hundreds of papers of
his estate, a receipt from James L. Haynes,
Clinton, Union Co., Ind., for $35.33 dated
Jan.4, 1861 stated that he received from
W.W. Sullivan (Nutter's administrator) for
his "distribute share" as one of the heirs
of Jefferson Haynes, decd.

Nutter's report was made to the Probate
Court of Union County, Winter Term 1856,
p.416 of Complete Record 1, 1853-1858.Here
the heirs were listed as they are in Ripley County, and the guardian charged himself with $267.50 cash received from Rip-
ley Common Pleas Court; also $110.21 re-
ceived from the estate of James Wheeler
plus interest of $8, a total of $385.71,
out of which he claimed disbursements of
$46.95. Separate accounts also appeared
for each child (pp.417-9), each child to
receive one-sixth or $64.28½ (accounting
not clear).

Charles W. Hunt was appointed third guardian of the Haynes children; he was a relative by marriage, as his wife's mother,Jane
Wales, was an aunt of the orphaned children. His report (Probate O.Bk.J, Complete
Record, p.361) was made in the Spring Term
of Court 1861 as guardian of Jasper N.,
Martha, Amanda, and Hester Ann Haines. He
charged himself with $179.34 as estate of
said orphans.

Probate O.Bk.K, 1863-1868, p.159:
    In the Court of Common Pleas, Winter Term
    1864, in Liberty, Union Co., Ind., Charles
    W. Hunt asked that he be discharged as to
    Jasper N. Haynes and Martha Haynes, since
    they had arrived at 21 years of age. They
    were paid off in full and filed their final
    receipts for same. The cause was continued
    for Amanda Haunes and Hester A. Haunes.
    Recorded Dec.26, 1864.

<u>Probate O.Bk.K</u>, <u>1863-1868</u>, p.323:
Court of Common Pleas, July Term, 1865,
in Liberty, Union Co., Ind., Charles W.Hunt
made his final report as the guardian of
Amanda Haynes, who had reached 21 years of
age. Recorded Jan.25, 1866.

On Nov.14, 1865 in Union County, Indiana,
Newton J. Haynes (he signed J.N.Haynes) and
Charles W. Hunt, guardian of Hester Ann
Haynes, gave a quit claim to James M. Haynes
and Robert N. Haynes for 50 acres in Clinton
County for the sum of $400 each, for the
north end of the W ½ of the NW Quarter of
Sec.16, Tp.22 N, Range 2 E. (This land was
purchased by their grandfather, Henry H.
Haynes, Feb.12, 1855.)

<u>Probate Court O.Bk.K</u>, <u>1863-1868</u>, p.600:
Court of Common Pleas, Dec. Term, 1866,
Charles W. Hunt presented his report and
resignation as the guardian of Hester Ann
Haynes. In this report of final settlement
Hester Ann Haynes received "by cash from
Henry, his estate -$4.00". (Although the
last name is not given, it is evident that
this is Henry H. Haynes because of the quit
claim deed. This amount possibly should
have been $400 rather than $4.00.) C.W.Hunt
resigned as guardian on the grounds that he
expected to be leaving the county. (No
other guardian was appointed even though
Hester was only 19 years of age. However,
this document was not recorded until Jan.4,
1868, when she would have been 21.)

<u>Note</u>: Biographical facts concerning Thomas Jeff-
erson Haynes compiled by his great-great-
granddaughter, Mildred Homann.

61 Margaret Jane Haynes, b. ca 1836
62 James L. Haynes, b. ca 1838
63 Louisa Haynes, b. ca 1839-40 in Ind.,
    d. Aug.1849 in Ripley Co., Indiana.
64 Jasper Newton Haynes, b. ca 1842
65 Martha W. Haynes, b. ca 1843
66 Amanda E. Haynes, b. ca 1845
67 Hester Ann Haynes, b. 1847

21.   Elizabeth Haynes, born ca 1817 in Rhea Co.,
       Tenn., married Henry Box in Union County,
       Indiana in 1837 (Bk.B, p.409). There is
       no proof that she was a daughter of Henry
       H. Haynes but all circumstances point to
       this probability. She was found in Indiana
       (Clinton Co.) in 1840, which further in-
       dicates that she was a daughter of Henry.
       (Inasmuch as Henry is shown with several
       daughters in the 1830 census of Rhea Co.,
       Tenn. and he was "of Union Co., Ind."when
       he was granted land prior to 1840 in Clin-
       ton Co., it is unlikely that Elizabeth
       could have belonged to any other Haynes
       family.)

22.   John T. Haynes, born ca 1820 in Rhea Co.,
       Tenn., married Marietta Campbell in Clin-
       ton Co. on Sept.18, 1846 (Bk.2, p.838).
       It is likely that he was one of the five
       boys living in the household of Henry
       Haynes in Clinton Co. in the 1840 census.
       There is no record of what happened to him
       nor any proof that he was a son.

23.   Robert N. Haynes, born ca 1823 in Rhea Co.,
       Tenn. No census or marriage record have
       been found to date, in Clinton County.That
       he was a son of Henry Haynes is shown by
       the quit-claim deed from his stepmother,
       Catherine Berry Haynes, on Sept.6, 1865,
       as previously mentioned.   On Jan.16, 1869
       James M. Haynes deeded him 50 acres in the
       W NW Quarter, Sec.16, Tp.22, Range 2 E
       (Bk.31, p.327). Whether this concerned the
       same land or an adjoining tract would take
       further study of the land transactions.
       Robert N. shared with his brother James M.
       Haynes the quit-claim deed given on Nov.14
       1865 by Newton J. (Jasper) Haynes and Chas.
       W. Hunt, guardian of Hester Ann Haynes
       (both children of Thomas Jefferson Haynes
       and therefore heirs to land left by Henry
       Haynes who d. 1865) for 50 ac. Pt. W NW
       Quarter, Sec.16, Tp.22, Range 2E (D.B.28,
       p.305), one of the tracts which a few
       months later James M. Haynes deeded to
       his brother Robert N. Haynes. There are

147

also deeds to R.H. Haines from Jackson
Lucas (D.Bk.31, p.42), and from John Petre
(op.cit. p.199), both in the 1860 period.
It is possible that Robert left Clinton Co.
before 1870, since his name is not found
in the 1870 census for this county; he may
have lived in an adjoining county.

25.   James Monroe Haynes, born June 22, 1828 in
Rhea Co., Tenn., died July 20, 1885, buried
in Laymon Cemetery, Clinton Co., Indiana.
He married (1) Jan.6, 1869 Miranda Parish
(Bk.C 4, p.739) who was born May 10, 1841,
died March 13, 1880, buried Laymon Cemetery;
he married (2) Oct.11, 1882 Joanna Calhoun
(Bk.C 7, p.223) who was born May 27, 1827,
and died aged 96 in Clinton Co., Feb.16,
1919 (Bk.H 24, p.259).(In the Census of 1870
James gave his age as 42, and birth place as
Kentucky, which could not have been correct
as his father was living in Rhea Co., Tenn.
in 1830.) James served in the Civil War,
Aug.22, 1861 to Sept.19, 1864.

68   Miranda Alice Haynes, b. Jan.29,1870
69   Richard Sherman Haynes, b.Dec.19,1872
70   Nancy Ellen Haynes, b. Feb.12, 1874,
Clinton Co., Ind., d. Nov.4, 1886,
buried Laymon Cemetery, Indiana.
71   Sylvester Nale Haynes, b. Aug.28, 1876
in Clinton Co., d. Aug.11,1877, buried
Laymon Cemetery, Clinton Co., Indiana.

(From Bible record of James M. Haynes, in
possession of Mrs. Effie M.Sheets, 1964.)

There are several land transactions in
Clinton County for James M. Haynes, son of
Henry Haynes (d.1865). Some of them were
listed under his brother Robert's name.On
April 3, 1866 he gave a warranty deed to
John DeFord for 30 acres Pt.W NW Sec. 16,
Tp.2, Range 2 E (Bk.28, p.458), and on June
2, 1867 a deed to Jonas Rathfon for 30 ac.,
Pt.W NW Sec.16, Tp.22, Range 2 E (Bk.30,
p.472). On Jan.13, 1866 he had received a
quit-claim deed from T.B.Lucas and Lucinda
his wife, Daniel Petre and Henry Petre, for

Pt. W SW Sec.16, Tp.22, Range 2 E (<u>D.Bk.28</u>, p.269) and one also on the same land from John W. Long and Margaret his wife, of Wayne Co., Indiana. (Note: Margaret Jane Long was one of the heirs of Thomas Jefferson Haynes; therefore a niece of James M. Haynes.) He also, for $500, received a deed for 20 acres from Alfred Transbarger and Martha A., his wife, on March 13, 1866, for the south end of the $W\frac{1}{2}$ of the NW Sec.16, Tp.22, Range 2 E (<u>D. Bk.28</u>, p.427), who also bought land in Sec.9, Tp.22, Range 2 E from Hiram and Rebecca Alspaugh his wife, in 1866, and sold 5 acres of the same to James M. Haynes in 1868. (Although payment is involved from Transbarger to Haynes, rather than quit-claim deed, one wonders if Martha A. Transbarger could have been Martha Haynes, daughter of Thomas Jefferson Haynes.)

James M. Haynes was involved in other land transactions; two of them were with John DeFord and Seth B. Slevens (<u>Deed Books 29</u>: 122; and <u>31</u>: 40 respectively).

This completes the list of children known or believed to have been sons and daughters of Henry H. Haynes and his wife Lucinda Neal, of which there were possibly five sons and six daughters as indicated by census records. Since their whereabouts were not learned of until recently, enough time has not elapsed to have located the majority of the descendants.

34.   William Haynes, born Jan.1, 1818 in Wayne County, Indiana, married Elizabeth Thompson March 27, 1839 (Bible record). Although the Bible record lists only the first three children of William Haynes, the 1860 census record of Stony Creek Tp., Henry Co., Ind., p.51, lists the additional ones:

72   Aaron Haynes, b. July 14, 1841, m. Mary M. Edwards Nov.30,1862
73   Delphina Haynes, b. March 16, 1842; m. Miles M. Pierce Dec.11, 1862
74   Silas S. Haynes, b. Aug.26, 1844, m. Sarah J. Howell Aug.18,1867, after he

returned from the Civil War (Company
E, 9th Regiment).

75 Lorenzo Haynes, aged 13.
76 Davis Haynes, aged 10. Davis M.Haynes
    m. Juliann Bales Aug.20, 1886
77 Orlando Haynes, aged 7. Orlando M.
    Haynes m. Sarah E.Jones, Dec.28,1883
78 Eunice Haynes, aged 1. Eunice A.
    Haynes m. George W.Hodson April 10,
    1904

35. Hannah Haynes, born Nov.15, 1819 (Bible re-
     cord), married William Reynolds Oct.3,1844
     (Bible record, also Bk.3, p.355). William
     Reynolds lived north of Amboy, Indiana.Two
     of his descendants were Mrs. Pliny Pitts,
     and Mrs. Pearl Elshire whose first husband
     was Dr.Goodrich.

36. Davis Haynes, born Nov.3, 1821, married
     Alice Gray Sept.13, 1849 (Bk.F, p.253, and
     Bible); they are shown in the census of
     1860 (p.61, Prairie Tp.) with the following
     children:

     79 John Haynes aged 9. He may be the John
         T. Haynes who married Mary E. LaRue,
         April 18, 1878
     80 Charles Haynes aged 5. He may be the
         Charles B. Haynes who married Ada M.
         Ice, March 26, 1878.
     81 Thomas Haynes, aged 3.

     Also living with them at the time of the
     census were John Gray, aged 60, and his
     wife Hannah, 63, both born in England.

37. Louiza Haynes, born Oct.10, 1823 (Bible);
     married William Sowash Sept.15, 1850 (Bk.F,
     p.312). She is shown as head of a household
     in Blue River Tp., Henry Co., in 1860 with
     the following children:

     82 John Sowash aged 7
     83 Davis Sowash aged 4, born in Iowa
     84 Wesley Sowash, aged 2, born in Iowa

In the 1870 census of Union County, Ind., Louiza Haynes is shown as a neighbour of Charles W. Hunt, grandfather of the compil-(#66) as Louisa Fletcher, head of a household, with John A. Sowash aged 19, Davis Sowash 15, Molly D.Fletcher 13, and George Fletcher 11. (The two latter were probably step-children.) A descendant, Mrs. Verne Feller of Marion, Indiana, supplied the Bible record of Richard Haynes Jr.

38.   Matilda Haynes, born Jan.27, 1826, married Abraham Davis Jan.21, 1844 (Bible) and had one child's birth recorded in the Bible.

  85   Louisa Davis, born March 20, 1845

40.   Susannah Haynes, born Jan.14, 1831,married James Chapman Jan.30, 1853. At one time she lived in Converse, Indiana, and her son was a printer.

41.   Richard Haynes III, born May 14, 1834 (B.R.) and he is designated as Richard Jr. in the Bible. No further trace of him was found.

47.   Martha Wales, born April 11, 1827, d.Aug.2, 1849, married Alexander McKillip. Issue:

  86   Richard McKillip, b. Aug.5, 1845, d. Oct.26, 1933
  87   William McKillip, b. May 18, 1849, m. Amazetta G. Tappen. No issue.

48.   Daniel Petre Wales, born Nov.19, 1828, died Dec.26, 1922, married (1) Sarah J. Pritchard and married (2) Oct.8, 1868 Almira Sering, (b. Jan.15, 1835, d. May 29,1895. Issue by first marriage:

  88   Martha A. Wales, b. Oct.9, 1850
  89   John Ellis Wales, b.Jan.30, 1853, d. 1876.

Issue by second marriage:

  90   Mary Wales, born Nov.5, 1866

91   Kitty Wales, b. Aug.22, 1870, d. May 22, 1922, m. George M. Stevens (b.Apr. 25, 1870, d. Oct.1961). No issue.

51.   Mary Jane Wales, born Jan.15, 1837, Union Co., Ind., died Sept.18, 1872 near Marion, Grant Co., Ind., married Nov.15, 1856 in Union Co. Charles White Hunt who was born Dec.18, 1832 in Hamilton Co., Ohio, and d. Aug.9, 1897, Converse, Miami Co., Indiana.

92   Abbie Hunt, b. Sept.9, 1857
93   James Franklin Hunt, b. March 31,1859.
94   Jennie Hunt, b. Nov.6, 1861
95   Dora Hunt, b. Feb.7, 1864 Union Co., d.s.p. June, 1926.
96   Charles White Hunt Jr., b.July 27,1866
97   Mary Olive Hunt, b. Sept.25, 1869

52.   Lorenzo Gard Wales, married Dec.8, 1864 Mary A. Oler.

98   Flora E. Wales, b. July 5, 1866
99   Charles Clement Wales, b. Oct.18,1867, d. Feb.1, 1895
100   James Samuel Wales, b. Sept.20, 1869
101   Jennie Wales, b. Aug.27, 1873
102   Ruth Wales, b. June 25,1884

53.   Charles Nutter Wales, b. Aug.16, 1845, d. June 26, 1928, married Sept.18, 1876 Clara Kimball (b.Nov.15,1856, d. Dec.13, 1938)

103   Infant
104   Nellie Fern Wales, b.Feb.1880, d.Aug. 13, 1881
105   Donald Richard Wales, b. Nov.1882, d. May 19, 1884
106   Frances Luella Wales, b. March 11,1885

61.   Margaret Jane Haynes, born ca 1836-7 Ind., married John Long (Bk.E, p.3) Feb.19,1860 in Union County. They lived on a farm near Centerville, Wayne Co., Indiana.

107   Nora Long, m. _____ Flagg and had a son Alvernus Flagg.
108   Perry Long. Lived in Richmond, Ind.

109 Olive Long, lived in Richmond, Ind.
110 Charles Long, lived in Richmond, Ind.
111 Frank Long, d. Aug.21, 1905 in Richmond, Ind., aged 40.

Margaret Haines, aged 15, born in Indiana, is listed in the Union County census of 1850 with the family of John Nelson. In Clinton, Ind., Dec.1857 Margaret Jane Haynes signed a receipt as one of the heirs of Thomas Jefferson Haynes. (This is the only place where we find the name Thomas used with Jefferson Haynes.) She signed a second receipt in 1859. On Jan.23, 1866 James M. Haynes (#24) received a quit-claim deed (recorded in Clinton Co., Ind.) from John W. Long and Margaret his wife, of Wayne Co., Ind., for Pt.W SW Sec.16, Tp.22, Range 2 E (D.Bk.28, p.269).

62. James L. Haynes, born ca 1838. The Civil War record in the National Archives shows James T. Haynes enlisted at Liberty, Ind. He said he was born in Marion Co., Indiana. He died at Jefferson Barracks, Mo., Feb.7, 1863. He served in Company G, 69th Regt.

64. Jasper Newton Haynes, born ca 1842 in Ind., died Jan.27, 1924 at the Masonic Home in Franklin, Ind., buried Elkhorn Cemetery near Richmond, Ind. He married Lydia Ellen Jones, Jan.1, 1873, Union Co., Ind. (Bk.3, p.405); she was born in Ind. and died July 22, 1912 at Richmond, Ind. (Wayne County Death Records CH 13, p.124).
In 1850 "Newt" was living with James Wheeler. In the 1860 census of Union County, he is shown in the household of James M. and Elizabeth Allen. In 1880 he was living in Abington, Wayne County. His occupation was "house carpenter".

112 Maude E. Haynes, m. Peter Maibach, Nov.11, 1902 in Wayne County.
113 Mary V. Haynes, m. Charles Heinbaugh March 10, 1897, Wayne Co., Indiana.

65. Martha W. Haynes, born ca 1843 in Indiana.
The 1860 census of Union Co., Ind. lists
Martha in the household of John and Delilah
Eikenberry as a servant,in a neighboring Tp.
to Harrison. She is said to have lived at
Abington and was raised by a Quaker family.
James M. Haynes for $500 received a deed
for 30 ac. from Alfred Transbarger and Martha A., his wife. It is possible that Martha Transbarger was formerly Martha Haynes
and that James M. Haynes was her uncle.

66. Amanda E. Haynes, born ca 1845 in Indiana.
It is thought that she was brought up by a
family in Cincinnati. She appointed Dr.G.R.
Chitwood of Liberty, Ind. as her agent in
the matter of the final settlement of her
father's estate.

67. Hester Ann Haynes, born 1847 in Indiana,
died Oct.8, 1898 at Woodberry, Illinois,
buried Mullin Cemetery near Montrose, Ill.
She married Sept.3, 1874 at Xenia (now
Converse) Indiana (Marriage Bk.C 5,p.183),
Alvis Gaston Mendenhall (b. June 25,1851
Miama Co., Ind., d. March 4, 1918 Wayne Co.
Ill., buried Egbert Cemetery, Burford,Ill.)
the son of Daniel and Martha D. (Hunt) Mendenhall. Martha D. Hunt's death certificate
shows her father as Asa Hunt. Factual evidence strongly indicates that she was the
daughter of Asa and Diana (Stanley) Hunt.
Known children of Asa and Diana are Rebecah
b. Dec.12, 1814; Lydia b. Feb.21,1817; Luzena b. May 1, 1819; Alvis b.1825; William
Gaston b. Feb.12, 1827; Eliza; and Emily.
Martha D., b. Aug.29, 1821 could easily fit
between Luzena and Alvis, and the D. stands
for Diana. Martha named a son Alvis Gaston,
naming him after two of her brothers. If
Martha is a daughter of Asa and Diana (Stanley) Hunt, and if Cynthia Wheeler was formerly a Hunt and a daughter of Zebulon and
Mary (English) Hunt, then Martha D. (Hunt)
Mendenhall would have been a second cousin
to Cynthia (Wheeler) Haynes.
In 1850 Ann Haynes lived with William Swaf-

ford of Union County, Ind., who was probably a brother-in-law of James Wheeler who married Sarah Swafford. In the census of 1860 she was living in Union Co.,Harrison Tp., Ind. with her great-aunt Jane Haynes Wales, also in 1870. After this date she probably went to Miami Co., Ind. to visit relatives, and there met Alvis Mendenhall. Hester Ann was known to relatives in Ind. as "Ann". Her children and their descendants knew her as Anna May, and only when the court records were checked was it learned that she was born Hester Ann. It is not known when or why she decided to change her name.

In a copy of Pinneo's Primary Grammar Book which belonged to Frances Wales Haycock's father, appear the handwritten names of "Annie May Haines, Liberty, Union Co.,Ind." and "Amanda Haines, Liberty, Union Co., Ind." along with that of Charles Wales,Aug. the 16th, 1860 (his 15th birthday). This would indicate that Hester Ann adopted the name "Anna May" at an early age, even though all legal documents carried her correct name.

114   Daniel Aurelius Mendenhall, b. Dec.7, 1875 in Converse, Ind., d.there 1876.

115   Dillon Coston Mendenhall, b.Dec.7, 1875 in Converse, Ind., d.there 1876.
116   Inez Mendenhall, b. Feb.17, 1878.
117   Stella Naomi Mendenhall, b.Dec.22,1880
118   Martha Edith Mendenhall, b.Feb.22,1883
119   Emma Luzena Mendenhall, b.July 31,1886
120   Hazel Mendenhall, b.Dec.8, 1890 Patton, Ind., d. Oct.5, 1899 in Illinois.

68.   Miranda Alice Haynes, b.Jan.29, 1870, Clinton Co., Ind., d. Aug.28, 1937, m. June 18, 1887 in Clinton Co. George Huffer Benge, (b.Sept.15, 1864, d. Nov.24, 1916).

121   Benjamin Harrison Benge, b.Feb.13,1889 Elwood, Ind., d.there June 12,1892.

122 Bessie Elizabeth Benge, b. Aug.7,1890
123 Effie May Benge, b.Sept.23, 1892
124 Robert Luther Benge, b.Sept.17, 1894
     in Clinton County.
125 Roy Dean Benge, b. June 29, 1897, m.
     Feb.5, 1919 in Clinton Co. Golda E.
     Rogers.
126 Jennie Alice Benge, b. Dec.15, 1899
127 Stanley Russell Benge, b? d. Indiana.
128 Dorothy Helen Benge, b.Jan.13, 1910
     Clinton Co., Ind.

69. Richard Sherman Haynes, b.Dec.21, 1871, d.
     Feb.1963 in Iowa, m. Dec.24, 1899 Effie D.
     Gray who d. June 1959.

129 A son b. March 18,1910, d. at birth.
130 James Monroe Haines, b.March 14, 1911
131 Richard Sherman Haines, b. Oct.11,
     1914, d.1933
132 Fae Effie Haines, b. March 7, 1918

86. Richard McKillip, b. Aug.5, 1845, d.Oct.
     26, 1933, m. Oct.23, 1877 Osea M.Tappen
     (b. Oct.14,1848, d. Sept.16,1927).

133 Martha McKillip, b.June 6, 1885

88. Martha A.Wales, b.Oct.9, 1850, d.Nov.23,
     1946, m. Feb.19, 1870 DeWitt Clinton Tappen
     (b. Feb.10,1850, d. Oct.23, 1922).

134 Jennie Tappen, b. March 12, 1871
135 Margaret Tappen, b.Jan.13,1873, d.1875
136 Daniel Wales Tappen, b.June 21, 1875
137 Bernard Tappen, b.May 20,1878, d.1880
138 Harry Lee Tappen, b. Dec.18, 1882
139 Myra Tappen, b.June 19, 1887
140 Helen Tappen, b. April 5, 1889, m.
     Joseph Barber.

90. Mary Wales, b. Nov.5, 1866, m. Aug.2, 1896
     Elmer E. Post (b.July 25,1870, d. March 21,
     1950.

141 Albert Wales Post, b. April 29,1897

92.   Abbie Hunt, b. Sept.9, 1857, Union Co.,
Ind., d.May 9, 1941 Tippecanoe Co., Ind.,
m. 1878 George Wolf (1855-1891).

     142 Charles Clarence Wolf, 1880-1942.
     143 Conrad Hunt Wolf, b.Nov.27,1882, d.
          Dec.4, 1971.
     144 Hallie Marie Wolf, b.Sept.15, 1891.

93.   James Franklin Hunt, b. March 31, 1859 in
Union Co., Ind., d.July 13, 1919, Marion,
Ind., m. Lauretta Simmons (b.March 3,1860,
d. Dec.20,1957).

     145 Frankie Hunt, b.Sept.1, 1888
     146 Darl Hunt, b.March 17, 1893, d.Sept.
          28,1971, m. Henrietta Eiler.
     147 Kenneth L. Hunt, b. Feb.25, 1895

94.   Jennie Hunt, b. Nov.6, 1861 in Union Co.,
d. Dec.26, 1936 near Marion, Ind., m.
Frank Creviston.

     148 Charlie Creviston, b. March 28,1882
     149 Mary Creviston, d. ca 1910, no issue.
     150 Howard Creviston, d.1950, no issue.

96.   Charles White Hunt Jr., b. July 27,1866,
Union Co., d.June 1926 Converse, Ind., m.
Maude Williams April 20,1904, n.i.

97.   Mary Olive Hunt, b. Sept.25, 1869, Union
Co., d.April 28, 1946 Indianapolis, Ind.,
m. Dec.25, 1890 at Xenia (now Converse)
Ind. Milton D. Macy (b.July 16,1857 Miami
Co., Ind., d.Jan.4, 1932 Converse, Ind.)
son of Oliver H.P. Macy and Elizabeth Hock-
ett. She m. (2) Albion Otis Wetherbee of
Needham, Mass., in St.Petersburg, Fla.,Feb.
25, 1940.

     151 Irene Elizabeth Macy, b.Sept.6, 1894
     152 Meredith Wales Macy, b. June 1, 1899
          Converse, m. April 18,1928 Grace
          Hiatt, b.Jan.14,1903, n.i.
     153 Oliver Wendell Macy, b. July 3, 1905
     154 John Milton Macy, b.April 17,1914,

Converse, m. Sept.9, 1939 Mary Jane
Grubb, b.Oct.26,1916, n.i.

98. Flora E. Wales, b.July 5, 1866, d.May 1935,
m. Nov.16,1892 Alfred V. McKillip (b.Nov.27
1863, d. Jan.1950).

155 Grace Margaret McKillip, 1893-1894.
156 Don Wales McKillip, b. Jan.2, 1896.

100. James Samuel Wales, b.Sept.20,1869, d.Jan.
23, 1941, m. May 18, 1899 Anna M. Willis
(b.Sept.2, 1871).

157 Charles Everett Wales, b. Aug.7,1900
158 James Willis Wales, b.Aug.26, 1907,
m. Mary Lou Phillips.

101. Jennie Wales, b.Aug.27, 1873, d.March 20,
1955, m. Feb.28, 1900 David E. Allebaugh.

159 Ralph Wales Allebaugh, 1900-1905.
160 Donald Meredith Allebaugh, b.June 25,
1907.

102. Ruth Wales, b. June 25, 1884, m. Dec.29,
1904 Arthur Hollingsworth,b.Feb.3,1879.

161 Elma Ruth Hollingsworth, b.Apr.1,1919

106. Frances Luella Wales, b.March 11, 1885, m.
June 12, 1912 Bruce Haycock, b.May 1, 1882,
d.March 4, 1955, son of William Arthur Haycock and Carrie O. Freeman Haycock.

162 Robert Wales Haycock, b.March 28,1913

116. Inez Mendenhall, b. Feb.17, 1878 at Converse, Ind., d.Feb.1, 1941, Montrose, Ill.,
m. (1) March 27,1899 Samuel Butler Kingery;
m. (2) Silas Fatoot Larison (b.June 4,1861
in Preble Co., Ohio, d.June 24, 1939, Montrose, Ill., son of Samuel and Mary (Fatoot)
Larison.
Issue by the first marriage:

163 Rosa May Kingery, b. Jan.28, 1900
164 Alvis Gaston Kingery, b.Dec.2, 1901

165 Ira Nelson Kingery, b.Oct.4, 1904,
     Ill., d.s.p. 1924
166 Guernsey Hubert Kingery, b.Mar.10,1908

Issue by second marriage:

167 Leslie Edward Larison, 1910-1912
168 Elsie Marie Larison, b.Jan.11,1913
169 Edith Lucille Larison, b.Apr.30,1915,
     d.1916.
170 Russell Clyde Larison, b.April 10,1917

117. Stella Naomi Mendenhall, b.Dec.22, 1880,m.
      Oct.3, 1900 Hector Lewis Baker (1875-1957)
      son of Sanford and Cynthia(Icenberger)Baker

      171 Alba Gaston Baker, 1901-1903
      172 Grace Lou Baker, b.Sept.30,1905, m.
           1938 at Atlanta, Ga. Clifton R.Thomas
           (b.July 9, 1875, Mableton, Ga.) n.i.
      173 Mary E. Baker, b. Feb.17, 1909
      174 Don Baker, b. Jan.25, 1911

118. Martha Edith Mendenhall, b. Feb.22, 1883,
      d.July 22, 1963, m. 1910 Grant Smith, n.i.

119. Emma Luzena Mendenhall, b.July 31, 1886 in
      Bloomfield, Ind., d. Aug.23, 1936 in Ill.,
      m. Charles Press Beason (1885-1959)

      175 John C. Beason
      176 Wayne Louis Beason, b.1910, d.1962,
           m. 1955 Charlotte Ann Wade.
      177 George P. Beason.
      178 Edith Beason, m. Kenneth Carter.
      179 Helen Beason.
      180 Curtis E. Beason.

122. Bessie Elizabeth Benge, b. Aug.7, 1890, d.
      May 13, 1949, m. 1913 in Clinton Co., Ind.,
      Frank Holland. Issue:
      Kenneth, b. 1914, m. 1937 Jewell Davis;
      children: Beverly and Patricia.
      Rutherford, b. 1915, m. 1935 Marcella Mich-
      els; children: Carolyn, and Joice who m.
      Robert Jones and has chn. Holly and Amy.

123   Effie May Benge, b.Sept.23, 1892 at Elwood
       Ind., m. (1) Alva Eikenberry who d. 1926,
       m.(2) Elby Sheets. Chn: (1st marriage)
       Wilbur, Mary, Betty, Paul, Joseph and
       Margaret.

124   Robert Luther Benge, b. Sept.17, 1894 in
       Clinton Co., Ind., m. 1918 Mary Finney.
       Chn: Lillian, Erma, Howard, Richard,John,
       Wilma, Luther, Georgia, Charles, Leona.

126   Jennie Alice Benge, b. Dec.15, 1899, d.
       1963, m. Roy Myers. Chn: Marjorie, Julia,
       Paul, Marilyn.

130   James Monroe Haines, b. March 14, 1911, m.
       Helen Rott. Chn: Elizabeth, John, Avon,
       Evelyn, Betty, James, Maralyn, Richard,
       Eldon, LeRoy, William, Sally.

133   Martha McKillip, b. June 6, 1885, m. Oct.
       25, 1905 Wayne G. Creek. Chn: Charles,
       Mary, John, Christabel, Jean.

134   Jennie Tappen, b. March 12, 1871, d.1951,
       m. Jan.1,1890 Edward J. Baird (1869-1953).
       Chn: Maurice, Donald, Harry, Hoyt.

136   Daniel Wales Tappen, b. June 21, 1875, m.
       1899 Ada Searle. Issue: Thelma b. 1901.

138   Harry Lee Tappen, b. Dec.18, 1882, d.1933,
       m. 1912 Myrtle Price. Chn: Lovenia and
       Darrell.

141   Albert Wales Post, b.April 29, 1897, m.
       1922 Florence Chapin. Chn: Samuel,Daniel.

143   Conrad Hunt Wolf, b. Nov.27, 1882, m.1905
       Minnie Macon. Chn: Marjorie, Mary,George,
       C.H., Madora, Charles, Warren, Eugene.

145   Frankie Hunt, b. Sept.1, 1888, m. 1912
       Homer Hensler. Chn: Dorothy and Homer.

147   Kenneth L.Hunt, b. Feb.25, 1895, m. 1917
       Fay Hardin. Issue: Jane.

148   Charlie Creviston, b. March 28, 1882, m.
       Lola Tomlinson. Chn: Mary Jo and John.

151   Irene Elizabeth Macy, b. Sept.6, 1894, m.
       (1) 1917 A.Wright Strieby (1895-1927); she
       m. (2) 1968 Randolph Norris Shreve of Pur-
       due University. One son Robert, b. 1919.

153   Oliver Wendell Macy, b. July 3, 1905, m.
       1932 Esta Harker. Chn: Donna, Jane, and
       Milton.

156   Don Wales McKillip, b. Jan.2, 1896, m.
       Bernice Johnson. They have dau. Patricia.

157   Charles Everett Wales, b. Aug.7, 1900, m.
       Pearl Mitchell. Chn: Betty and Virginia.

160   Donald M. Allebaugh, b. June 25, 1907, d.
       1952, m.Thelma Conrad. Chn: Judith, Jane.

161   Elma R. Hollingsworth, b.1919, m. Herschel
       Boll. Chn: Mary and John.

162   Robert Wales Hancock, b.1913, m. Doris
       Givens. Chn: Brian, Rebecca and David.

163   Rosa M. Kingery, b. 1900, m. (1) Luther B.
       Warden, m. (2) August Shaefer, d. 1941.

164   Alvis G. Kingery, b. 1901, m. 1922 Mary F.
       Runyan (1903-1949). Chn: Robert, Roberta,
       Alvis, Inez, Evelyn, Alma, Arthur, Carl,
       Thelma.

166   Guernsey H. Kingery, b.1908, m. (1) Cora
       Walker, chn: Violet; m. (2) Marjorie
       Sadlier.

168   Elsie M. Larison, b. 1913, m. 1929 George M.
       Hensley. Chn: Mildred, George, Irma, John,
       Norman, James,Delbert, Albert, Fern, Peggy,
       Linda, Beverly.

170   Russell C.Larison, b. 1917, m. (1) Rose Vau-
       ltenberg, (2) Virginia Pinnell, one child
       Peggy by this marriage, m. (3) Frieda Finks,
       4 chn. by this marriage.

173   Mary E. Baker, b. Feb.17, 1909, m.1931 Hoyt
       Ellerbee. One son, Earl Ellerbee b. 1933.

                    ****

JASPER HAYNES   (see p.68)

WILL OF JASPER HAYNES, CULPEPER COUNTY, VIRGINIA:

In the name of God Amen. I, Jasper Haynes of the
County of Culpeper and State of Virginia being
very low and weak but of sound memory and calling
to mind the uncertainty of this life and that all
flesh must yield unto death when it shall please
God to call, do make and ordain this my last Will
and Testament in manner following:

My soul I recommend to Almighty God who gave it
me trusting in the merits of my Saviour to Rise
again to Life Eternal my body to be buried in a
decent manner at the Direction of my Executors
hereafter mentioned and as to my worldly goods I
give and bestow in manner as followeth:

Imprimus, I lend to my beloved wife during her
natural life or widowhood that part of my Estate
hereafter mentioned viz: One negro man named Sam,
one negro woman Dinah and one negro girl named
Jenny, also the half of my stock of all kinds
also Two Feather Beds and furniture, also a Black

Walnut Table and Desk and one Chest and half of
my pewter and one Large Iron Pott and a flax and
cotton wheel and half of my Plantation working
tools.

Item the 1st. I give and bequeath unto my son
JOSEPH that part of my land lying and being between Dark Run and White Oak Run joining Bobo,
Powel and Ryner to him and his Heirs forever. I
give to my said son one young cow to him and his
Heirs forever. I give and bequeath to my two sons
JASPER and STEPHEN the Residue of my land in Culpeper County to be equally divided between them,
my son Jasper having sold his right with my Consent to my son Joseph, I give and bequeath this
my son Jasper's part to my son Joseph to him and
his Heirs forever.

2ndly. And the Residue of my Estate not already
given (including those I have lent my beloved
wife, except the stock of all kinds and household
furniture) I give and bequeath unto the rest of
my children: Elizabeth, Moses, Benjamin, Mary,
James, Anne and William to be Equally divided
among them in manner as followeth, that the Negroes and other part of Estate to be set up at
Public Auction, no person admitted to bid but my
Children the whole of them having equal right to
bid one against another and the amount of the estate to be equally divided after they having done
Bidding and each part or proportion I give to each
of them each of their Heirs & forever.

It is my will and desire that all my Estate be appraised at the old Rates valued in Hard money and
sold the same way and that the whole of my children have an equal part of all my Stock and Household furniture. And Lastly I do hereby Constitute
and appoint my sons JOSEPH and JASPER HAYNES my
Executors of this my last Will and Testament and
do hereby revoke all former Wills by me made and
do Declare this my last Will and Testament.

In Witness whereof I have hereunto set my hand and seal this 19 day of June, 1779.

(signed)   JASPER HAYNES

Signed sealed published and Declared in presence of
Alexr Waugh   Humphrey Sparks   Wm. Phillips

At a Court held for Culpeper County the 21st day of January 1782 this last Will and Testament of

Jasper Haynes deceased was Exhibited to the court by the Executors and was proved by the oaths of Alexander Waugh and Humphrey Sparks, two of the Witnesses thereto and Ordered to be Recorded. And on the motion of the said Executors, Certificate was granted them for obtaining a probate thereof in due form, they having sworn to the same and giving bond and Security according to Law.
Teste: John Jameson, Cl. Crt.

****

Children Of JASPER HAYNES (compiled by Virginia Beal and published in the Haynes Eagle, Dec.1963):
Note: Jasper Haynes was born ca 1715 and lived in Caroline County, Virginia 1746. He had bought land in Spottsylvania, Hanover, and Louisa Counties by the year 1739. His wife was Elizabeth, surname uncertain; possibly a Powell or a Sparks. (Tyler's Quarterly XIII:1, pp.23-43; Towle and Clark Families, by William R. Newman; Richard Haines and His Descendants, by Capt.John W.Haines, pp. 353-357; also individual records.)

1. Capt. Joseph Haynes, b. Aug.3, 1742, d. Aug.3, 1815 Botetourt Co., Va.; m. Oct.9, 1779 Jannet Young, b. 1751, d.1822. Child:
    a. Major William Henry Haynes, b. Aug.30,1785, m. Polly Hill. Issue: William, Joseph, John, Henry, and Polly.

2. Jasper Haynes Jr., d.1827; m. (1) _____
   Powell, m. (2) 1790 Elizabeth Roberts; their
   daughter Lucinda m. John Beadles.

3. Stephen Powell Haynes.

4. Elizabeth Haynes m. William Sparks. Chn:
   John, William, Joseph, Humphrey, Jasper,
   Mary, Elizabeth and Sary.

5. Moses Haynes, d. 1829 in Georgia, m. Sarah
   _____. Chn: Stephen, William, Moses,Nancy,
   Elizabeth who m. Leonard Keeling, Polly,
   Sarah, Jane, and Thomas who m. Lettie Duncan.

6. Benjamin Haynes, who lived in Botetourt Co.,
   Va. 1783-1787, and in Allegheny Co., Va. until
   ca 1824. Chn: William, Jane who m. George
   Boggess in 1793, and Sarah who m. William
   Johnston in 1800.

7. James Haynes who m. 1786 Sarah Jackson. They
   had a son William Haynes.

8. Mary Haynes, who m. 1787 George Waite.

9. Ann Powell Haynes, b. Feb.21, 175- in Culpeper
   Co., Va., m. Jan.14, 1774 Joseph Clark (1752-
   1839). Children:
   a. Frances b. Feb.13, 1775, no issue.
   b. Martha Clark, b. May 17,1777, m. a
      cousin, Reuben Clark.
   c. Larkin Clark, b. Oct.27, 1778, m. Jan.30,
      1797 Rebecca Bell.
   d. James Clark, b. Sept.16, 1780, lived in
      Elbert Co., Georgia.
   e. Mary Clark, b. Nov.21, 1782, m. Col.
      Heard of Georgia.
   f. Ann P. Clark, b. Nov.2, 1784, m. John C.
      Easter.
   g. Elizabeth M. Clark, b. Oct.7, 1786, m.
      Col.Thomas White. Their dau. Eunice m.

James H. Holland.

  h. Sarah T. Clark m. Lewis Shisler.
  i. Bathsheba S. Clark, b.1791, d.s.p.
  j. William David Clark, b. Oct.13, 1793, m.
    March 16, 18 5 Jane H. Eliason.
  k. Tabitha Clark, b. Feb.5, 1796, m. Cuthbert
    Reese; their dau. Elizabeth m. George W.
    Holland.
  1. Eunice H. Clark, b. Jan.9, 1798, m. Solomon
    H. McIntyre.

10. William Haynes, b. Dec.18, 1763, d. May 1,1819,
    m. Feb.7, 1790 Catherine Shanklin. Chn:

  a. James M. Haynes, b.Feb.17,1794 Greenbriar
    Co., West Virginia, m. Sept.20, 1821 at
    Union, W.Va., Isabella Dunlap.
  b. Agnes Haynes, b. 1797, m. Michael Erskine.
  c. Andrew S. Haynes, b. 1799.
  d. William T. Haynes, b.Aug.2, 1802.
  e. Thomas N. Haynes, b. 1805.

****

Will of WILLIAM HAYNES, Bedford County, Virginia:

In the name of God Amen. I William Haynes being
in the full exercise of my reason and memory
(Thanks be to Almighty God) and calling to mind
the mortality of my Body ---- and knowing that
it is appointed for all men to die, do make and
ordain this my last will and testament.

IMPRIMUS. I will that out of that Estate with
which it hath pleased God to bless me in this
life all my just debts be punctually paid and
after the payment thereof - I give devise and
dispose of the same in the following manner Viz:

I give to my son-in-law Stephen Sanders the land
and Plantation whereon I now live containing 200
acres to him and his Heirs forever, only reserving

to John Otey one acre whereon his mill now stands
provided the said Otey, agreeable to a former bargain, shall keep the said mill in repair and grind
all the grain the said Sanders shall want for the
use of the said Plantation, or any other person
into whose hands the said Land may fall toll free
and on failure the said acre of Land is to revert
to the said Sanders his Heirs and Assignees.

ITEM. I lend to my daughter Ann Ferril two negroes to wit Lucy and Jean during her natural life
and at her decease to be equally divided between
her two daughters Mildred and Elizabeth, also I
give to my daughter Ann Ferril one feather bed
and furniture.

ITEM. I give to my son John Haynes and to my
daughter Frances Smith one negro boy Peter to be
equally divided among them.

ITEM. I give to my daughter Elizabeth Leftwich
one negro boy Ceazer to her and her heirs, also
a sorrel horse named Pompey.

ITEM. I give to my son William Haynes one negro
man named James to him and his heirs.

ITEM. I give to my daughter Mildred Sanders one
negro woman named Peg to her and her heirs.

ITEM. I give to my daughter Mary Long one negro
girl named Judith to her and her heirs.

ITEM. I give to Elizabeth Sanders oldest daughter of Stephen Sanders and Mildred his wife, one
negro girl named Sall to her and her heirs.

ITEM. I give to my son Henry Haynes one bay horse
and all the residue of my estate I give to be
equally divided between my daughter Elizabeth Leftwich and my son Henry Haynes - giving the said
Henry one feather bed and furniture, he accounting
with the said Elizabeth for the value thereof in
the above division.

And I do constitute and appoint William Leftwich and Stephen Sanders Executors of this my last Will and Testament. In Witness thereof I have here-unto set my hand and Seal this Eighth day of April One Thousand Seven Hundred and Eighty.

William W. Haynes   SEAL
(his X mark)

Teste:
Merry Carter
Frances Carter (her X mark)
Mary Carter

At a Court held for Bedford County the 25th day of June 1781. This last Will and Testament of William Haynes deceased was proved by the Oaths of Merry Carter and Frances Carter witnesses thereto Subscribed and Ordered to be Recorded and on the Motion of William Leftwich Gent. one of the Executors therein named who made Oath thereto Certificate is granted him for obtaining Probate in due form giving security whereupon he together with David Wright and Merry Carter his securities entered unto and acknowledged their bond in the penalty of three hundred thousand pounds for the said Executors due and faithful administration of the said Decedents Estate and performance of his will - Liberty being reserved the other Executor mentioned in said Will to join in the Probate thereof when he shall think fit.

Teste   J. Steptoe
Clk.

A copy Teste V.W.Nichols
Clerk

****

Children of William Haynes (compiled by Virginia Beal and published in The Haynes Eagle, Dec.1963)

Note: William Haynes, b. ca 1710, d.1781 in Bed-form Co., Va., m. 1734 Elizabeth _____. He was

a private in the Bedford County Militia in 1758.
(Refs: Hopkins, Turner-Leftwich, pp.200,219,220;
Hendricks and Their Kin; D.A.R.Marriage Records.)

1. Mildred Haynes, m. Sept.29, 1768, Bedford Co.
   Va.,Stephen Sanders.
2. Ann Haynes, m. ____ Farrel. Had at least 2
   children - Mildred and Elizabeth.
3. John Haynes, b. 1753 Hanover Co., Va., d.1840
   Bedford Co., Va., m. Joicey Anderson. Will
   probated Nov.23, 1840. Children: Dudley;
   Thomas who d. 1806 and had a daughter Millie
   who m. a Karr of Franklin Co., Tenn.; David;
   Edward; Patrick; John; Lucy who m. Dec.2,
   1816 in Bedford Co. James Hogan; Betsy who m.
   Charles Graham; and Anderson Haynes.
4. Frances Haynes who m. a Smith.
5. Elizabeth Haynes who m. Col.William Leftwich
   in 1757.
6. William Haynes, b. Aug.4, 1740, Amhurst Co.,
   Va.; d. Aug.3, 1827, Ohio Co., Ky. He was
   Capt. in Bedford Co. Militia and Pvt. in 11th
   Va. Regt. He moved to Kentucky ca 1796. He
   m. (1) in 1764 Hannah Ellis, and (2) Sarah
   Tully New (no issue of this marriage).
   Children of the first marriage:
   a. Hardin (or Thomas Harding) Haynes.
   b. Charles Ellis Haynes, b. 1765, m. Nancy
      Goodrich. His children were identified
      through Ohio Co. Estate File Box 1053E:
      Lucy b. 1786, m. a Morris; John, 1788-
      1871, m. Elizabeth McQuire; William,
      1788-1849, m. Jane McQuire; Hardin, 1793-
      1876, m. Lucinda Walker; Charles E. Jr.,
      1796-1849, m. Ann McQuire; Barton;Jesse;
      Nancy, 1797-1859, m. William Nichols;
      Polly, m. Joseph Wallace; Bethena who m.
      a New.
   c. William Haynes Jr.
   d. Jesse Haynes m. Mildred Tinsley.
   e. Susannah Haynes m. George McDonald.
   f. Elizabeth Haynes m. Henry Searcy.

g. Josiah Haynes, m. Judith New.
h. Sarah Haynes m. John Felix.
i. Hannah Haynes m. a Mr. Thomas or Thompson.
j. John Barton Haynes m. (1) Rhoda Huff.
7. Mary Haynes, b. July 22, 1751, d. Jan.17,1825,
    m. Aug.3, 1772 John Long who was a Revolution-
    ary soldier. Moved to Woodford Co., Ky. in
    1789. (See Ky. Historical Register, Oct.1954)
8. Henry Haynes Jr., b. ca 1745, d.1816 in Bed-
    ford Co., Va. His will dated Aug.6, 1816 was
    probated Nov.25, 1816. He m. (1) March 22,
    1768 Bathsheba Hampton; m. (2) May 20, 1784
    Tabitha Turner (Hinshaw 6:930).
    Chn. by the 1st marriage:
    a. Mary (Polly) Haynes, m. 1793 William
        Stratton. Chn: Betsy, Sally, Henry,
        William, John and Polly.
    b. Betty Haynes, m. 1788 Thomas Smith.
        (Hinshaw op.cit.912)
    c. Hampton Haynes, m. March 6, 1793 Mildred
        Farrell (ibid,930).
    d. William Haynes, b. 1773, d.Meade Co.,Ky.
        July 28, 1856.
    e. John Haynes, m. Sept.25, 1804, Elizabeth
        Scott.
    f. "Old" Henry Haynes, b. 1778, d.1858 in
        Breckenridge Co., Ky., m. Phebe Hatcher.
    g. Milner Haynes, b. 1781, d. 1856, m. (1)
        in 1808 Nancy Pate; m. (2) in 1840 Sarah
        Richardson. He d. Meade Co., Ky.
    h. Francis Haynes m. 1806 Elizabeth Terry.
    i. Bathsheba Haynes, m. 1803 John Whitely.
    j. Milley Haynes, m. 1805 William Whitely
    k. Sally Haynes m. 1804 Warner Cobbs (id.694)

    Chn. by 2nd marriage:
    l. Nancy Haynes, m. 1822 John Cobbs.
    m. Frances Haynes m. 1819 Samuel Mead.
    n. Joel Haynes m. Patsey Greer.
    o. Stephen Haynes.
    p. Matilda Haynes, m. Edward Lazenby.
    q. Rhoda Haynes.

Note: See Hinshaw 6:930, for some other Haynes
        marriages; e.g. "Old" Henry Haynes m. (2)
        Mary H. Smith, Feb.5, 1816; some marriages
        found only under the name of spouse.

Addenda, p.127 this chapter:
        Louisa Hanes m. Lemuel Carmichael in Jeff-
        erson Co., Tennessee, June 23, 1841 (Bk.2,
        1840-1870), married by Lynn Snodgrass, J.P.

                        ****

            Edited from data compiled by:

                Irene Macy Strieby Shreve
                West Lafayette, Indiana

                Frances Wales Haycock
                Converse, Indiana

                Mildred Hensley Homann
                Macon, Georgia

THE MASSEY FAMILY

with

CURETON CONNECTIONS

The Massey-Cureton relationship was shown briefly in Historical Southern Families, Vol.XII, p.138, where Elizabeth Rives married (1) James Massey, and (2) William Massey, sons of Joseph Massey of Kent County, Maryland.

The name occurs with great frequency in early English records. There are various spellings - Massy, Massey, Massie, also Maci, Macy, deriving from the Flemish family Masci, who came from the village of the same name in Normandy, about twelve miles from Dieppe, across the English Channel from Hastings.

Four members of the family accompanied William the Conqueror to England in 1066, namely Hamo (or Hamon) de Masci and his three sons, Rame, John and Robert. They held important commands in William's army and in recognition of this service, Hamon was given vast estates in Cheshire, and the title of "Baron of Dunham" was bestowed upon him.

Part of an old deed, quoted from a history of Cheshire, reads: "I, William, King of England etc. do give unto Masci all my right and title to the hopps and hoppsland from me and mine to thee and thine, to hold of me and mine with bow and arrow, where I shoot upon Yarrow. And in witness of this sooth, I seal with my tooth. In presence of Mauld

and divers others." Whatever talents William may
have had, the gift of poetry was not among them.

The land referred to lay near Liverpool of
the present day and was held before the Conquer-
or's time by Gherbord, a nobleman of Flanders, as
Earl of Cheshire.

It is not known when the spelling of the name
Masci changed to Massie, Massey and various other
forms, but it is believed they all derived from
the same Masci of Normandy.

Descent of the Massies of Tatton:

1. William Massy, younger brother of Hamon Massy
    (Masci), Baron of Dunham-Massy. (Chart of
    Massy of Rixton in Baines' History of Lanca-
    shire, Vol.IV, pp.412,413.)
2. William Massy, son of William, to whom Alan,
    son of Alan of Tatton, gave the lands called
    Bruchel in Tatton - bounding the same in his
    deed; rendering a pair of white gloves on the
    feast day of the Nativity of St.John the Bap-
    tist. He married Margery, perhaps the daugh-
    ter of Hugh Mainwaring. He was styled Sir
    William Massy in 1270 and had issue: Richard,
    son and heir; Robert of Rosthorn, second son
    and afterwards heir to his brother; Thomas,
    another son who was living in 1270; and Ha-
    wise, a daughter who married Richard de Fern-
    eley.
3. Sir Richard Massy of Tatton, son and heir of
    William, married Isabel _____; he died without
    issue and was succeeded by his brother Robert.
4. Robert Massy of Tatton, who married and had
    issue: William Massy; Hamon Massy who married
    Katherine, daughter of Alan Rixton of Rixton
    and his heir (Hamon was later styled Sir Hamon
    Massy in 1347 and was the progenitor of the
    Massies of Rixton in Lancashire); Adam Massy,
    another son to whom his father gave custody
    of the lands in Tatton belonging to Raufe
    (son of William de Moberley) until Raufe came

of age in 1327; Robert Massy, another son who died ca 1328.

5. Sir William Massy of Tatton, Knight in 1335, son and heir to Robert, died May 2, 1338. He married in 1307 Margery, daughter of Thomas Legh of High Legh. Issue: Hugh, son and heir; Oliver of Denfield in Rosthorn; John; Richard; a daughter Ellen who married (1) Gilbert Hassall of Hassall in Lancashire, and (2) Sir William Brereton of Brereton in Cheshire.

6. Hugh Massy of Tatton, died 1371. He married Alice _____ and had issue: Richard, son and heir, who married Alice, daughter of Gilbert de Haydock in Lancashire in 1342 but died without issue and was succeeded by his brother John.

7. Sir John Massy of Tatton, named heir to Hugh, was sheriff of Cheshire in 1387 and 1390. He and Thomas his eldest son were attainted by Henry IV. He died in 1403, probably slain at the Battle of Shrewsbury fighting with Henry Percy against the king. He married Alice, sister and heir to Sir Geoffrey Worsley in Lancashire; she died in 1427.
From Baines' Massey of Tatton and Worsley, Vol.III, p.284: "The Worsley estates passed to Alice, sister and sole heir of Geoffrey Worsley of the eleventh generation of the Worsley family, who conveyed it to Sir John Massey of Tatton, son and heir of Hugh Massey of Tatton, who, with Thomas his eldest son by this marriage, was attainted by Henry IV in 1400. In the same year Robert de Worsley, half brother to Sir Geoffrey Massey, presentedd a petition to the King and Council, preferring claims to the estate and Manor of Worsley near Barton and Halton, Lancashire."
Issue of Sir John Massy and Alice (Worsley):
a. Thomas, eldest son who married Margaret _____ but died without issue in 1420; Margaret afterwards m. Sir John Gresley.

b. Geoffrey who succeeded his brother Thomas as heir.

c. Richard.

An old pedigree mentions also sons Hugh, John and Lawrence; also daughter Joan who married (1) Sir William Venables, and (2) Sir Oliver Stanley; and daughter Margery who married Sir John Bromley in Cheshire.

8. Sir Geoffrey Massey, son of Sir John and heir after his brother Thomas; he married Margaret daughter of John Hulton of Farnsworth in Lancs. He died in 1427 at the age of 70, without lawful surviving issue.

9. William Massey Esq., of Tatton, son of Richard and nephew of Sir Geoffrey, married a daughter of Sir Geoffrey Warburton and had issue: Geoffrey, Thomas and Richard. He died 1467.

10. Sir Geoffrey Massey of Tatton, son and heir of William, married in 1453 Isabel, daughter of Sir John Botelet of Bewsy near Warrington in Lancashire. They had only one daughter, Joan. Sir Geoffrey was living in 1475, and Joan, his heir, married Sir William Stanley of Tatton; they had one daughter, Joan (or Jane).

11. This Sir William Stanley of Tatton (in right of Joan his wife, daughter and heir of Sir Geoffrey Massey) was son and heir of Sir Wm. Stanley of Holt Castle in Denbighshire, who was Lord Chamberlain to King Henry VII, and brother to Thomas Stanley, first Earl of Derby.

12. Joan, who died at the age of seventy-seven in 1570, was the only child and heir to William Stanley by his wife Joan (Massey); she married (1) Thomas Ashton, son and heir of Sir Thomas Ashton of Ashton-super-Mersey in Cheshire. He died young and Joan married (2) Sir Richard Brereton who died at Islington, Middlesex, in 1557. Their son and heir was:

13. Geoffrey Brereton, who married Alice, daughter of Piers Leicester in 1551 and had issue Richard, son and heir, and a daughter who died

without issue. Geoffrey Brereton died in 1565 aged thirty, and his widow married Robert Charnacke; she died in 1572.

14. Richard Brereton of Tatton, son and heir of Geoffrey, married in 1572 Dorothy, daughter of Sir Richard Egerton of Ridley in Cheshire, and died without issue in 1598. Dorothy married Sir Peter Legh and died in 1637.

    Richard Brereton of Tatton settled all his estates on Sir Thomas Egerton, Lord Chancellor of England, from whom the Earls of Bridgewater descend. Sir Thomas was Solicitor-General in 1581 and held many important posts. His heir was Thomas Egerton who died without issue and the estates passed to his sister Hester, widow of William Tatton. They are now held by the present Lord Egerton.

Note on Egerton:

Saxon rights, after the Battle of Hastings, were transferred to Hugh, surnamed Lupus, created Palatine Earl of Chester. The place Malpas was chosen as headquarters for Lupus. (Mala-passu was the pass-out from Wales into England, referred to by the poet Drayton, and was within the original boundary of the township of Egerton.) Earl Lupus built various fortresses at Malpas to strengthen the Welsh border, and created his natural son Fitz-Hugh as Baron of Malpas about 1093. There were two daughters, Letitia and Matilda, and the line of Egerton sprang from Matilda's marriage to William Belrard. A son, Philip, who took up his abode at Egerton, eventually used "Egerton" as his surname. Much later, another Philip Egerton, along with John Masci of Tatton. William de Legh, Knt., and Peter Dutton, were appointed to go with the followers of Richard II to overthrow the Duke of Lancaster in 1399, and to go with the Cheshire bowmen to Ireland. Richard II returned with the bowmen to the Welsh coast, to his castles of Caernarvon, Beaumaris, and Conway; they were stormed by Henry IV and Richard was made prisoner, deposed, and in 1400 killed by order of King Henry IV. In 1403 Philip Egerton married Matilda, daughter of David de Malpas.

From Croston's History of Lancs. and Cheshire, p. 304:

"Thomas Hesketh was called in 1446 to take up his knighthood, but declined. He married Margaret, co-heiress of Hamon de Masci of Rixton. One son, Robert, married Alice, daughter of Sir Richard Boothe, Baron of Dunham-Massey. Their son, Thomas Hesketh, married (1) Elizabeth, daughter of William Flemming, Lord of Croston and Mawdeslegh in Lancashire, and (2) Grace, daughter of Sir Richard Townley (1492) of Townley; he married (3) Catherine Briers of Lathom but died without issue."

Note: In 1532 a controversy arose between Mr.Massy of Puddington in Cheshire and the Mayor, as Massy had brought several Spaniards to Chester Castle, and some murders resulted. In 1594 one Hesketh came representing the King of Spain to the Earl of Derby, offering him the Crown of England. Hesketh was hanged.

The pedigree of Briers (Bryers, Brers) in Dugdale's Visitation of Lancashire, p.59, shows descent from Roger Byers of Walton and his wife Blanche (daughter and heiress of Richard Cross of Liverpool) to Lawrence Bryers of Walton- to Roger Bryers and Anne Harrington - to Lawrence Bryers of Walton and wife Elizabeth (daughter of Richard Molyneux of Hawkley) - to Roger Bryers of Walton who married (1) Margerie, daughter of Robert Fazerkley of Walton, and (2) Alice Holme of Lancaster County. Issue of the first marriage was a son Lawrence, who died 1662, and who married Mary, daughter of Sir Cuthbert Clifton of Lancs. It is of interest that Richard Cureton (will dated 1627) of Shropshire, who married Margaret Taylor June 16, 1608, asked Roger Bryers (Brers) to help his widow after his death. Richard and Margaret (Taylor) Cureton had a son, William of Prees and Grinshill, and one of his sons was Richard Cureton who emigrated to Philadelphia in the "Rebecca", Aug.31, 1685, with his wife Margaret (Embrey). (H.S.F.XII, p.108.)

Note: Tatton and Dunham-Massey, frequently mentioned in this chapter, are adjacent in Cheshire, about ten miles S.E. of Manchester and about thirty miles east of Chester. Hamon de Masci had the original land grant after he accompanied William the Conqueror from Normandy, as has been shown.

From Ormerod's History of Cheshire, Vol.II:

"In Clutton (adjacent to Coddington in Cheshire) William Massey recovered land here in a suit against William Aldersey of Chester. In the eighth year of the reign of Queen Elizabeth (1566) Thomas Massey held this manor, "200 acres, 100 in orchard and 100 in woods, from the Queen --- and other lands including Carverden, etc."
Note: The Coddington Massies migrated to Philadelphia - Thomas, William and Humphrey. Their wills were recorded in Philadelphia County. A Humphrey Massey shows in the will of Isaac Ashton (Phila.Co., 201A -1699) where Isaac Ashton paid cash to Humphrey Massey and John Moore.

In 1582 the arms of the Massie family of Coddington were painted on the windows of the parish church there, and can be seen today.

An old pedigree book of Chester in the British Museum (MSS #5528) shows a marriage of William Massey of Grafton to Anne, daughter of John Massey of Coddington; the two families were closely related. Another William Massey, Mayor of Chester in 1591, married Alice, the "Maid of Chester", daughter of Thomas Baurn.

Note: The Massey and Cureton families present the researcher with the same difficulty, namely, that the given names of William, Richard, John and

Thomas occur frequently in every generation.

By the year 1563, a William Massey was settled at Puddington (Visitation of Cheshire, p.172), where he was sheriff of Cheshire. In turn his sons succeeded him in this office - Richard (1569), William (1573) and Nicholas (1583). (Ormerod's Hist. of Cheshire, p.441.)

William Massey died as a Catholic in Chester Castle, April 2, 1579, his wife Ann having died at Puddington Nov.30, 1568.

From Croston's Hist. of Lancashire: In 1581 the persecutions against Popish recusants were pressed (that is, nonconformists of various denominations who differed from the established religion of the country), including Richard Massey and Lady Katherine Egerton, whose daughter married Sir William Curteyne, as shown on a descent placque now hanging in Tatton Hall, the ancient home of the Massey family, later occupied by the Egertons.

An impressive memorial placque in the church at Burton-in-Wirrill, Cheshire, reads:

"This tablet is erected to replace monuments formerly in the Massey Chapel.

William Massey of Puddington, died April 2, 1579, and Anne his wife, and to honour the Barons of Massey, of Dunham-Massey, and their descendants the Masseys of Puddington, Lords of Puddington for 800 years, in all wars."

The placque was erected by George Massey of New York City.

1583   Organization for the Defense of Queen Elizabeth in Lancashire: Catholic signatures include Henry Bannister (who married Alice Cuerden, daughter of John Cuerden), and John Massey.

1588 Names of those who contributed to the De-
      fense Against the Spanish Armada included
      Wm. Massye (25 pounds), Roger Brers (son-
      in-law of Richard Cuerton) and John Carerden.

1660 From Baines' Hist. of Lancashire: The list
      of Papists who surrendered their estates in
      Lancashire include many who later appear in
      Virginia: Harrison, Massey, Cureton, etc."

1678 Elizabeth Massey of Rixton, widow of Rich-
      ard, indicted at Lancaster.

Religious persecutions of the time undoubtedly
led to the migration of these and other families
to America.

From Memorials of the Civil War in England, by
James Hall:
p.41 Capt. (Wm.) Massey of Coddington was taken
      prisoner by the King's forces at the Battle
      of Middlewich. (Note: After this, William
      Massey seems to have moved into the Wem
      section, and his records appear in the Wem
      Parish Register.)
p.61 John Massey, son of William Massey of Cod-
      dington, drunct so much ale he could not go
      home, and the next day he died.
p.67 Aug.5, 1643, Richard Massey, trooper, was
      buried - he was slain by a Royalist cannon-
      ball.

Visitation of Cheshire, 1663, p.77, shows John
Massey, born Feb.3, 1582, died Sept.18, 1619,
married Anne, daughter of Richard Grosvenor of
Eaton. Issue (among others): John, eldest son,
d.s.p.; Roger, born ca 1614, married Mary, daughter of Roger Middleton of Denbighshire, Wales
(they had a son John born ca 1654); Edward, a
Major in the Parliamentary Army but later changed
and supported the king; he was sent to Ireland
and died there, unmarried, and buried in the Abbey

of Leix, Dublin.

The old Massey home is described in the book
Cheshire and Its Welsh Border, pp.19-23, by Herbert Hughes:

"Puddington Hall, on a commanding site on the
Wirrill shore of the Dee, just above Shotwick -
home of the race of the Masseys, a great name
divided among many branches, as William Webb described them about 1600.
From the Conquest to the 18th century, the
Masseys of Puddington dwelt at the Old Hall, and
had a turbulent time of it too, until the last of
them perished in the dungeon of Chester Castle. If
the shade of this sad, imprudent William Massey
returns to the scene of his old home (a Jacobite)
he will find a great deal of it preserved in the
present building, which is a fine example of careful restoration..... The Masseys were notoriously
adventurous.... the family were always Cavaliers,
Loyalists and Catholics in the old cause. They
were in the "Nest of Papists" (Masseys, Stanleys,
Pooles, Whitmores and Bunberies) who helped defend
Chester for the Royalists. After the war, William
Massey was compounded (to pay to the Parliamentary
Treasury) 1210 pounds down and 34 pounds per annum
- a lot of money in those days."

It was a tragedy in 1678-79 when Catholic
priests were hunted down in Cheshire and Father
Plessington, who ministered to those at Puddington
Hall, was captured in the old Massey home. He was
chaplain to Edward Massey.
Dr.Thomas Cartwright, Bishop of Chester 1686-
89, relates in his diary some of the gossip at Mr.
Massey's, Sir James Poole's, Sir Rowland Stanley's
and Sir Thomas Grosvenor's houses. "Sir Thomas and
Lady Grosvenor differed on religious matters which
was the cause of some dissention between them, and
the lady was much visited by Mr.Massey" (a zealous
Catholic, father of Sir William Massey who was to

end in the dungeon of Chester Castle; the cause which he supported was the Jacobite uprising of 1715).

This William Massey had been in Lancashire in secret meetings with the Jacobites. The rebels entered Preston on Nov.11, 1715 and were routed by the King's forces on the 14th. William, scorning surrender, got away and rode to Speke Hall; there he made his horse swim three miles across the Mersey, and thence 45 miles to Puddington, where the horse fell dead near the drawbridge. Sir William was eventually arrested and confined in Chester Castle where he died, as previously mentioned, and was buried at Burton. He willed his estate to his godson Thomas Stanley, who assumed the name Massey upon succession. The combined Massey-Stanley estates were sold in the nineteenth century; Massey Hall is presently owned by Mrs. Olive Higgin, who entertained the writer there in 1970.

By the Act of 1592, all Popish recusants were considered to be traitors of a kind, and about this time William Mascy and wife Jane (Standish) were in Leyland Parish, where Jane is listed as a "convicted recusant". This was the home town of the Cuerdens until about 1604, when John Cuerden disappeared (his death place or date have never been ascertained), but his daughter Mary, wife of Sir George Chadderton, stayed at Cuerden Hall at various times until the Civil War broke out.

This William Mascy was a son of Richard Mascy of Rixton and wife Anne, daughter of Thomas Middleton of Middleton Hall in Westmoreland. Another son of Richard and Anne was Hamlet Mascy of Rixton who married Dorothy, daughter of Roger Bradshaigh of Lancaster County. Richard Mascy, son of Hamlet and Dorothy, married (1) Alice, daughter of Sir Cuthbert Clifton of Lancaster County, and it was their son Richard who emigrated to America and whose will is found in Brunswick County, Virginia (Dugdale's Visitation of Lancs., 1664-65).

The English and Welsh background of the Masseys and Curetons is shown in H.S.F. XII, when they settled at Wem, Grinshill, Moreton Corbet, etc., close to the Welsh border in Shropshire. Plague devastated Wem in 1650, and the town was completely destroyed by fire in 1677.

Massey entries in the Parish Registers include the following:

In Moreton-Corbet Parish in Shropshire, about 8 miles NE of Shrewsbury:

Francis, son of Thomas Massey, bapt.Jan.1,1586
Jane, dau. of Thomas Massey, bapt. May 19, 1588
Anne, dau. of Thomas Massey, bapt.July 5, 1590
Rychard, son of Thomas Massey, bapt. Nov.11,1592

Ann, dau. of Arthur Corbett of Moreton, wife of Mr.Thomas Heath, died in childbirth but the son Thomas Heath is bapt. June 8, 1696. (Note: The close intermarriages between the Heaths, Masseys, and Curetons in Virginia and in North and South Carolina is shown in H.S.F.XII. James Cureton m. Betsy Heath in Virginia, p.136.)

The Massey entries in the Registers of Wem are as follows:

June 7, 1591	Isabell Massey, buried
March 20, 1616	Thos. buried, son of John Massey
June 20, 1616	Sara, wife of John Massey,buried
June 29,1617	John Massey and Mary Downes of P. of Hodnet, married
Feb.1664	William a young child of William Massey, died
Nov.30, 1664	Richard Massey m. Frances Brayne
Feb.2, 1668	Mary, dau. of Wm.Massey and Elizabeth, bapt.

From the records of Moreton-Say in Shropshire (next to Audlem where Richard Cureton, Canon of Lilleshall Abbey made his will in 1540):
Records begin in 1650 and include the following:

1685   Apr.6: Mr.Nathaniel Cuerton was admitted
        to the Cure at Moreton-Say.
        Note: William and Elizabeth Massey died in
        this parish in 1679 and were buried in the
        adjacent parish of Hodnet, where the Rev.
        Nathaniel Cuerton was minister (H.S.F.XII,
        p.108). He was the brother of Richard
        Cureton, bapt. Sept.29, 1642 at Grinshill,
        who migrated to the Quaker colony in Phila-
        delphia, 1685, in the "Rebecca", with his
        wife Margaret (Embrey), settling first in
        Merion, Pa., and later joining the Masseys
        in the Duck Creek area.

1702   Alice, daughter of Elizabeth and William
        Ratcliff, bapt. (Note: The Ratcliff family
        came in the "Rebecca" with Richard Cureton
        and family.)

1792-1800
        John Churton is Asst.Curate in the Church
        of Moreton-Say (presumably the son of John
        Churton who died at Grinshill in 1789). He
        was a brother of William Churton of Edenton,
        Virginia, surveyor for the party which went
        into western North Carolina in 1746; he was
        an employee of Lord Grenville, proprietor
        of the Grenville District, N.C., and was
        elected to the N.C. Legislature in 1761 for
        making excellent "first maps" of the area.
        He died at Edenton in 1769, apparently un-
        married, and willed his property in Virginia
        to his brother John Churton in Cheshire and
        to his sisters Dorothy and Sarah.

                    ****

Lineage of HENRY MASSEY SR. (Compiled by Eula
                                Starr Massey)

In 1631 a Jeffrey Massey came to America from
England and settled near Salem, Massachusetts.
During the following years, until 1711, a number
of others of this same name came from England and
are recorded as settling in Virginia. In the
first U.S. Census, they are found in Maryland,
Virginia, North and South Carolina, with various
spellings of the name; altogether they numbered
nearly a hundred heads of families.

It has not yet been established which of this
group of Virginia settlers was the direct ancestor
of Henry Massey Sr., but investigation may determine this eventually.

Thomas Massey, of Marple, Chester County, Pa.,
whose will is recorded in Philadelphia Co., Pa.
(W.Bk."C", p.144, March 24, 1707/8)names his sons:
Mordecai Massey the eldest son, and wife, who get
the plantation and "all smith tools"; sons James
and Thomas Massey get ₺100 each, and "black walnut
chest to Thomas". "My wife, if widow, to have
lower room in brick house during her maternal
life". To James and Thomas "all land in Willis-
town, 417 acres". The four daughters, Estes,Mary,
Hanna and Phebe divide the household goods with
Phebe his wife, who is named Executor, with Henry
Lewis of Haverford, Pa.

The fact that his family was living in Brunswick County, Virginia, prior to 1760 is shown by
the will of JOSEPH MASSEY, recorded there in 1761.

Will of JOSEPH MASSEY of Brunswick Co., Virginia
(W.Bk.3, 1761, p.368; Inventory 1761, p.374). His
earlier records show in Kent County, Maryland.

In the name of God Amen. I,Joseph Massey of
Meherin Parish, County of Brunswick, being very
weak of body but of sound and perfect mind, of

good memory and disposing attitude, thanks be to
God for the same and calling to mind the mortality of my body and knowing that it is appointed
for all men to die, do make and ordain this to be
my last will and testament in manner and form
following hereby, revoking all other wills and
testaments by me formerly made.

I commend myself into the hands of God who
gave it and for my body I commend to the earth in
a Christian manner by my Executors being herein-
after named.

1. I give and bequeath to my son John the land
between my path abounding by the said to the end
of his lane then along Page's path to the Middle
Creek and all in that bounds called the neck between the two creeks and to his heirs and assigns
forever. I give and bequeath to John one negro
man Jack.
2. I give and bequeath to my daughter Sarah Avent
   negro boy Ned.
3. I give to Amy Avent 20 shillings.
4. I give to my daughter Rebecca Wise 20 shillings.
5. I give unto my daughter Agnes Richardson 20
   shillings.
6. I give unto my daughter Mary Wise 10 shillings.
7. I give and bequeath unto my son Joseph Massie
   5 shillings.
8. I give and bequeath unto my son William Massie
   280 acres of land whereon he now lives and a
   negro boy named Junius, also a negro girl
   named Doll and all the hogs belonging to the
   plantation and cattle and house and all the
   housing stuffs and after my death all my
   saddle and housing.
9. I give unto my son Thomas Massie one half of
   my land not before mentioned and my son James
   to divide as he thinks fit - also bed and
   furniture, iron pott, ½ dozen new plates and
   my bay stallion and his saddle and bridle and
   new housing, and my MILL and a dish - and a
   negro boy George and a negro girl Phyllis.

10. To my son James Massie I bequeath the plantation whereon I now live with 500 acres of land being the lower part of 1000 acres other than that I have given to my son Thomas Massie - also negroes Bob and Hannah.

11. I give unto my daughter Winifred a negro man Jacob and boy Simon.

12. I give to my daughter Lucy a bed and furniture and flat iron pott and a negro boy Minge and another named David.

13. To daughter Betty I bequeath a bed and furniture and iron pott and a negro wench named Sarah and a negro boy Benson.

14. To daughter Frances I bequeath a bed and furniture and iron pott, and a negro boy Abraham and a negro girl Fib.

15. To my beloved wife Elizabeth (Lee, daughter of William Lee) during her widowhood, all my estate both real and personal and negro boy Sam.

16. To my great-granddaughter Charlotte Massie negro Sam.

17. William and Thomas, my sons, should buy a horse apiece.

Signed: Joseph Massie

Wit:
John Hoseman
James Clark
Bethiah Hoseman

Proved: 26 May, 1761
John Robinson, Clk.

Joseph Massey's son James married Elizabeth Rives (born ca 1745, died after 1786), the daughter of George Rives and Sarah (Cook) Rives. (H.S.F.XII, p.138.) James died in 1763 and his will was recorded in that year in Brunswick Co. (correction of information given in op.cit.). In November of the same year his widow bore a son and named him Henry Massey. Later, she married James's brother William, and in 1774 they, with their children (of whom later) came to the Wax-

haws and settled on what is thought to be a King's
Grant of land, though this has not been proved.
Several hundred acres of this land are still in
the possession of their descendants. The original
homestead was called the Red House place, and one
can still see the foundations of the stone chim-
neys and corner pillars remaining from the old
house. Nearby is the family burial plot surround-
ed by a stone wall and containing the remains of
William and Elizabeth and several of their children and grandchildren. It is to be regretted that
this part of the land passed out of the family
about 1866.

Henry Massey was allowed a pension for service
in the Revolutionary War (File 180103) on an application executed Aug.30, 1832, while he was a resident of Mecklenburg County, North Carolina. He
stated that he was born in Brunswick Co., Va., in
1763 and removed to S.C. in 1774 with his parents,
and resided there in the Waxhaw settlement, where
he served with the S.C. troops as follows:

He first served one month under Capt.William
Simpson and Col.Marshall, and was discharged a
few days before the Battle of Stone. He volunteered again under Capt.Robert Crawford; joined Gen.
Sumter in the Indian Land, S.C.; was in the Battles
of Rocky Mount and Hanging Rock; served two months;
was discharged; volunteered under Capt. Drennan
and was in the Battle of Fish Dam Ford; served 2
weeks and was discharged; volunteered under Col.
Henry Hampton and was in the Battle of Blackstocks
Plantation on Tyger River in which General Sumter was wounded, served two weeks (file 18-103-2);
enlisted in July 1781 under Lieut.James Thews in
Col.Maham's Regiment of Cavalry; served one year
and was discharged at Manry's Ferry, Santee River.

From Indents of the Revolutionary War:
#454, Bk."P" Issued on the 6th May 1785 to Mr.
      William Massey for ninety-eight pounds,5s.
      43/4d. sterling for sundries for Cont'ls
      and Militia in 1779,1780,1781,1782,1783, as

per one acc't in whole and in part audited.

        Principal   ᖯ98. 5s. 4-3/4d
        Annual interest ᖯ6.17s.6-1/4d

#28 Lib."O": Issued 19 Jan.1785 to Col.William
    Massey for twenty-two pounds ten shillings
    sterling, pay as Muster-Master-General for
    the State of South Carolina in 1779 and 1780.
    Balance and account audited.

        Principal ᖯ22. 10s.
        Interest   1. 1 s.10d.

           ****

Children of William and Elizabeth (Rives) Massey
(not in chronological order)

1. Henry Massey Sr., born 1763 (probably the son
   of Elizabeth's first marriage to William's
   brother James). Henry married in 1782 at the
   close of the Revolutionary War, Betsy Cureton,
   daughter of James Everett Cureton of Prince
   George and Sussex Counties, Va., and wife
   Betsy (Heath). James Cureton later moved to
   Brunswick Co., Va., then to the Waxhaw district, S.C. He was representative of Prince
   George Co., Va. to the Legislature with Henry
   (Lighthorse Harry) Lee in 1791-1805.
   From Genealogy of the Witherspoon Family, by
   James C. Wardlay, pub.1910: "Many of the Waxhaw men were numbered among the patriots of
   the Revolution..... Major Robert Campbell,
   Major Jno. Barkley, and Henry Massey. Waxhaw
   Church was a general place of rendezvous for
   the patriots, and at the time of the Revolution, that time which tried men's souls, the
   men of the congregation .... were conspicuous
   and even the boys as Henry Massey and Andrew
   Jackson were found in martial array in defense
   of their home and country."

Henry and his wife Betsy (Cureton) settled on
land adjoining her father's, or perhaps it was
part of her father's place given her on her marriage. This land lay partly or entirely in North
Carolina, as the state line ran between it and
the Cureton land. In his application for a pension in 1832, Henry Massey stated that he was a
resident of Mecklenburg Co., N.C. He was a member of the North Carolina House of Representatives
from Mecklenburg County in 1811 and 1812, and
State Senator in 1831 and 1832, as shown in Dr.
J.B.Alexander's History of Mecklenburg County.

Children of Henry Massey Sr. and Betsy (Cureton):
i.   James Cureton Massey, b. 1785, m. Sarah
     Blakeney and moved to Florida in 1851. Issue:
     John Philpot Curran Massey, m. in Florida;
     Thomas Massey, served in Mexican and Civil
     Wars; Mary Massey, m. Robert Colbert; Char-
     lotte Massey, m. a Heath of Chester County;
     Rosa Massey, m. a Heath of Chester County.
ii. William Massey, b.1802, m. _____ Heath.
     Issue: Jane, Elizabeth, and Sarah who d.s.p.;
     Rebecca who m. Dr. James Rufus Bratton and
     had chn. William, Andral, John, Moultrie and
     Hattie; William Heath Massey who m. Melissa
     Hicklin and had several chn., moved to Torza
     in York Co. and then to Texas.
iii.Charlotte Massey, b.1788 and m. Benjamin S.
     Massey her first cousin. Chn. given under
     James Massey family later.
iv. Betsy Massey, m. Jack Massey, son of James,
     and lived only a short time.
v.   Henry Massey Jr., b.1794, m. Elizabeth Porter
     his first cousin, daughter of Reese and Tem-
     perance Porter. Two chn: Mary, who m. Samuel
     Buckner Massey (son of Benjamin) and had chn.
     Samuel, Henry, Alice and Emma; and Henry
     Reese Massey who m. (1) Margaret, daughter of
     Thomas W. Huey and had chn. Henry, Martin,
     Frances and Benjamin; he m. (2) Mary, daugh-
     ter of Professor Robert Henry, and had chn.

Charles and Samuel; after Mary's death he m.
(3) Mrs. Harriet (Sims) Campbell, and they had
chn. William and Minnie.

vi. Everard Massey, b.1796, m. Mary Knox Harper,
one child Benjamin Harper Massey. After Ever-
ard's death Mary m. as her second husband
James Stewart and had two sons, John P. and
James H. Stewart.
Benjamin Harper Massey, b. 1819 in the Wax-
haws, m. Nancy Catherine, daughter of James
Cureton Haile (who was the son of Benjamin
Haile, discoverer of the Haile gold mine in
Lancaster Co. and a Revolutionary soldier).
They were the parents of nine children.

vii. Mary Rebecca Massey, b. 1808, m. John Massey
her first cousin, and died early.

2. James Massey, son of William and Elizabeth
(Rives) Massey, was a soldier in the Revn. He
was administrator of his father's estate ca
1816. He m. Polly Sykes of Virginia. Issue:
Benjamin Sykes Massey who m. Charlotte Massey,
daughter of Henry Massey. Issue:

i. Lycurgus Herschel Massey, m. Lucinda
Miller, dau. of James and Sarah Miller.

ii. James R. Massey, m. (1) a first cousin,
Miss Bass, no issue. He m. (2) Elizabeth
Perry, 7 chn.

iii. Polly Massey, m. (1) a Daniel, and (2)
Osmus Lanier, they had Tabitha and Osmus.

iv. William Massey m. Margaret Crockett,
one child, Nancy.

v. John Massey, m. (1) a daughter of Henry
Massey (either Rebecca or Betsy, who d.
a few months later); he m. (2) a Mrs.
Mills and had chn. Mary, Rosalind, Cornelia and John.

vi. Charlotte Massey, m. Thomas Kirk Cureton.
She lived only a short time and he marr-
ied as his second wife Elizabeth Rives
Massey, dau. of Benjamin. Children listed

in Benjamin Massey family.

3. William Massey, son of William Massey and
    Elizabeth (Rives) was a soldier in the Revn.
    War. He was made guardian of the orphan of
    his brother George after 1817; a receipt
    dated Jan.7, 1832 for the sum of $5721.55
    was given to John Benjamin Massey by William
    for his part of his father's estate (Joseph
    Massey was administrator). He probably moved
    to Tennessee about this time, for Joseph
    Massey and his son James brought news of the
    prosperity in Tennessee after a trip there
    in 1831, which caused most of the family to
    move west in 1837 and 1838. William Massey m.
    Betsy Marshall; there were two sons, William
    and Thomas. The family was lost sight of
    after they left South Carolina.

4. Charlotte Massey, daughter of William and
    Elizabeth Massey, married William McDaniel
    and had four children: Tom, Mary, Henry and
    Daniel. The McDaniel family is now represent-
    ed by some of that name in Chester County,
    S.C., and by the Browns in Lancaster County.

5. Polly Massey, daughter of William and Eliza-
    beth Massey, m. (1) Roger Gibson and had one
    child Sam, who married a Cureton and had chn.
    Jane and Jeremiah. Polly m. (2) Ben Peoples
    and had chn. Ann, George and Ben; they moved
    to Georgia.

6. George Massey, son of William and Elizabeth
    Massey, born 1771, died 1815 in York Co.,S.C.
    He held a commission in Co. of Infantry, 1st.
    Battalion, under Col.William Hanna in 1803.
    He and Thomas Davie were agents for the Cat-
    awba Indians. He was administrator of the
    estates of James Cotton and Curtis Kirk, and
    guardian for Joshua Kirk at the time of his
    death. He married (1) Rebecca Kirk Cotton

(widow of James Cotton and daughter of George
and Curtis Kirk). George and Rebecca had four
children: Joseph, Kirk, Charlotte and Henry.
Joseph married Jane, daughter of Benjamin
Massey, and moved to Alabama; Charlotte, born
Nov.3, 1804, married John P. Cook in 1825;
Henry boarded with his father's brother James
for three years after the death of his parents; he married Amelia Johnson and moved to
Florida.
George Massey married (2) Mary Brumfield Morr-
ison, who had one or two daughters by her
first husband. She and George Massey had three
children: John Benjamin Massey, born March 29,
1810, Harriet, born Dec.26, 1811, who married
James H. Gilmore, and Elizabeth, born Dec.17,
1813, who married _____ Haguewood.

7. Joseph Massey, son Of William and Elizabeth
    Massey, born 1773 in Brunswick Co., Virginia,
    died Jan.19, 1836. He married Aug.6, 1806
    Martha Hood, daughter of Allan Hood from Scot-
    land. Martha was one of ten brothers and sis-
    ters; the Hood family lived near Rock House
    which John Massey built about a mile and a
    half north of Waxhaw Presbyterian Church,where
    they all held their membership. The Masseys of
    Virginia were Church of England, but became
    Church of Scotland after moving to the Wax-
    haws. Joseph Massey and his wife were the
    parents of nine children, three dying in in-
    fancy. Martha Hood Massey was born 1783, and
    died June 6, 1826.
    Joseph Massey, under the command of Capt.Sam-
    uel Dunlap, Lieut.Col. William Simpson, and
    Adj. Thomas Lee, was appointed to drill and
    form companies of men for the War of 1812;
    they included four Hood Brothers and Everard
    Massey.
    Children of Joseph and Martha (Hood) Massey:
    (1) James Madison Massey, b. Nov.30, 1808, d.
        May 10, 1893, m. Dec.31, 1835 Hattie

Shanks Spratt (b. Feb.15, 1817, d. March 28, 1905), daughter of Andrew Spratt Jr. and Esther Shanks. They lived in the Rock House until their removal to Desoto Co., Mississippi, where they settled on the east side of Cold Water River, Sec.1,T4, R7, 1838. James Massey was appointed Capt. of Chickasaw Volunteer Regt., March 17, 1840, Miles Cary Col.Comdt. 51st Regiment, E.W.Andrews, Adjt. James was a farmer and always lived where he settled; the home is now owned by his granddaughter Annie Jane Hurt.

Children of James Madison Massey and wife Hattie:

i. James Spratt Massey, b. Feb.5, 1838 in the Rock House, S.C., d.s.p. Oct.29,1862; served in the Civil War.

ii. Elizabeth Greer Massey, b. March 9, 1840 in Desoto Co., Miss., d. Oct.31, 1898,m. William Porter Howell (son of Starling Howell and Polly Porter Crawford). N.I.

iii. William Henry Massey, b. Aug.12, 1842, d. Sept.27, 1877, m. Dec.12,1865 Margaret A.J.Miller (daughter of Dr.Joseph Doby Miller and Margaret Amelia White). They were the parents of 6 chn: Hettie, Annie, Mary, Minnie, Joseph and Addie.

iv. Joseph Benjamin Massey, b. July 2, 1844, died young.

v. John Madison Massey, b. July 23, 1849, d. Jan.13, 1932, m. (1) Alice Ewing Miller. Chn: John Ewing Massey, b. March 18, 1879, m. Hattie Odell and had 7 chn.; and Mabel Elizabeth Massey, b. Aug.2, 1881, m. Kenneth H. Wann and had 3 children. John Madison Massey m. (2) Martha P. Lauderdale, Sept.26, 1889; chn: Sarah b. Jan.15, 1893, m. O.F.Mathis; James M. b. July 27, 1894, m. Lulu Garnett and had one child; Joseph A., b. Aug.21, 1896, m. Cora Harris, 6 chn.; Frances Massey, b.

Dec.12, 1897, m. Arch Carter; 2 chn.;
Winifred Massey, b. June 30,1899, m.
Clarence Gartrell; Mildred P. Massey,
b. Aug.27, 1901, m. Dr.Cecil Mathis,
one child.

vi. Nancy Jane Massey, b. Aug.30, 1851, d.
Oct.27, 1917, m. Sept.6, 1871 Samuel
Urbane Johnston. Chn: Odie, Minnie, Urbane, Leonard, Samuel, William, Ernest
and Eva.

vii. Allan Drew Massey, b. Dec.16,1853, d.s.p.
22 April, 1878.

(2) Elizabeth Anna Massey, daughter of Joseph
and Martha (Hood) Massey, was b. July 10,
1811, d. Aug.29, 1883, m. Nov.12, 1829 to
John McColough Spratt who was b. March 2,
1808, d. May 5, 1884. Children:

i. Martha Jane Spratt, b. March 25, 1831,
d. 1921, m. (1) Thomas Montgomery of
Mississippi. Chn: Cora and Bob. Thomas
d. Feb.21, 1855 and Martha m. Dr.Weir.

ii. Nancy Elizabeth Spratt, b. Feb.2, 1833,
d.1869, m. Samuel C. Stevens of Miss.
Chn: Reese, Lizzie, Lula, Conrad, Ovie
and Walter.

iii. Joseph Massey Spratt, a Civil War veteran, b. April 22, 1835, d.s.p. Oct.20,1914.

iv. John James Spratt, b. Sept.3, 1837, d.
1930, m. with children.

v. Sarah Roxanna Spratt, b. April 26, 1839,
d. June 26, 1872, m. Oliver McReynolds
of Dangerfield.

vi. Artimesia Amanda Spratt, b. 18 July,1841,
d. Jan.26, 1899, m. Dr.William Harrison
in 1865. Eight children.

vii. William Andrew Spratt, b. Jan.27, 1844,
a Civil War veteran, d.s.p. Apr.6, 1920.

viii. Frances Susannah Spratt, b. July 27,1845,
d. Dec.1, 1919, m. Thomas Massey, son of
William H. Massey and wife Sarah (Montgomery). Eight children.

    ix.   Helen Spratt, b. Nov.2, 1847, d. ca 1916,
         m. Whit Hess and had children.
     x.   Robert Benjamin Spratt, b. Feb.20, 1850.
         No further information.
    xi.   Flora A.S.Spratt, b. Oct.24, 1854, d.
         Dec.17, 1914.

(3) William Henry Massey, son of Joseph and
     Martha (Hood) Massey, b. April 3, 1813, d.
     ca 1865, m. Dec.8, 1844 Sarah Montgomery of
     Mississippi, moved to Texas and died leaving
     six children.

(4) Jane Artimesia Massey, daughter of Joseph
     and Martha Massey, b. Dec.24, 1814, m. Alex
     Carnes Dunlap. Five children.

(5) Allen Alonzo Massey, son of Joseph and Martha
     Massey, b. Feb.20, 1817, d. May 9, 1900, m.
     Susan Tillery Greer (1821-1882) in Desoto
     Co., Miss. Dec.14, 1842. Eleven children.

(6) Joseph Benjamin Massey, son of Joseph and
     Martha Massey, b. Nov.27, 1820, m. Nancy,
     daughter of Andrew Spratt and his second wife
     Jane White Wren. Nine children.

8.   Betsy Massey, daughter of William Massey and
    his wife Elizabeth (Rives), m. Aquilla Greer
    and moved to Tennessee with their son Will-
    iam Massey Greer. No further record.

9.   Robert Massey, son of William Massey and
    Elizabeth (Rives).

10. Jane Massey, daughter of William Massey and
    Elizabeth (Rives), b.1783, m. William Porter
    and had a daughter Polly, b. ca 1807, who m.
    (1) a Crawford and had one daughter Jane who
    m. George Gill of Lancaster Co. and had four
    chn. Polly m. (2) Starling Howell and had
    twelve chn.

11. Benjamin Massey, son of William and Elizabeth
    Massey, b.1785, d.1832, m. Mildred Chew Rob-
    inson, daughter of John Robinson and wife
    Jane (Downs). Jane Down was the daughter of
    Henry Downs of England and his wife Jane
    Douglas of Scotland who came to America and

settled in Orange County, Virginia. Their son
Henry Downs m. Frances Chew, daughter of Colonel
Chew, and their daughter Jane Downs m. John Robinson and had children: James, Henry, Thomas, Mildred (shown above) and Sam; possibly others.

Children of Benjamin Massey and his wife
Mildred Chew Robinson:

(1) - (6) Sons William, John, Joseph, Thomas,
James and George, never married.

(7) Elizabeth Rives Massey, m. Thomas Kirk
Cureton. Elizabeth (b.1807, d.1862) and
Thomas Kirk Cureton (b.June 3, 1803, d.
July 3, 1857) are buried in the Massey-
Cureton graveyard in the Waxhaws, S.C.
Children: Thomas, James, John, Virginia
and Eliza. (Details shown in H.S.F.XII,
pp.120-122.)

(8) Jane Downs Massey m. Joseph Doby Massey,
son of George Massey and Rebecca (Kirk).
No children.

(9) Dr.Benjamin Franklin Massey m. Amelia
Jones, and died leaving a son Bartlett
Franklin Massey. Amelia m. (2) Dr. Edw.
Hooper and moved to Alabama where she d.
leaving chn. Theresa and William Hooper.

(10) Samuel Buckner Massey, m. Mary Eliza
Massey, daughter of Henry Massey and Eliz.
(Porter). Chn: Samuel, Henry, Alice and
Emma. Alice m. James Everard Massey, son
of Benjamin, and had four chn: James Jr.,
Eula, Ida, amd Janie.

(11) Frances Amanda Massey, m. Dr.Franklin
Kilgore. They had several chn. including
Harriet, Frances, Annie, and son Massey.

12. Temperance Massey, daughter of William Massey
and Elizabeth (Rives), married (1) Reese Porter and had one daughter, Elizabeth, who married Henry Massey and had chn. Mary Eliza and
Henry Reese Massey. Mary Eliza Massey m. Samuel Buckner Massey as previously shown. Henry
Reese Massey m. (1) Margaret Huey and (2)

Mary E. Henry and (3) Harriet Campbell. Family
shown under Henry Massey.
Temperance Massey m. (2) Joseph Gilespie and
had children: Polly who m. Bela Sizer and had
Anson, Elvira, and Mary Jane; Millie who m.
James Cunningham and had six chn.; and Minnie
who m. Samuel Schooley and had four children.

****

The Massey family appears to have been trans-
planted from Philadelphia and its environs about
1708, to a small hamlet named Massey, which lies
about ten miles north of Dover, Delaware, near the
source of Duck Creek, which empties into Chesa-
peake Bay. It was apparently founded by Samuel
Massey and his wife Sarah (Wight) of Cork, Ireland.
Their records were found in Kent County, Maryland,
(W.Bk."D", 1720, p.167, will 196). Sarah was the
daughter of Thomas Wight of Cork County, Ireland
(Myers' Quaker Arrivals in Philadelphia, 1682-
1750). William Cureton, son of Richard, and these
Masseys were engaged in cutting the canal through
the Maryland - Delaware peninsula.
     Sarah Massey, wife of Samuel Massey, decd.,
purchased the property of John Foes in 1709 (Bk.
TS 112, Kent Co.,Md.) and named it Massey. She
sold her property to Henry Evans in 1721 (Bk.TS
99, Kent Co., Md.).
     Sarah (Wight) Massey was a witness and signed
the marriage certificate of William Cureton (immigrant) and his second wife Susannah (Shoemaker)
Price, widow of Isaac Price of Plymouth who died
1705. Susannah married William Cureton March 27,
1708 (Radnor Monthly Meeting, RS 358, p.235).She
signed William Cureton's Quaker certificate with
Mordecai Massey. This William Cureton represented
Duck Creek in the Quaker National Assembly at
Philadelphia in 1733.
     Abstract from the Quaker Records of Duck
Creek, Delaware:

p.112 (Monthly Meeting, Haverford, Pa. 14th of ye
8th. Mo., 1714:

Our friend William Cureton and Susannah his wife
soon after their removal from these parts requested
a certificate on their behalf to friends there,but
some difference happening between him and some of
his late neighbours at Plymouth hath been ye occas-
ion that they have been detained as long without
any recommendation and our friend as appears to us
having endeavoured to remove all reasonable object-
ion that was made, by submitting to ye rules established among friends at that base. Therefore we
think it is our duty to certify in his behalf that
among his neighbours where he has lived many years
he has appeared a good neighbour, a peaceable man
of sober conversation, and his teaching being of
good and sound words we hope may be of service
where his lott may be cast, also his wife being of
good report and in unity with us, we recommend
them to you, desiring their welfare in every way
but more especially their perseverance in ye truth
that have been in some measure manifested unto
them that thereby they may be servicable among
God's people. And hereafter receive ye award of
come ye Blessed, with so much love we remain your
friends in ye Fellowship of ye Gospel.

Signed at our monthly meeting at Haverford, Pa.,
14th of ye 8th month, 1714.

Signatures include several of the Jones family,
who were connected by marriage with the Curetons,
as shown in H.S.F. XII.

****

Miscellaneous Masseys and Curetons

One of the emigrants to Philadelphia ca 1682 was Thomas Massey, son of William Massey, a nonconformist minister whose records are shown in the Wem Register, and who was the son of an older William Massey, listed as "Parson of Wigan", who lived for a time at Preston. During the Civil War he was "Preacher to the Parliamentary Soldiers", and settled near their headquarters at Wem. He had a daughter Susannah who married John Cuerton of Prees.

In 1755, Daniel Massey bought land of David Witherspoon (Records of Kent Co., Md.) and sold to Henry Clarke in 1758. In 1765 Catherine Massey sold land to Joseph Massey (Bk.DD 2,167). In 1761 Elijah Massey bought land of Dennis Delaney and in 1766 Ebenezer Massey bought land from Joseph Massey (ibid, p.337). It is interesting to note that Joseph went to Georgia in 1766 and petitioned for land there, but his petition was refused and he returned to Brunswick Co., Va.,and probably remained there until he died. He had sons James and William, as has been shown.

William Massey, son of Joseph, was a member of the second Provincial Congress for the District Eastward of the Waterree River (now Catawba River). The ten representatives from this district were: Col. Richardson, John Kershaw, Matthew Singleton, Thomas Sumter, Aaron Loocock, Capt. Wm. Richardson, Capt. Robert Patton, Rev.William Tennant, James Bradley, and William Massey Esq.

Some Masseys remained in Kent County, Maryland as in 1802 Benjamin Massey sold land to Winder Massey (Bk.BC 7, p.309), and in 1822 Bunker Massey traded land.

Richard Cureton, born 1698 in Merion, Pa., removed to Edgecombe County, N.C. and his will at Halifax dated 1760 names his three sons: Thomas, John, and Richard Jr. This Thomas Cureton is the father of James Cureton (ancestor of Thomas Kirk Cureton, compiler of this lineage) who took his family to the Waxhaw District in 1788 and later returned to Virginia. James Cureton was elected to the Legislature in 1791, and stayed at Bland- ford in Virginia until after he left the Legis- lature about 1803. His real home was in Sussex County, Va., about thirty miles south of Peters- burg.

In 1766, Richard and William Cureton (grand- sons of William Cureton of Broniarth, and sons of William Cureton Jr. [b. July 22, 1699] and his wife Martha Hales) left the area of Duck Creek, Delaware, and moved to Wilkes County, Georgia, where they are shown living in Capt.Samuel Alex- ander's district.

Note: The Flemish origins of the Curetons (Cuer- ton, Curton, etc) were shown in H.S.F.XII.

In 1180 Arnold de Curton gave property to Richard Belmeis who became Bishop of London. The land was situated at Fyfield in east London and was used as an Augustinian House for Abbesses. This same Bishop Belmeis established Lilleshall Abbey in Shropshire, and it is therefore not sur- prising to find the Cureton family continuing their association with it. Records show that for many generations, the Curetons held important ecclesiastical offices and served the church with distinction.

William Cuerton, father of Richard Cuerton of Lilleshall Abbey, was minister of St.Alkmund's Church in Shrewsbury in 1540, and later Dean of St. Mary's in the same city; he later retired to Grinshill where he was minister of St. Audlem's (placque on wall).

From <u>Annals of the Bodleian Library</u>,1840, 2nd.ed.
    Clarendon Press, Oxon:

p.329 William Cureton, D.D., Sub-Librarian of the
    British Museum, 1840, in charge of Ancient
    Manuscripts:
    On July 5, Convocation confirmed the nomin-
    ation of Rev. William Cureton, M.A. of
    Christ Church, Oxford (afterwards so well
    known for his Syriac studies, which gained
    him the patronage of the Prince Consort and
    a Canonry at Westminster Abbey, and who
    died 17th June, 1864) to the Sub-Librarian-
    ship of the British Museum vacated by Rev.
    E. Hawkins.

p.336 Rev. Herbert Hill, M.A. (Fellow of New
    College, Oxford), now Master of Lord
    Leicester's Hospital, Warwick, was approved
    by Convocation, Oct.26, 1840, as Sub-Librar-
    ian in the room of Mr. Cureton, who removed
    to the British Museum.

p.489 Rev.William Cureton, M.A. in 1834 served the
    British Museum; assistant to Mr. Hawkins.

From Edward Carpenter's <u>A House of Kings</u>, London:
    John Baker, 1966:

p.283 In 1852 those who went on the Progress to
    Worcestershire were Mr. Frere (Treasurer of
    Westminster Abbey), Mr. Jennings (Rector of
    St.John's) and Dr.Cureton (Rector of St.
    Margaret's Church and Steward of Westminster
    Abbey).
    <u>Note:</u> St. Margaret's Church adjoins West-
    minster Abbey, and is the official church
    for members of the British House of Commons
    (Parliament).

p.296 "Ordered that there shall be a Sunday Even-
    ing Service in the Nave of the Abbey from

202

the first Sunday in January; the Service
shall be the usual evening Service with a
Sermon, the Dean to make arrangements for
the Preachers, and Dr. Cureton to be a
Committee to make the arrangements. Bring,
if you can, the poor, the profane, the
careless, and the ignorant."

****

This research has clearly shown the origins
of the Massey and Cureton families and their
close association from the time when Richard de
Masci married in 1421 Margaret, daughter of
Oweyn de Caurthyn (Welsh for Cuerton, in Flemish
Cawarden).

In 1538, at the dissolution of the great
Lilleshall Abbey near Donnington, Shropshire,
among the eight Canons who were equally 1/8
owners, were William Massey and Richard Cuerton.

A John Massey was Abbot of Combermere Abbey
ca 1540, and John Cuerden, of Cuerden and Leyland
Parish, Lancashire, died near there.

A William Massey was Rector of Ellesmere Parish, about two miles from Grinshill, home of the
Curetons.

From Chester Pedigree Book, British Museum,
MSS 5528: Hamon de Masci of Dunham (died 1567)
married ca 1543 Alice, daughter of Henry de Cuerden of Malbank Hall (near Combermere Abbey).

From Joseph Hunter's Agincourt: A Contribut-
ion Towards an Authentic List of the Commanders
of the English Host in King Henry V's Expedition
to France in the Third Year of his Reign: (Brit.
Museum MSS 24, 704). This shows William Curton,

Robert Curton, and Nichus Massey serving under
Sir John Blount in France.

The families were associated in America
from approximately 1700, in the areas of Merion
and Haverford, Pennsylvania, and Duck Creek,
Delaware, then to Brunswick and Sussex Counties,
Virginia, then on to their common graveyard
(Massey - Cureton) and the Family Association in
the Waxhaw section of South Carolina, about twelve
miles north of Lancaster, South Carolina.

****

Research by:
Dr. Thomas Kirk Cureton
501 E. Washington Street,
Urbana, Illinois

WARRENS of SURRY COUNTY, VIRGINIA

with related family

RICHARDS

The progenitors of this family were the Warrens of Kent County, England. As shown in Boddie's Virginia Historical Genealogies, p.238, and Southside Virginia Families II, p.369, their pedigree has been well authenticated from the latter half of the fifteenth century, when William Warren was principal Customs Officer of the Cinque Ports, and was recorded in the Municipal Records as Mayor of Dover in 1493. He died in 1506 and was buried in the Church of St.Peter in Dover. He was apparently a man of considerable fortune, and left all his houses and lands to his wife Joanne for life, and thereafter to his son John.

Visitation records confirm that his only surviving son was John, who married Jane Moninges and was three times Mayor of Dover; he also represented Dover in Parliament between 1529 and 1541. He acquired land in the Parish of Ripple, Kent, about five miles from Dover, but seems to have continued to live in Dover, where he died in 1546 and was interred beside his father in St. Peter's church. His wife survived him for many years (will proved 1572) and was buried with her

husband.
Thomas Warren, son of John, born ca 1510, married Maria Christian Close of Calais. Like his father, Thomas also served in Parliament and as Mayor of Dover. He seems to have spent his latter years at Ripple, where he died April 23, 1591 at the advanced age of eighty, and was buried in the church of St.Mary the Virgin. The only surviving son was John born ca 1561, shown in the Visitations. John Warren married Anne, daughter of Sir William Crafford, at Great Mongham, Aug.2, 1591, and they had twelve children. John died Jan.21,1612, aged fifty, and his widow married Edward Boys in 1621.
William Warren, son of John Warren and his wife Anne (Crafford), born ? died 1631, baptized at Ripple March 7, 1596/7, married in 1619 Katherine, daughter of Thomas Gookin of Ripple Court, Kent. Children, according to the Parish Register, included Thomas Warren who emigrated to Virginia with his cousin Daniel Gookin.

Smith's Fort Plantation:

The oldest brick house in Surry County,Va., is the one built by Thomas Warren the immigrant in 1651-52, on land purchased by him from Thomas Rolfe. There is no doubt about the authenticity of its ownership and age, which are clearly proven by the records. The house is located about half a mile from a high bluff on Gray's Creek, situated on a bend in the creek.
Thomas Warren, in a marriage settlement made Sept.23. 1654 with Mrs.Elizabeth Shepard, daughter of Ancient Planter William Spencer, and widow of Major Robert Shepard, described himself as "Thomas Warren, Gent., of Smith's Fort" (Bk.I, p.56). This plantation lay next to the 550 acres granted Thomas Gray in 1635 (H.S.F.XVII, p.81). Thomas Warren seems to have settled on the eastern branch of Smith's Fort Creek in 1640. His

206

original grant was for 450 acres, and payment for
same was to be made seven years after entry. This
is set forth in a grant for 290 acres made to him
by William Berkeley, July 3, 1648 (Pat.Bk.,p.146):
"grant unto Mr. Thomas Warren two hundred and
ninety acres of land lying at the head of the
easternmost Branch of Smith Fort Creeke being in
the County of James City bounded as followeth:
from a poplar along the bounds of Goodman Spil-
timber north by east half westerly seventy chaines
along the bounds of Mr. John Corker .... the
said land being due unto said Thomas Warren as
followeth (viz) being part of a patent of four
hundred and fifty acres formerly granted unto the
said Warren the 3rd of February 1640 to have and
to hold etc. to be held etc. yielding etc. which
payment is to be made seven years after the date
of the 3rd of February 1640 and not before etc.
Dated the 3rd of July 1648."

Thomas Warren served in the House of Burgesses Oct.1, 1644, thus becoming a member at
the early age of 22, which is exceptional though
not unknown. He married three times. The name of
his first wife is not known; he married as his
second wife Mrs. Elizabeth Shepard (Surry D.& W.
Bk.I, 1652-72, p.56). His third wife was Jane,
widow of John King. Thomas made his will March
16, 1669, probated April 21, 1670. (Ibid, p.169,
deposition of Thomas Warren, aged 40, May 3rd.,
1661.)

Thomas Warren, son of Thomas the emigrant
and his third wife Jane, was born Jan.9, 1659
and died 1721; will probated Aug.16, 1721 (Bk.5,
p.362). He married Elizabeth _____, whose
will was probated in 1730, in which she names
four sons: William, John, Joseph and Robert,also
grandson James Davis, the son of daughter Elizabeth.

Surry Deeds & Wills, 1715-30, p.241:
Thomas Warren and Elizabeth his wife, 1 Feb.1719:
To Benjamin Chapman for 5 shillings, land where
Marmaduke Johnson now lives in Surry County,

containing 200 acres, adjoining land of Thomas
Woodhouse.
Feb.17, 1719: Released for Ten Pounds all that
tract of land formerly exchanged by George Foster
and Elizabeth his wife and Samuel Plaw, conveyed
to Elizabeth Warren by deed 3 Dec.1695, 200 acres.
(Note: Samuel Plaw married Jane, widow of Thomas
Warren the emigrant, as her third husband.)

John Warren, son of Thomas and Elizabeth
Warren, mentioned in his father's will and be-
queathed land "called Rich Neck where he now
lives", was born 1676 and died ca 1700 in Old
Rappahannock County, Virginia. He married Rachel
Sergent (daughter of William Sergent) who died
1707 in Essex County, Virginia (Wills & Deeds,
Bk.12, 1704-1707). Their son, Thomas Warren of
Surry County, Va., was born 1700 and died 1759.
His will, dated April 25, 1759 and probated June
19, 1759, mentions wife Lucy, sons John and Thom-
as, and daughters Mary, Lucy and Rebecca. (W.Bk.
1754-68, p.197.) The will of Lucy Warren, dated
March 29, 1783 and probated Nov.22, 1785 (W.Bk.12,
p.86) mentions daughters Mary Batts, Rebecca
Davis, Charity Smith, also sons Thomas and John
Warren and son-in-law Richard Rowell.(Note:for
text of wills, see H.S.F. IX, p.231.)

Thomas Warren, son of Thomas and Lucy and
great-great-grandson of Thomas the emigrant, was
born prior to 1740 in Old Lunenburg County, Va.,
and died in Franklin County, Va. in 1801. He
served as Captain of Infantry, Virginia Line, in
the Revolutionary War (War Dept., Vol.176, p.23).
He married Jane Browne, and names his sons in the
following deeds:

TO ALL to whom these presents shall come
Know Ye that I Thomas Warren of Franklin County
and State of Virginia for and in consideration of
the natural love and affection which I have to my
son Jesse Warren and also for the further consid-

ation of six shillings in hand paid by said Jesse
Warren the receipt whereof is hereby acknowledged
have given granted bargained and sold to my said
son Jesse Warren a certain negro woman named Lucy
which negro I do hereby warrant and forever defend from the lawful claim of any person or persons whatsoever, unto my said son Jesse Warren,
his heirs and assigns forever. In witness whereof
I have hereunto set my hand and seal this eleventh
day of June in the year of our Lord one thousand
seven hundred and ninety nine.

                    Thomas Warren   (Seal)
Teste:
John Stewart, Charles Stewart
Wilson Maddox

Received June 11th 1799 of Jesse Warren six
shillings in full satisfaction for the within
mentioned negro by me.
                    Thos. Warren

Teste by John Stewart, Charles Stewart
Wilson Maddox

At a Court held for Franklin County at the Courthouse in October 1799:
This bill of sale and receipt from Thomas Warren
to Jesse Warren was acknowledged by the said Thos.
Warren and ordered to be recorded.

                    J.A. Callaway, C.C.

Note: Above deed is found in Franklin Co. D.Bk.4,
       p.214.

The following deed is found in Franklin Co. D.B.4,
pp.184-214:
        TO ALL WHOM THESE PRESENT shall come Know
Ye I Thomas Warren of Franklin County and State of
Virginia do hereby give and grant that all the

209

property which I now possess with the <u>track</u> of
land whereon I now live with two negroes namely
Daniel and Grace, with the household furniture
of every kind, which land, negroes, property and
furniture I do hereby give, grant and deliver to
my five sons, namely Zachariah, Ambrose, Drury,
William and Elijah Warren, to be equally divided
amongst the said five sons, at the decease of
myself and my said wife Jane Warren, which land,
negroes, property and furniture I do hereby warrant and forever defend from the lawful claim of
any person or persons whatsoever. In witness
whereof I have hereunto set my hand and seal this
twelfth day of August in the year of our Lord
1801.

     Thomas Warren (Seal)

Teste:
James (his X mark) Holloway
Wilson (his X mark) Maddox
Elizabeth Maddox, Jesse Warren
Rhoda Warren

At a Court held for Franklin County at the Courthouse in September 1801:

  This deed of Gift from Thomas Warren to Zachariah, Ambrose, Drury, William and Elijah Warren
was proved by oath of Wilson Maddox and Jesse
Warren, two of the subscribing witnesses and
ordered to be recorded.

     J.A.Callaway, C.C.

    ******

  Jesse Warren, son of Thomas and Jane Warren,
was born in Virginia and died in Robertson County,
Tennessee in 1840. He married Rhoda Richards in
Franklin County, Virginia, the daughter of Edward
Richards and wife Elizabeth. (Wingfield, <u>Marriage
Bonds of Franklin Co., Va.</u> 1786-1850, p.235:
Jesse Warren and Rhoda Richards, Feb.13,1790.

Surety. Elijah Warren. Minister, Thomas Douglas.)
Note: The discrepancy in the date of the marriage
and the birthdate of their son Sibert may be due
to the change of calendar; the marriage date was
probably Feb.13, 1789/90.

Edward Richards, father of Rhoda, was born
before 1745 in Old Lunenburg Co., Va. and died in
Franklin Co., Va. 1812; will probated April 6,
1812, Rocky Mount, Franklin County. He lived in
Old Lunenburg during the Revolutionary War, and
enlisted Feb.28, 1778 as a private in Major Jonathan Clark's Company, 4th Va. Regiment, commanded
by Col.James Wood. On April 30, 1785, a certificate for the sum of Ł102.8.10d was issued for
the balance of his pay. (Ref: War Dept.; NSDAR
#378158, #459664, and #467429.

Will of Edward Richards, dated Dec.1803 and probated April 6, 1812 (W.Bk.I, p.11):

In the name of God Amen. I Edward Richards of
the County of Franklin being of sound mind and
memory do make this my last Will and Testament
hereby revoking all former Wills by me heretofore made.
First: I give to my son Shadrach Richards one
negro girl named Vicie, besides what I have
already given him & his heirs forever.
Secondly: I give to my grandson Joel Richards,
oldest son of my son Shadrach, one negro girl
named Peggy to him and his heirs forever.
Thirdly: I give to my son Wortman Richards over
and above what I have already given him, one negro
man named Julius, also one negro woman named Sole
and her child named Barbary, also one tract of
land adjoining the lines of the land on which he
now lives, supposed to contain one hundred and
thirty acres to him and his heirs forever.
Fourthly: I give to my son Edmund Richards one
negro man named Andrew, also a negro woman named
Charlotte, and the child named Linda, also a

negro girl named Juda and also a negro boy named
Martin with the whole of the land and plantation
whereon I now live, together with two new surveys
adjoining thereunto, also one hundred acres of
land adjoining the lines of John Hargar together
with all my household furniture, plantation uten-
sils & stock of all kinds to him and his heirs
forever and whereas I now possess a tract of land
and mill on the north fork of Chestnut Creek containing about three hundred and thirty acres, my
will and desire is that the aforesaid tract of
land together with the mill and all the apparatus
thereunto belonging, be sold on credit of eight-
een months and the money arising therefrom be
equally divided between my daughters Nancy Hargar,
Charity Stuart, Roda Warren, Betsy Maddox, and the
children of my deceased daughter Susan Jones --
and whereas I have given to my son Edmund Richards
a greater proportion of my estate than I have given
to my other children, I therefore direct and it is
my express will and desire that he shall support
and maintain my wife Elizabeth Richards during her
natural life or widowhood with all things necessary, such as good wholesome diet, clothing, lodging
such as she has heretofore been accustomed to and
that she have the use of my mansion house without
molestation and that she have the use of my negro
girl Juda during her natural life and after her
decease to go as before directed to my said son
Edmund and his heirs forever.

AND lastly I appoint my sons Shadrach Richards
and Edmund Richards, Executors of this my last
Will and Testament. In witness whereof I have
hereunto set my hand and affixed my seal this
X day of December, 1803.

                    (Edward (his X mark)
                    (Richards   (Seal)

Signed sealed published and declared as & for the
Last Will and Testament of the above named Edward

Richards in the presence of us: Ste.Smith, Thos. Thompson, Zachariah Warren.

At a Court held for Franklin County, April 6,1812: This last Will and Testament of Edward Richards deceased was proved by the oath of Stephen Smith, and Thomas Thompson, two of the witnesses thereto and ordered to be recorded.

And at a Court held for Franklin County, June 1, 1812, on the motion of Shadrach Richards and Edmund Richards, the executors named in the last Will and Testament of Edward Richards deceased, who made oath as the law directs and together with Jonathan Patterson and Wateman Richards their securities entered into and acknowledged their bond in the penalty of five thousand dollars, conditioned according to law. Certificate is granted them for obtaining a Probate in due form.

Teste: James Callaway
CFC

****

From <u>Will Book 10</u>, p.530, Springfield, Tenn.

Isaiah and Sebirt Warren, letter Testamentary State of Tennessee, Robertson County, Court Term 1840

To Isaiah Warren and Sebirt Warren citizens of Robertson County. It appearing to the Court that Jesse Warren is dead and having written a will in which you are appointed executors which has been duly proven in open court and you having given bond and qualified according to law and it having been ordered by the said court that letters testamentary be issued to you. These are therefore to authorize and empower you the said Isaiah Warren and Sebirt Warren to enter upon the executors of said will and take into your possess-

ion all the property and to make to the next
court a perfect inventory thereof and a collection
of all debts and after paying all just demands
against the testators and setting up the business
of the said estate according to law you will pay
over and deliver the property and effects that
may remain in your hands and do all other things
that may be required according to the provisions
of the said Will and laws of the land.

Wit: Joseph E. Winfield
         Clerk of said Court at office this 8th day
                                of Oct.1840.

Teste: Joseph E. Winfield, Clk.

****

Will of Jesse Warren:

In the name of God Anem.
I, Jesse Warren, of Robertson County and State of
Tennessee, being of sound mind do make this my
last will and testament hereby revoking all former
wills heretofore by me made.
And first I give to my wife Rhoda Warren after
death my negro girl named Catherine and her bed
and furniture, also a good feather bed and sufficient furniture for two beds for own benefit and
comfort during her natural life.
I give to my daughter Rhoda Warren one feather
bed and sufficient furniture for two beds.
I also give to my daughter Rhoda Warren 30 dollars
beside equal part of my estate with the rest of
my children and after my death I will that all my
property excepting my lands be sold to the highest
bidder on credit of twelve months and money arising from such sale be equally divided between my
wife and my daughter Rhoda and all the rest of my
children and my three motherless grandchildren,
namely Emily England now Emily Choat, daughter of
Titus and Susannah England, also Moses Standley
son of Ulinney (?) and John Standley and also

Martha Jane Robins, daughter of Samuel and Nancy Robins.

And all my lands I leave it with my executors whom I shall appoint to sell it the way they may think best and the money arising therefrom be equally divided amongst my wife and children and grandchildren as above stated.

I want if Moses Standley and Martha Jane Robin should die before they come of age for my part of the estate I want it to be equally divided amongst my own kin.

And after the death of my wife Rhoda Warren I will that my negro girl Catherine be sold by my executors, not to the highest bidder but to some person supposed to be good to slaves, for such sum as may be had or as they may think proper to take and the money to be divided as the rest. And the rest of the property held by my wife she may dispose of as she thinks.

And lastly I appoint my two oldest sons, Sebirt Warren and Isaiah Warren as my executors. In witness whereof I said Jesse Warren have set my hand and affixed my seal this day of July in the year of our Lord 1840.

Signed and published in the presence of us:
Chas. Ellison
Andrew Ellison

                              Jesse (his X mark) Warren

N.B. I will that whatever I hold of cash notes and money that after my death my executors collect the money for the notes and my wife Rhoda Warren have a comfortable support out of it for one year and the balance to be equally divided between her my wife Rhoda Warren and all the above named children and grandchildren.

Written before signed or witnessed.

A paper believed purporting to be the last Will and Testament of Jesse Warren was presented in open court for probate and thereupon came Charles

Ellison and Andrew Ellison subscribing witnesses thereto who being sworn acpose (?) and say that they were acquainted with Jesse Warren in his life time and that he acknowledged the execution of said paper in their presence to be his last will and testament that he was in proper mind and that they attested the same at his request the same as therefore to be recorded.

And thereupon came Sibert Warren and Isaiah Warren the above named executors and entered bond with Tuunties (?) in the sum of three thousand dollars conditioned as the law Anech (?) and acknowledged their bond Executors qualified agreeable to law.

****

Isaiah Warren, son of Jesse and Rhoda (Richards) Warren, was born 1793 in Virginia and died Nov.23, 1862; buried in Old City Cemetery, Nashville, Tennessee (Acklen's Tombstone and Bible Records). He married ca 1819 in Tennessee Permelia Ann Phillips, born 1803 in North Carolina and died in Fannin County, Texas, 1885. She was the daughter of Ezekiel Phillips, who was born in Maryland and died in Tennessee, wife Mary _____ born ca 1778 in N.C., died in Tennessee. Isaiah Warren died intestate but in the March term, 1865, Robertson County Court, an allowance was made to his widow Permelia.

Order Book 1859-1866, p.648:
Mrs. Permelia Warren's Year's Allowance:

We the undersigned having met at Mrs. Isaiah Warren's and made the following allowance for the widow, Permelia Warren, in accordance to said order, to wit: Pork 650 pounds, wheat 15 bushels, sack of salt, sugar 50 pounds, coffee 35 pounds, molasses 10 gallons, $3.00 for spences, all of which is respectfully submitted.

Signed: Wm. W. Moss
C. Jones
Wm. McCarly

Robertson Co. Court, March Term, 1865.

The foregoing year's allowance of Mrs. P. Warren was presented to the Court and examined and the same was confirmed and ordered to be recorded.

Signed: R.H.Murphy, Clk.

Isaiah Warren Jr. was born Oct.10,1843 in Robertson Co., Tenn. and died in Hunt County, Texas, Feb.22, 1899. He married Frances Lourisie Capps, born 1848 in Robertson County, and died 1879 in Fannin County, Texas. She was the daughter of Ewing Capps (b. 1817 in Tenn. and d. ca 1860 in Tenn., m. Mary Pitts who d. after 1879 in Robertson Co., Tenn.). Ewing Capps was the son of William Capps who was b. in Virginia and died in Tenn., will probated Tenn. Oct.1835.

Mary Ellen Warren, daughter of Isaiah Warren, was born in Fannin Co., Texas, April 15, 1872 and died at Fort Worth, Texas Jan.28, 1961. She m.1892 William C. Schultz, b. Lamar County, Texas 1872 and died March 3, 1904 in Paris, Lamar Co., Texas.

Viola Schultz, daughter of William and Mary (Warren) Schultz, was born Oct.4, 1896, married 23 Sept.1914 John Raymond Hopkins, born in Ohio 1880 and died in Mercedes, Hidalgo Co., Texas Oct. 16, 1957.

Mary Fay Hopkins, daughter of John and Viola Hopkins, born Aug.16, 1915 in Dallas, Texas, marr. Lonnie Connor Rushton at Mercedes, Texas Oct.20, 1935.

Mary Ann Rushton, born June 30, 1938 at Mercedes, Texas, married Joe A. Hoppe, Feb.4, 1961.

Nancy Martha Rushton, born Jan.16, 1945 at Mercedes, Texas, m. Jere Paul Parrish, Sept.4,1965.

Correction: S.V.F.II, p.369:
    Richard Swift was born April 2, 1767 in N.C.
    and married Katherine Moss, Nov.2, 1781.
    (Caswell County, N.C. Marriage Bonds.)

    Ibid, p.371:
    Paul Rees Ratliffe, b. Nov.1, 1900,
    d. July 7, 1960.
    Sybil Warren Seeley, b. Oct.5, 1903,
    d. Nov.14, 1962.

                    ******

The foregoing data complete the information published in Southside Virginia Families, Vol.II,
p.371, which was contributed by Merle E. (Warren)
Ratliffe, a great-granddaughter of Sebirt Warren.
Research also by Mrs. Viola Schultz Hopkins who
descends from Isaiah Warren, and her daughter Mary
Fay Rushton; and by Mrs. Zoe (Hill) Warren.

                    ******

Descent of the immigrant Thomas Warren from
Charlemagne: (previously published in HSF,Vol.I)

Charlemagne, Emperor of the West, d.814, married
Hildegarde, daughter of Count Gerold:

Louis, Emperor of the West, d.840, married Judith
daughter of Welf, Duke of Bavaria:

Charles, Emperor of the West, d.877, m. Ermin-
trude, daughter of Odo, Count of Orleans:

Louis, Emperor of the West, d.879, m. Adelaide:

Charles, King of France, d.929, married Eadgifu,
daughter of Edward, son of Alfred the Great.

Louis, King of France, d. 954, m. Gerberga, dau.

of Henry, Emperor of Germany:

Charles, Duke of Lower Lorraine, d. ca 994, m. Bonne, dau. of Godfrey, Count of Verdun and Ardennes:

Gerberga of Lorraine m. Lambert, Count of Louvain who d. 1015, of the lineage of Charlemagne:

Maud of Louvain, m. Eustace, Count of Boulogne, d. ca 1049:

Lambert, Count of Lens, d.1054, m. Adelaide, dau. of Robert, Duke of Normandy, of the lineage of Charlemagne:

Judith of Lens m. Waltheof, Earl of Huntingdon and Northumberland, d. 1076:

Maud of Huntingdon m. (2) David, King of Scotland d. 1154, of the lineage of Alfred the Great; m. (1) Simon de St.Liz, Earl of Huntingdon:

Henry, Earl of Huntingdon, d. 1152, m. Ada, dau. of William de Warenne, Earl of Surrey, of the lineage of Charlemagne, of Alfred the Great, and of William the Conqueror:

Ada of Huntingdon m. Sir Henry de Hastings of Ashill, d. 1250, of the lineage of Charlemagne:

Hillaria de Hastings m. Sir Wm. de Harcourt of Stanton Harcourt, d. 1271, of the lineage of Charlemagne and of Alfred the Great:

Sir Richard de Harcourt, of Stanton Harcourt, d. 1283, m. Margaret, dau. of John, Lord Beke of Eresby:

Sir John de Harcourt of Stanton Harcourt, d.1330, m. Ellen, dau. of Sir Eudo la Zouche of Haryng-worth of the lineage of Charlemagne, of Alfred

the Great, of Brian Boru, King of Ireland, and of
Llewellyn, Prince of North Wales:

Matilda de Harcourt, m. Henry Crispe of Standlake,
Esq., d. after 1387:

John Crispe of Kingston, Esq., d. after 1404, m.
Anne, dau. of Wm. Phettiplace of Kingsey, Esq.

Henry Crispe of Cobcote, Esq., d. ca 1426, m.Joan,
dau. of Nicholas Dyer, Esq., of Rotherfield:

John Crispe of Whitstable, Esq., d.1475, m. Joan,
dau. of John Sevenoaks of Sevenoaks:

John Crispe of Canterbury, Esq. d. ca 1503, m.
Agnes, dau. of John Queke of Quex-in-Thanet, Esq.

John Crispe of Quex-in-Thanet, d. ca 1534, m.Alice
dau. of Thomas Denne Esq., of Kingston:

Margaret Crispe m. John Crayford (Crafford) of
Great Mongham, Esq., d. ca 1535:

Edward Crayford (Crafford) of Great Mongham, Esq.
d. 1558, m. Mary, dau. of Henry Atsea of Herne:

Sir Wm. Crayford (Crafford) of Great Mongham, d.
1623, m. Anne, dau. of John Norton of London:

Anne Crafford m. John Warren Esq. of Ripple, d.
1612:

William Warren Esq. of Ripple, d.1631, m. Catherine, dau. of Thomas Gookin of Ripple Court:

Their son was Thomas Warren the immigrant, as
shown previously.

****

I N D E X

Delaney Dennis 199
Devin William 101
DeWitt Laron 14
Dickenson John 79
Dikes Henry 88
Dillard James 101,John 102,
    Thomas 79
Doherty James 90,122, Jim
    133, William 133
Dorman Joseph 120
Dowell John 82,83, Thomas
    83, William 83
Downs Henry 195,196, Jane
    195,196
Dudley Adria 73, Eliz. 73,
    Sally 73
Duncan Keziah 96
Dunlap Alex.195
Durrett Richard 82,84,
    William 79

-E-

East Hester 12
Easter John 164
Edwards Pauline 113
Egerton Dorothy 175,
    Katherine 178, Philip
    175,176, Richard 175,
    Thomas 175
Eley Jesse 76
Ellis Hannah 168
Ellison Andrew 215 Chas.215
Embrey Margaret 177,183
England Emily 213, Susannah
    213, Titus 213
English Chas.74, Dinah 70,
    George 74, Henry 73,75,
    James 74, John 74, Par-
    menas 74, Stephen 73,
    86,89, William 73
Evans Henry 197

-F-

Farley Harold 115
Farr Susan 13
Farrell Mildred 169
Fatherlee Mary 43
Fazerkley Margerie
    176, Robert 176
Felix John 169
Ferril Ann 166
Floyd Lauranna 73
    Margaret 96, Wm.96
Foes John 197
Foster Elizabeth 207
    George 207
Fountain R.G. 37

-G-

Gerry Mary 129
Gibson Jane 191,Jeremiah
    191, Roger 191, Sam 191
Gilbert Bristow 110
Gillasby Jacob 119,
    John 119
Gillespie Joseph 197
Gilmore James 192
Goodall James 82
Goodrich Nancy 168
Gookin Daniel 205, Thos.
    205
Gough Ralph 80
Gravely Page 115
Graves Lewis 21, Wm.103
Gray Alice 149, Effie 155
    Hannah 149, John 149
Greer Ann 70, Aquilla 71,
    76,102,195, Delia 76,
    Henry 77, James 77,Mary
    70, Patsey 169, Sarah
    75, Susan 195, William
    70,75,77,195
Gresley John 173
Grosvenor Anne 179,
    Richard 179

-H-